SIMPLE FORMS

SIMPLE FORMS

ANDRÉ JOLLES

TRANSLATED BY PETER J. SCHWARTZ

VERSO
London • New York

This translation is based on André Jolles's *Einfache Formen: Legende, Sage, Mythe, Rätsel, Spruch, Kasus, Memorabile, Märchen, Witz*, 2nd edn (Tübingen: Niemeyer, 1958) and is published by kind permission of Walter de Gruyter GmbH.

1 3 5 7 9 10 8 6 4 2

Verso
UK: 6 Meard Street, London W1F 0EG
US: 20 Jay Street, Suite 1010, Brooklyn, NY 11201
versobooks.com

Verso is the imprint of New Left Books

ISBN-13: 978-1-78478-493-5
ISBN-13: 978-1-78478-494-2 (UK EBK)
ISBN-13: 978-1-78478-495-9 (US EBK)

British Library Cataloguing in Publication Data
A catalogue record for this book is available from the British Library

Library of Congress Cataloging-in-Publication Data
Names: Jolles, Andrãe, 1874-1946, author. | Schwartz, Peter J., 1967-
translator.
Title: Simple forms / Andrãe Jolles ; translated by Peter J. Schwartz.
Other titles: Einfache Formen. English
Description: English-language edition | New York : Verso, 2017. | Includes
index.
Identifiers: LCCN 2016038474| ISBN 9781784784935 (pbk. : alk. paper) | ISBN
9781784784928 (hardback : alk. paper)
Subjects: LCSH: Literary form.
Classification: LCC PN45.5 .J613 2017 | DDC 808—dc23
LC record available at https://lccn.loc.gov/2016038474

Typeset in Minion by Hewer Text (UK) Ltd, Edinburgh
Printed in the US by Maple Press

Contents

Foreword

It is a cause for celebration to have Jolles's classic *Simple Forms* in English after some eighty-five years; it took sixty-five for Shklovsky's *Theory of Prose* to reach us. Propp's *Morphology of the Folktale* took only thirty, thanks to Svatava Pirkova-Jakobson, but in that instance 1958 was the optimal time, at the onset of the structuralist revolution and in particular of so-called 'narratology'.

Simple Forms came too late for that, even in France (1972), and in any case, along with some other reasons, to be examined later on, there was always the fundamental incompatibility between Germanic philosophy and the French tradition (enlivened by Jakobson). What we had in the Anglophone world was Northrop Frye (*Anatomy of Criticism* appeared in 1958 as well), whose Jungian archetypes have a rather different flavour than Jolles's more simple forms. Meanwhile, Jolles has inevitably been compared to the great German Romance philologists (most notably Spitzer and Auerbach), who made their impact as American exiles; but in fact Jolles was initially an art critic, and his formation lay rather with the morphology of the Warburg circle.

Narratology has meanwhile become as specialized and abstruse as film studies, so it is good to have this pioneering return to such popular forms as the joke, the riddle and the saying. The fairy tale has reached a professional status of its own after the combined onslaughts of Propp, anthropology and semiotics, while after Lévi-Strauss myth has become so privileged a category – torn between Jung and structuralism – that it is hard to propose it as a topic without suspicion, confusion or both together. Jolles's book is a kind of genre study (he would himself no doubt have wanted us to see it as an investigation into the origins of genre rather than as a contribution to yet another already constituted discipline); but we miss its impact if we do not realize that at least one of its originalities (and secret aims) is to displace all the classic and traditional categories of myth, lyric, tragedy, comedy, with some new ones, fresher and closer to the everyday social life in which they were practised. Meanwhile, Peter J. Schwartz's translation gives us welcome access to the informal language with which Jolles makes his way through these problems, thinking aloud, and frankly breaking off where he can see no immediate solution. This is a great book, always stimulating, and exhilarating in its speculative leaps, its shrewd insights, its wilder guesses.

Jolles's conception of the structure of the 'simple form' deploys the classic hermeneutic opposition between outside and inside, surface appearance and inner essence, deep structure and realization, meaning and its expression. We begin with the positing of some primordial 'verbal gesture', from which the simple form emerges. This form then produces a number of texts – the lives of the saints in the first instance, the sagas in the second – and it is subsequently appropriated as a literary art form, an artificial or derivative genre, by individual artists or intellectuals in a later historical period. There are, no doubt, authentic and inauthentic versions of such cultural appropriation, and Jolles has something to say about that. But the 'verbal gesture', and the 'mental disposition' from which it springs, is theoretically and structurally less clear. For one thing, each of these complexes is radically different from the next – in function, in elements, in form – so that universal and quasi-anthropological structures can as little be deduced from them as from the scattered components of daily life: What would brushing one's teeth have to do with greeting an acquaintance, buying a trolley ticket, or punching a time-card? For another, in all these cases, we are working backwards, from the individual texts to the hypothetical underlying 'gesture' they share: so that it is only some general theoretical account of the structure that 'begins with' the latter. Meanwhile, we have omitted another curious detail of the process: Jolles will try to link each of these forms with an object, such as the relic of the saint or the 'rune' of the riddle. 'The simple form can always transfer its power to an object, charging the object with the power of the form.' This is the iconographer speaking, rather than the literary formalist; and the programme here remains incomplete and unfulfilled, to say the least, but adds a pleasing and idiosyncratic heterogeneity to the work itself.

In what follows, I will be less attentive to these structural features of the theory, and more interested in the content of the forms themselves, not least in their relationship to one another: Can they possibly make up that 'system' for which the conclusion calls? Can they somehow be generated from within rather than, as here, empirically collected and botanized? And to begin with, how many of them are there? Can one imagine more of them? Or disqualify this one or that on the grounds of structural inadequacy?

To be sure, nine is already a very large number to hold together in the mind: one thinks of Lacan's question, 'How high can the Unconscious count?' He reached, I think, the number six as the outer limit. For most of us, however, I suppose that something like four constitutes the magic number (in theological hermeneutics, the seven levels of meaning were generally understood to be reducible to four in the long run); and four marks the framework of the Greimas square (to which I am committed), itself derived from Aristotle. In that case, we will have to see what we want to do with the other five.

The opening four chapters do indeed present a coherent set of logical oppositions. Legend, a term Jolles borrows from the 'Legends of the Saints', generates a simplified paradigm of an individual life which can be offered for 'imitation' to the reader or listener (in the sense of the 'Imitation of Christ'). It is to be strictly distinguished and differentiated from biography, not merely by way of its elimination of empirical detail and its adherence to a well-nigh Proppian sequence of structural events; but also in the spirit of an attack on 'facts' and a general onslaught on empiricist historiography which will be a significant leitmotiv throughout the whole book. The work can thereby be resituated within a wholesale attempt to rethink history in this period, from the Warburg circle's emphasis on iconology to Heidegger's new historicity (derived from Dilthey and Count Yorck von Wartenburg). We will come back to it shortly.

The next section, which singles out the form of the Norse and Icelandic saga as a unique narrative archetype, then gives us the fundamental clue to both method and thematics here. Its emphasis on the collective as opposed to the focus of 'legend' on the exceptional individual supplies us with our first (rather banal) opposition. Its designation of the Scandinavian family or clan as the materialist basis or 'social equivalent' for this particular form is a hermeneutic gesture that will be familiar to non- or anti-formalist readers; and it adds a missing link to the standard sociological list of narrative forms as they move from tribal myth to ancient epic and on to the individualism of the bourgeois novel, reminding us of the problematic nature of most of our evocations of feudalism which exclude Icelandic democracy (itself perhaps a better candidate for Marx's Germanic mode of production than the usual ones).

This is then the moment to return to Jolles's own theoretical positions on the nature of the 'simple form' itself, which he calls a *Sprachgebärde*, or what we might translate as a 'verbal gesture' or *gestus*, a term not fully assimilable to the common 'gesture' of English usage, which is most often a simple physical movement. Here Jolles offers an interesting parallel to Brechtian usage, where the *gestus* is a whole unity of situation and reaction captured as a unique act. But where, in Brecht, such a unity (ideological, political, even philosophical) is an act to be captured on stage by the enlightened play of actors trained in the *Verfremdungseffekt* – or 'estrangement effect' – in Jolles what results is a proto-literary form, which I would designate as narrative (despite its embodiments in such things as riddles and sayings). This is the deep or Ur-level of Jolles's identification of his forms, the proto-formations or phyla of his literary archaeology. It can know authentic exemplifications, as in the Grimms' collection of their fairy tales: but it will be – each of these forms – better known to us by its cultural and artificial elaborations, by the modern elaboration of named artists and writers. The whole debate is recapitulated in the folktale chapter, and familiar from the way in which it tormented several generations of German writers: Schiller's *Naive and Sentimental Poetry* will come to mind, in which Schiller managed to reassure himself as to his own literary validity by opposing a modern or self-conscious, reflexive type of literature (the 'sentimental') to Goethe's 'naive' or primordial lyric talent – a quintessential 'force of nature'.

Jolles's own position on this would seem to waver; at times he feels that his own notion of deep forms and their actualization or artificial appropriation somehow solves the dilemma at work here (probably more deeply rooted in the German ideological tradition than in the Western countries). At the same time, however, the polemical force of his work is surely at least implicitly directed against aesthetic artificiality and effete glorifications of the individual artist or creator. Was Homer a real person? I doubt if the Barthes–Foucault position on the death of the author really lays this question to rest. At any rate, this particular preoccupation will form one pole of the ideological polemics that drive Jolles's theorizations here; we will meet the other one shortly.

The next pair of chapters then shift from the enunciatory subjects to the speech act itself (although, to be altogether strict, the saint or hero – the object of a popular 'imitation' – was never an individual speaker but rather always an object of collective contemplation). The riddle was of course always grasped as a form of speech, addressed to a puzzled listener; but in what sense can 'myth' be said to imply a primordial communication system of this kind? Here we find one of those striking originalities that unsystematically light up Jolles's uniquely personal writing as he thinks his way through this thicket of literary problems. Normally, for most of us, myth means a kind of metaphysical statement (if not, as in the Greek source-word, and for an ethnographer like Lévi-Strauss, a string of narrative episodes). For Jolles it is always what in our more limited national-popular idiom we call a 'just-so story', namely the answer to a question, and a question about the existence of things at that. So, not 'How did the leopard get its spots?' but rather, 'Where did the world come from?' And now the great opening words of creation take on a different tone and voice: not Kant's thunderous and sublime pronouncement in the void: 'Let there be light!'; but rather the reply of a storyteller, 'In the beginning, God . . .' The words are no longer phatic but rather conversational, around a fire; and the concrete social situation re-emerges together with its simple form, just as it did in the two opening chapters.

As for the riddle, however, a more sinister situation begins to disclose itself: not a harmless party game, but Wotan interrogating Mime for his head and life. The riddle becomes the discourse of authority, the questioning of a judge, the very instance of judgment itself and of ultimate knowledge and the knowledge of secrets (itself a new social situation, that of Freemasonry and the secret, potentially revolutionary, society).

At this point we will overleap the chapter on sayings and arrive at the 'casus' itself, the official juridical situation, in which the event must be measured up to the letter of the law. It was one of Jolles's most brilliant insights to have discovered and named the uniqueness of this simple form, secretly or implicitly present in so much of moralizing literature, when not outright drama itself: since the Greeks a proto-form of judgment, a call to the audience to make up its own mind on the basis of the evidence, as most overtly in Brecht himself.

And with a little ingenuity, I would like to shoehorn the chapter on sayings into this general category as well: for is not the folk-saying as such also an element in the wisdom of the community, a sentence that sums up the experience of the group in question, which has its own unique way of formulating what perhaps every group knows, but expresses differently? 'Life is not like crossing a field': Schwartz is himself most ingenious indeed in identifying English versions for his German aphorisms. (Here, of course, the debate about author and collective anonymity returns with a vengeance: How many popular Italian and English proverbs are not in fact derived from Dante or Shakespeare?)

So now, in this latest series – riddle, saying, casus – we find a new set of themes emerging: the social, not just the family or clan, but the secret society or in-group, the 'people', the law and the norm; and a new type of source, which Jolles shares with Walter Benjamin and in a different way with Raymond Williams, namely the category of experience: collective experience, not merely the tacit knowledge of the group but the very mark and symptom of its coherence, its existence as a social unity.

Experience, as a category or a concept, is an admirable mediator between objective situation and subjective reaction or response: including in itself the more profound questions of memory and habit as well as those of praxis. In the post-structuralist period, however, this subjective entity (if it is one) has fallen under the opprobrium reserved for all the humanisms and all the versions of the centred subject and conscious mastery. Existentialism used it extensively, as *l'expérience vécue* – lived or authentic experience as opposed to the other kind, which Sartre characterized with ferocity as an instrument of domination in *La nausée*. For Walter Benjamin, meanwhile, experience (*Erfahrung*) constituted the collective lore of older social formations (and their literary expressions), which the *Erlebnisse* or shock effects (also generally translated as experiences) administered by modernity and the big city tended to weaken and dissolve, resulting in alienation, as well as modernism in the arts. For Raymond Williams, too, experience designated the essentially collective life everywhere threatened by capitalism. In philosophy, the stronghold of the category of experience is clearly phenomenology as such, whose mauling by poststructuralisms of all kinds has perhaps not altogether rendered it extinct: a concept as inadmissible as it is indispensable.

But 'experience' is a productive concept only when it is articulated in terms of an opposition between form and content, for it must in fact be identified with both. Experience is an inchoate yet original subjective substance which is then shaped and named, and in effect given form, by pre-existing social and collective categories – words and expressions (sayings!) that seem to organize it, named emotions which appear to identify it, articulations familiar to others (familial, group, ethnic, even universal–philosophical) and which now allow me to see what has happened to me in relatively accessible signifiers, however much I want to give them a more unique and distinctive twist and slant, a personal mark, a kind of singularity I can own or defend as belonging (in public) to a privacy and a self.

At this point, we are in a position to conjecture the preconditions necessary for the existence of such an inchoate experience, at the same time that we can separate out its social forms of expressivity (which to be sure have their own historical preconditions); and something like a *gestus* or a simple form becomes historically visible. Jolles's unspecified but rather traditional frame of reference allows him to elude such historical specification and to frame his typology in terms of some general human nature (never theorized in any dogmatic or philosophical fashion), thereby leaving history on the side of the artificial and the modern-individualistic exploitations which such archaic forms underwent in what for Germany would be Enlightenment or post-Enlightenment times. The distinction thus lies at the intersection of two ideological thematics which it might be well for the moment to keep distinct from one another: the first a historical or *historial* one, in which the primordial or archaic is separated from the modern 'or civilizational', the other a subjective distinction (related to the *Bildungsroman*) in which the naive is opposed to the sentimental, to use Schiller's famous language, or the popular-spontaneous to the reflexive or 'intellectual' (in its social as well as its mental sense).

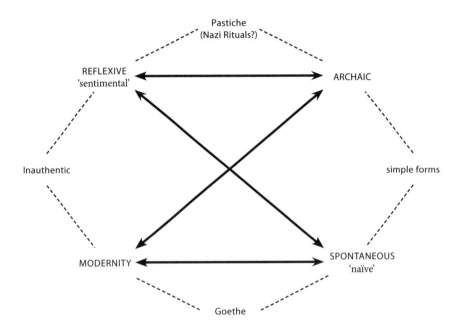

What is productive and what for the moment we want to retain from Jolles is the distinction between form and content constantly at work in his descriptions, rather than the mythical positing of some simpler and more natural era.

To be sure, I here read the chapter sequence as a kind of discovery procedure in which, by his choice and then his reasoning, which he shares quite openly with us, Jolles is in the process of thinking something through, thinking something else through, coming to awareness of the very object of his own meditation. This presupposes, of course, what I do not know, namely the order of the original lectures, or better still, the order of their composition. And it raises the interesting question of exclusions: Were more such simple forms conceivable (he says so, but does not suggest any)? Could one add to the list? Are there some he discarded or declined to consider, to admit to the fundamental sequence?

For at any rate it is a fact that, with our next form, the *memorabile* (which I loosely translate as 'anecdote'), the thematics begin to alter, and what I have called the hidden polemic acquires a new target. To be sure, it was always there implicitly from the myth chapter on, in which Jolles rapidly dismisses the rivalry of myth with history as such. But here, in the memorabile, the quarrel with 'real' history becomes overt, and he gives us his memorabilia in two versions, the simple form and the historically correct one. At this point I begin to find the chapters less satisfying. I would myself, for this one, have preferred the category of the *fait divers*, and any self-respecting structural or narratological analysis would at once have perceived two distinct narrative lines intersecting in the well-nigh Kluge-like anecdote of the councillor's suicide and the apartment of Asta Nielsen next door. And there is always Roland Barthes' notorious 'reality-effect' to designate the contingencies of the non-functional detail – the stray and gratuitous descriptive element, clothes, furniture, unnecessary personnel – that lend 'verisimilitude' to the historical anecdote. But Barthes has an explanation for it: it serves the bourgeois ideology of realism, something Jolles senses and seems to resist, but would certainly not identify in those terms.

Meanwhile, the newspaper (the morning prayer of modern man, as Hegel put it), the public sphere, might have served as a more convincing form-context; while the medieval conception of an event does not seem complete without Walter Benjamin's notion of the memorable – what is so striking as to be retained in memory, and in 'folk memory' at that.

So what the memorabile chapter does begin more powerfully to achieve is rather the denunciation of modernity and of its tyranny of the fact; preparing the wholesale defence of Jacob Grimm's theory of the collective origin of the fairy tale in the anonymous *Volk* itself. There is a certain ideological transfer at work when Jolles describes Grimm's fury and indignation at the artificial revision and tampering with authentic fairy tales and poems by Brentano and Arnim in his own generation.

And this indignation has its echo in the content of his analysis as such: for what Jolles rightly identifies as the ground tone of the fairy tale, the ground bass, the generative element, is the feeling somehow that the world is not right, that this world as it is now is not as it should be, that there is a fundamental injustice at work in the daily life and worldly experience of the tellers and the listeners of the original fairy tales (he never calls them 'peasants' by name). Here is the political impulse par excellence: it is not only the time that is out of joint, it is the world order itself, whether in medieval times or our own. And the miraculous, as it most profoundly characterizes the fairy tale, is not only a protest against that bad actuality and a Utopian correction of it; it also forms a kind of enclave within that fallen reality: the form is a social form as well, like a cabin or clearing in the woods. It affords an instant of other-worldliness, a line of flight, a place of momentary salvation. We have reached the political nerve of Jolles's great book, which it will be an inevitable task to examine further.

And what of the last chapter? What of the simple form which is the joke or *Witz*, in which Jolles might have rivalled so many distinguished modern theorists on this interesting and profoundly social matter, beginning with Freud himself (and Bergson)? It is a disappointing amalgam of very different types of discourse, from comedy itself to satire, irony, wit, caricature, all of which deserve their own independent scrutiny. But the conclusion is telling: the humorous unbinds; comedy, the joke, put an end to the social and its mechanisms, they dissolve society as such. He here rejoins Hegel, who sees comedy and laughter as the ultimate stage in the dissolution of ancient society and its gods. Here, presumably, it is that bad modernity Jolles has been denouncing in the preceding chapters which is thereby dissolved like Prospero drowning his book. It is as though Jolles, coming to the end of his great project, reaches a moment of disgust with it and scatters its pages to the winds.

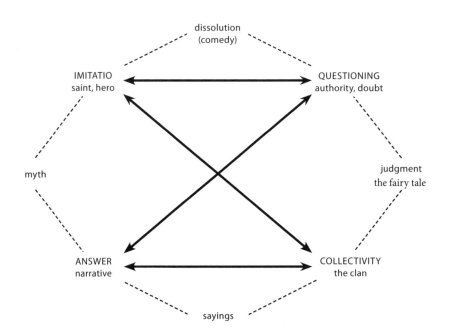

But maybe Weimar is no longer amusing; maybe this is a moment of the *passage à l'acte*, of the need for commitment, for praxis and action. And so we reach the rise of National Socialism and that fateful Nazi party-card he shared with Heidegger. But that was the most superficial thing they had in common.

In that spirit, I want to conclude by taking a closer look at the archaism that motivates Jolles's great book, and that animated so many of his contemporaries, like Heidegger himself. The lurid Nazi rituals must have been, for both of these cultivated scholars, an intellectual's fantasy of things to come, of a profound social transformation (or moral regeneration, to use a more modern political reference) of which the marches and symbols turned out to be a broken promise.

Anti-modernism is to be sure not only an ideology but a most ambiguous ideology indeed, available to both Right and Left. The Luddites, the communes of the 1960s, Winstanley, revolutionary fantasies about the Russian *mir*, are as easily classifiable under that catch-all rubric as the traditionalists of the late Qing or the neo-Monarchists of the Action française. Meanwhile, the category has the additional drawback of no longer being topical or current at all: religious fundamentalists, whether American or Islamic, are none of them anti-technological any longer, whatever they think of Darwin or of infidels. I suspect that at least two distinct lines of ideological affiliation need to be distinguished here: one has to do with agriculture and country versus city; the other has to do with nationalism. The obsession with 'the soil' that reappears in both is a coincidence in name only; and in a postmodernity from which nature has been eliminated, these once burning issues reappear under the utterly different guise (no less urgent and obsessive) of ecology as such, where the nation is no longer a meaningful category but ownership and extraction surely are.

In this respect the mid-to-late twentieth century now seems a transition period between heavy industry and information technology. Heidegger's fantasies about modernity took the form of a reversion to pre-Socratic philosophy, in which Being was respected by the right kind of forgetfulness, along with that Ur-Germanic language in which a proximity to the soil and to being was as densely preserved as in ancient Greece itself – the only two languages he seemed willing to acknowledge as non-mongrel. In a classic work, Jean Paulhan analysed what he called 'la preuve par l'étymologie', in which he argued (tongue in cheek no doubt, and with one eye on the initial inroads of Heideggerianism in postwar France) that the uncovering of an 'original' meaning by etymology is no less philosophical a 'proof' than the syllogism: historical and phenomenological rather than logical. Thus the old German *buan* means 'to dwell', but is also related to the words for building and being itself. The deep past of language is more authentic than its fallen uses in the modern newspaper.

Something of this search for a lost authenticity is certainly present in Jolles's hypothesis of the simple forms that continue their subterranean work beneath the artificial decoration of a modern fallen speech. This is why Jolles is not really to be classified as a philologist, but finds his homeland in iconology, in the transmission of what I strongly resist calling archetypes. It is a method, indeed a whole mystique of history, and an ethos, with profoundly nationalist implications, but which need not be utterly incomprehensible in a non-national 'melting pot' like our own: witness socio-biology, whose scientific elaboration could scarcely mask its longing for the recovery of the true, the fundamental human animal, but which, in the absence of the right political movement, had to be satisfied with the gym and the tanning salon.

Jolles's enthusiastic endorsement of Nazism – and in the absence of biographical detail we cannot go much further than that, although significantly we know that, like Heidegger, he was certainly active in the political and racial sanitizing of his own university (Leipzig) – tarnished his reputation forever and discouraged translation of his book for many years (unlike the extraordinary recovery of Parteigenosse Heidegger). But only those who desperately try to wish away the political and ideological ambiguities of human life will want to ignore the riches of his landmark text.

Fredric Jameson

Translator's Introduction

Who was André Jolles?[1] Born in Den Helder in 1874; raised in Amsterdam; in his youth a significant player in the literary Movement of the Nineties (Beweging van Negentig), whose organ was the Dutch cultural weekly *De Kroniek*; a close friend of Aby M. Warburg's and Johan Huizinga's, Jolles studied art history at Freiburg beginning in 1902 and then taught art history in Berlin, archaeology and cultural history in occupied Ghent during World War I, and Netherlandic and comparative literature at Leipzig from 1919 until shortly before his death, in 1946.[2] A man of extraordinary intellectual range – his publications include essays on early Florentine painting, a dissertation on the aesthetics of Vitruvius, a habilitation thesis on Egyptian–Mycenaean ceremonial vessels, literary letters on ancient Greek art, and essays in German and Dutch on folklore, theatre, dance, Boccaccio, Dante, Goethe, Zola, Ibsen, Strindberg, and Provençal

---

1   On Jolles generally, see Walter Thys, 'Uit het leven en werk van André Jolles', *De Nieuwe Taalgids* 47 (1954), pp. 129–37, 199–208, translated into German by Tilli Wolff-Mönckeberg as 'Aus dem Leben und Werk von André Jolles (1874–1946)', in *Intra & extra muros: verkenningen voornamelijk in de neerlandistiek en het comparatisme* (Delft: Eburon, 2008), pp. 13–34. See also Walter Thys, *'Gebildeter Vagant': Brieven en Documenten* (Amsterdam/Leipzig: Amsterdam University Press/Leipziger Universitätsverlag, 2000), pp. 1–17; Antoine Bodar, 'Jolles, Andreas Johannes', in J. Charité and A. J. C. M. Gabriëls, eds, *Biographisch Woordenboek van Nederland*, vol. 4 (The Hague: Instituut voor Nederlandse Geschiedenis, 1994), pp. 219–20, and 'De Schoonheidsleer van André Jolles: Morphologische Beschouwingen', PhD diss., self-published (1987), pp. 8–26; Frans Hinskens, 'André Jolles – Van vagant tot ontheemde', *Nachbarsprache Niederländisch* 17: 1–2 (2002), pp. 66–82.

2   It remains in question whether Jolles's death was suicide, provoked by despair at the end of the war. Barbara Wackernagel-Jolles, 'Hommage à mon père André Jolles/Herinneringen van de middelste dochter', *Maatstaf* 41: 1 (1993), p. 72; Thys, *Gebildeter Vagant*, p. 6.

and Renaissance Italian poetry – he was also an amateur playwright and an outspoken champion of modern trends in dramatic art and stage design. To his friends, he could be something of an intellectual midwife, helping Warburg to formulate what would become a signature concept, the 'pathos formula',[3] and Huizinga to conceive *The Waning of the Middle Ages* (1919).[4] Jolles's chief work, the one for which he is best known, is *Simple Forms* (*Einfache Formen*, 1929), a collection of lectures delivered in German at Leipzig in 1927–28, and then revised.[5]

Simple Forms has been called a significant precursor to structuralist and narratological literary theories, although it lies outside their main lines of development. It is often mentioned alongside the work of the Russian and Czech formalists, especially Vladimir Propp's

---

3   Ernst Gombrich, *Aby Warburg: An Intellectual Biography*, 2nd edn (Chicago: University of Chicago Press, 1986), pp. 105–27; Bernd Roeck, *Florenz 1900: Die Suche nach Arkadien* (Munich: Beck, 2001), pp. 229–41; Claudia Wedepohl, '"Wort und Bild": Aby Warburg als Sprachbildner', in Peter Kofler, ed., *Ekstatische Kunst – Besonnenes Wort: Aby Warburg und die Denkräume der Ekphrasis* (Bozen: Edition Sturzflüge, 2009), pp. 32–43; Silvia Contarini, '"Botticelli ritrovato": Frammenti di dialogo tra Aby Warburg e André Jolles', *Prospettiva* 68 (1992), pp. 87–93, and 'Nello specchio di van Eyck: Warburg, Jolles, Huizinga', *Intersezioni* XXI (August 2001), pp. 301–33.

4   Antoine Bodar, 'Clio en Melpomene herbeschouwd: Over de theorieën van Johan Huizinga en André Jolles', *Spektator* 16 (1986/87), pp. 407–20; Silvia Contarini, 'Huizinga, Jolles e la prosa nell'autunno del Medioevo', in Gian Maria Anselmi, ed., *Dal primato allo scacco: I modelli narrativi italiani tra Trecento e Seicento* (Rome: Carrocci, 1998), pp. 265–83, and 'Specchio'; Anton van der Lem, 'De Tovenaar André Jolles', in his *Johan Huizinga: Leven en werk in beelden & documenten* (Amsterdam: Wereldbibliotheek, 1993), pp. 193–210.

5   The book was released in October 1929, although the title page bears the date 1930. The final text was produced by Jolles in collaboration with two of his students, Elisabeth Kutzer and Otto Görner, who synthesized a rough, written version with their own precise notes from his lectures at Leipzig. Jolles is supposed to have destroyed the entire manuscript during the summer of 1929 in a fit of frustration with its rejection by a Dutch publisher; fortunately, Kutzer and Görner retained a second copy. See Ulrich Mölk, 'Bemerkungen zur Genese von André Jolles' Konzept der einfachen Form', in Michaela Weiß and Frauke Bayer, eds, *Einfache Form und kleine Literatur(en): Für Hinrich Hudde zum 65. Geburtstag* (Heidelberg: Universitätsverlag Winter, 2010), pp. 19–21; Walter Thys, 'Toelichting van de Vertaler', in André Jolles, *Eenvoudige vormen: legende, sage, mythe, raadsel, spreuk, casus, memorabile, sprookje, grap*, transl. Walter Thys (Delft: Eburon, 2009), pp. 22–5. I have omitted Kutzer and Görner's unsubstantial and somewhat fawning short foreword to *Simple Forms* from my translation.

Morphology of the Folktale (1928), with which it shares a debt to Goethe's ideas on morphology.[6]

The book's aim is to describe the nine elementary narrative structures underlying, as Jolles thought, all literary production: legend, saga, myth, riddle, saying, case, *memorabile*, fairy tale, and joke. He viewed these 'simple forms' as structuring principles operative in language before their 'actualization' in specific legends, sagas, fairy tales, and so on, or as components of more complex narrative types. Jolles construed each simple form as the reflection in language of a particular mode of human engagement with the world: the *legend* as a response to the human need for ideals of conduct; the *saga* as an approach to problems of family, blood ties, and inheritance; the *myth* as a form of cosmological inquiry; the *riddle* as a matter of social inclusion through sharing of special knowledge; the *saying* as a way of transmitting folk experience; the *case* as a form that relates human action to norms and values; the *memorabile* as a way of representing history in its concrete factuality; the *fairy tale* as an image of a just world unlike the real one; and the *joke* as a dissolution of what we find inadequate or reprehensible.[7]

Simple Forms (which is extensively discussed in specialist genre studies and in reflections on genre and narrative, though less in English than in other languages) has long been recognized as a classic of genre theory.[8] Critics have, however, made several objections to it: that it is grounded on a metaphysics of language inherited from German idealism or on indefensible anthropological presuppositions; that it has

---

6 Klaus W. Hempfer, *Gattungstheorie: Information und Synthese* (Munich: Wilhelm Fink, 1973), pp. 80–2; Jurij Striedter, *Literary Structure, Evolution and Value: Russian Formalism and Czech Structuralism Reconsidered* (Cambridge, MA: Harvard University Press, 1989), pp. 29, 54–5; K. Beekman, 'Over het klassificeren van genreconcepten: Propp's *Morfologija Skazki* en Jolles' *Einfache Formen*', in T. van Deel and Nico de Laan, eds, *Staalkaart: Opstellen over Letterkunde* (Amsterdam: Huis aan de Drie Grachten, 1984), pp. 9–18.

7 A good short summary of the book as a whole is provided in English in Robert Scholes, *Structuralism in Literature: An Introduction* (New Haven: Yale University Press, 1974), pp. 42–9.

8 The book is now in its eighth German edition (2010), and has been translated into French (1972, reprinted 1991), Spanish (1972), Portuguese (1976), Croatian (1978, reprinted 2000), twice into Italian (1980, retranslated 2003, reprinted 2008), twice into Japanese (1997, 1999), and most recently into Dutch (2009). On its translation history, see Thys, *Gebildeter Vagant*, 1,025–6, and 'Toelichting', 32–3.

been superseded by later theories; that its claim to comprehensiveness as a theory of literature is questionable; and that its descriptions of genres are vague or otherwise unsatisfactory.[9] On the other hand, several scholars, including Hans Robert Jauss, have defended Jolles or worked to develop his project,[10] while many genre specialists simply avail themselves of, or slightly modify, his definitions. The question of the work's value is complicated by Jolles's enthusiastic and principled decision to join the National Socialist German Workers' Party in May 1933, which was followed by years of active commitment to the reorganization of scholarship at Leipzig University along Nazi lines.[11]

According to Jauss, the main utility of Jolles's book lies not in its systematic conception – 'a conception not even represented rigorously by Jolles himself' – but in the heuristic value of its idea that the simple forms 'are not established in each period and all literatures, but rather can be conceived, exhausted, forgotten again, reconcretized, rearranged, and extended as an open class of possibilities' which 'can be selected, realized, or also not realized according to cultural codes and social conditions', thus allowing the researcher to infer 'the particularity of a period's and literature's cultural code from the particular historical constellation of the forms'.[12] This is made possible by the way Jolles derives each simple form

---

9   For balanced critical accounts of Jolles's theory and its reception, see Hermann Bausinger, 'Einfache Formen', in *Enzyklopädie des Märchens: Handwörterbuch zur historischen und vergleichenden Erzählforschung*, 15 vols (Berlin: De Gruyter, 1977–2015), vol. 3, pp. 1211–26; K. Beekman, '"Enkelvoudige vormen" en hun nawerking', *Spektator: Tijdschrift voor Neerlandistiek* 12: 5 (1982/83), pp. 329–44; Leander Petzoldt, *Dämonenfurcht und Göttervertrauen: Zur Geschichte und Erforschung unserer Volkssagen* (Darmstadt: Wissenschaftliche Buchgesellschaft, 1989), pp. 75–8.

10   See especially Hans Robert Jauss, 'The Alterity and Modernity of Medieval Literature', transl. Timothy Bahti, *New Literary History* 10: 2 (1979), pp. 181–229, and the revision of Jauss by Regula Rohland de Langbehn, 'La teoría de las "formas simples" de André Jolles (1874–1946): Una reconsideración', *Hispanic Research Journal* 3: 3 (2002), pp. 243–60; also Kurt Ranke, 'Einfache Formen', *Journal of the Folklore Institute* 4: 1 (June 1967), pp. 17–31; Rüdiger Zymner, ed., *Handbuch Gattungstheorie* (Stuttgart: Metzler, 2010), pp. 306–7; Michaela Weiß and Frauke Bayer, eds, *Einfache Form und kleine Literatur(en): Für Hinrich Hudde zum 65. Geburtstag* (Heidelberg: Universitätsverlag Winter, 2010); Walter A. Koch, ed., *Simple Forms: An Encyclopaedia of Simple Text-Types in Lore and Literature* (Bochum: Brockmeyer, 1994).

11   On Jolles's Nazism, see Thys, *Gebildeter Vagant*, pp. 4–7; Bodar, 'Schoonheidsleer van André Jolles', pp. 20–6; Hinskens, 'André Jolles'.

12   Jauss, 'Alterity and Modernity of Medieval Literature', pp. 213, 215.

from a particular mode of engagement with the world – from its characteristic *Geistesbeschäftigung* or 'mental disposition'. Legend, for instance,
arises from a *Geistesbeschäftigung* that he calls *imitatio* – a concern with
producing models of virtue for emulation, as a response to the human
need for ideals of conduct. The often historical figure about whom a
legend is made – such as a saint – is cast by the form as a model of virtuous
conduct. Jolles also constructs a reverse type, the 'anti-saint', with whom
the criterion of imitability appears as a warning *not* to imitate. Among the
saints we find for example St George, who originates in the age of
Diocletian in response to the persecution of Christians and is later transformed, in a Christianized Europe, from martyr to militant dragon-killer.
Among the anti-saints there is the figure of Faust, whose story appears
initially as legend (in the *Faustbuch* published by Johann Spies at Mainz in
1587 and its antecedent sources), but is then converted by Christopher
Marlowe into a tragedy (*Doctor Faustus*, c. 1592). In the *Faustbuch*, Faust's
damnation is clearly a warning. Not so with Marlowe, who pilfers an
English translation of Spies's text for the Faust material, but makes something different of it. Unlike the anonymous author of the *Faustbuch*,
Marlowe casts his protagonist not as a warning but as a paradigmatic
example of a moral and psychological conflict. Faust is no longer an *imitabile*: he has become, so to speak, a problem. Given this distinction, we can
read the *Faustbuch*'s ambivalence as a *symptom* of the conflict between
Renaissance religiosity and Renaissance humanism, and Marlowe's play as
a *thematization* of the same conflict. This formal shift can also help us
perceive the historical transition from a medieval cultural code amenable
to legend to a modern one more disposed to tragic form. These are useful
distinctions – and ones independent of metaphysics.[13]

   In the German context, the charge that Jolles's theory may be rooted in
an outdated metaphysics of culture or language, or in a dubious anthropology, necessarily resonates with the problem of his political commitment to National Socialism, despite the fact that his interest in Hitler

---

   13 'Jolles's antiquated metaphysics of language, which hypostasizes language as
a self-acting being, should not lead us to disregard the fact that in characterizing the
simple forms, he succeeds in showing how particular verbal gestures become subordinate to a unitary pattern, and that in this way he comes to grips with transphrastic
principles of organization that remain relatively concrete, unlike (for instance)
contemporary attempts to define the lyric genre.' Hempfer, *Gattungstheorie*, p. 166.

apparently postdates the book's publication by three years.[14] To begin with the metaphysics of Spirit: in its Hegelian usage, particularly, the Idealist concept of *Geist* (mind, intellect, spirit) has had negative overtones since the Second World War. The Nazis, in fact, had little official use for Hegel's philosophy.[15] But because the metaphysical postulate of the advance of Absolute Spirit through world history could all too easily be misapplied to the Third Reich as the supposed highest expression of the German *Weltgeist* (world spirit), the practice of *Geistesgeschichte*, or intellectual history understood as the manifestation of a collective human mind, spirit or intellect identified with a *Volk* or people, fell into disrepute after the war.[16] The question remains whether including the word *Geist* in *Geistesbeschäftigung* commits Jolles to *Geistesgeschichte*, to *völkisch* nationalism, or to a metaphysics of language or history. Although at least one commentator has identified the *Geistesbeschäftigung* as an 'objectively active force in the Hegelian sense',[17] the one overt reference to Hegel and *Geistesgeschichte* in *Simple Forms* is critical. Jolles seems to be fully aware of the methodological circularities involved in construing cultural artefacts as expressions of a World Spirit definable only in terms of such artefacts, and he distinguishes his own approach from this one.[18] Where he does cite a theoretician of *Geist* with approval,[19] it is not Hegel but a close

---

14   Thys, *Gebildeter Vagant*, p. 826.

15   'Hegel was rarely cited in the Nazi literature, and, when he was referred to, it was usually by way of disapproval.' Walter Kaufmann, 'The Hegel Myth and Its Method', in his *From Shakespeare to Existentialism* (Princeton: Princeton University Press, 1980), p. 104. On the incompatibility of Hegel's views on law and the state with Nazi ideology, see ibid., pp. 109–13. On the complex relationship of Hegel's philosophy to its political reception, see Ernst Cassirer, 'Hegel', *The Myth of the State* (New Haven: Yale University Press, 1946, pp. 248–76).

16   'Despite all the transformations of the concept of the spirit of a nation [*des Volksgeistbegriffes*], this category has survived as the indispensable means of interpretation in the human sciences [*geisteswissenschaftlicher Deutung*].' Hans Freyer, *Theory of Objective Mind: An Introduction to the Philosophy of Culture*, transl. and with an introduction by Steven Grosby (Athens, OH: Ohio University Press, 1998), p. 4; *Theorie des objektiven Geistes: Eine Einleitung in die Kulturphilosophie* (Leipzig: Teubner, 1923), p. 4. On the ideological taint adhering to *Geistesgeschichte*, see Max Wehrli, 'Was ist/war Geistesgeschichte?', in Christoph König and Eberhard Lämmert, eds, *Literaturwissenschaft und Geistesgeschichte 1910 bis 1925* (Frankfurt am Main: Fischer, 1993), p. 23.

17   Alfred Schlossig, cited in Hermann Bausinger, *Formen der 'Volkspoesie'*, 2nd edn (Berlin: Erich Schmidt, 1980), p. 62.

18   Jolles, *Simple Forms*, pp. 4–6.

19   Ibid., p. 9.

friend and colleague at Leipzig, the conservative sociologist Hans Freyer, whose theory of culture as 'objective mind' (*objektiver Geist*) rejects the teleological metaphysics of the Hegelian Absolute Spirit while still embracing the antimodernist reification of the *Volk* as historical agent characteristic of *Geistesgeschichte*.[20] Despite the fact that Jolles and Freyer were among the first German professors to join the NSDAP in 1933,[21] Jolles's thinking in the late 1920s diverges significantly from Freyer's on several key issues. *Simple Forms* does not make the chauvinistic distinction of 'culture' from 'civilization' so dear to interwar German romantic conservatives, among them both Freyer and Weimar's best-known morphologist of culture, Oswald Spengler.[22] Though it has been suggested that Jolles's morphological method may be indebted to Spengler, both the fact that he does not refer to Spengler in *Simple Forms* and his express agreement with Huizinga's merciless critique of the first volume of *The Decline of the West*

---

20   Jolles clearly owes a debt to Freyer's theory, as in the concept of *Bündigkeit* ('concision': 'a term for the automatic consolidation of elements of content in a creative process') – Ernst Cassirer, *Zur Metaphysik der symbolischen Formen. Nachgelassene Manuskripte und Texte*, vol. 1, ed. John Michael Krois and Oswald Schlemmer (Hamburg: Meiner, 1995), p. 356 n. 383 – and possibly also the idea of the 'objectivation of autonomous worlds out of any of the active ways of the mind' – Freyer, *Theory of Objective Mind*, p. 36. On Jolles and Freyer, see Antoine Bodar, 'De Schoonheidsleer van André Jolles', pp. 145–210. Although Freyer observes in 1923 that the metaphysical basis of Hegel's system 'is definitely shattered' and 'the charm of the dialectical method . . . irrecoverably exposed', still he advocates its application to scholarship 'as a formal model', and looks forward to the re-grounding of *Geisteswissenschaft* on a new metaphysics. Freyer, *Theory of Objective Mind*, pp. 12–14. See also Bodar, 'De Schoonheidsleer van André Jolles', p. 149. The term 'objective mind' originates with Georg Simmel. On Freyer's debt to Simmel, see Jerry Z. Muller, *The Other God that Failed: Hans Freyer and the Deradicalization of German Conservatism* (Princeton: Princeton University Press, 1987), pp. 46–9.

21   Muller, *The Other God that Failed*, p. 230.

22   Oswald Spengler, *Der Untergang des Abendlandes*, 2 vols (Munich: Beck, 1918–23). See Jeffrey Herf, *Reactionary Modernism: Technology, Culture, and Politics in Weimar and the Third Reich* (Cambridge: Cambridge University Press, 1984), pp. 49-69 (on Spengler), 122–9 (on Freyer). On Freyer, see also Muller, *The Other God that Failed*, pp. 88–100, esp. p. 96. Martin Jesinghausen-Lauster, *Die Suche nach der symbolischen Form: Der Kreis um die Kulturwissenschaftliche Bibliothek Warburg* (Baden-Baden: Valentin Koerner, 1985), pp. 246–8, reads Jolles's project as championing the *Kultur* of the simple forms over the *Zivilisation* of their actualizations, but it seems to me that Jolles does not *value* the simple forms over the latter; his aim is to distinguish them objectively.

(1918) suggest that the point is open to question.[23] Indeed, Jolles explicitly rejects the anthropomorphic hypostasis of national cultural forms as agents within an epochal model of history characteristic of Spengler.[24] In any case, the notion of 'objective mind' (or 'objective culture' – the term is originally Georg Simmel's) can theoretically be detached from metaphysics. For Simmel and Freyer, 'Objective mind' (or 'spirit') is what human intellect creates in the world, then must confront as a precondition for further activity: 'The spirit [*Geist*] produces countless constructs which continue to exist in a peculiar autonomy, independent of the soul that created them as well as of any of the others that accept or reject them.' Among such constructs we find language, art, literature, architecture, religion, law, states, technology, science, customs – in other words, everything that is the proper object of *geistesgeschichtliche* study.[25] These are all products of a collective cultural endeavour that need not necessarily be called *Geist*, identified with a *Volk*, or assigned a particular historical trajectory.[26]

---

23 Johan Huizinga, 'Twee Worstelaars met den Engel', *Verzamelde Werken* (Haarlem: Tjeenk Willink, 1948–53), vol. 4, pp. 441–96. See also Frank Ankersmit, *Meaning, Truth and Reference in Historical Representation* (Ithaca, NY: Cornell University Press, 2012), pp. 212–13. 'I have read your article on Spengler with pleasure; you do a good job of conveying the fluctuations of the soul [*ziele-schommelingen*] that we experience while reading it – also the seasickness caused by those fluctuations. It irritates me that the whole thing is so badly written.' Jolles to Huizinga, 19 June 1921, in Johan Huizinga, *Briefwisseling*, ed. Léon Hanssen, W. E. Krul and Anton van der Lem, 3 vols (Haarlem: Veen/Tjeenk Willink, 1989–91), vol. 1, p. 338. Antoine Bodar's argument regarding Jolles's debt to Spengler – 'Vorm en geestelijke occupatie', *Forum der Letteren: tijdschrift voor taal- en letterkunde* 24: 4 (December 1983), pp. 260–78 – is overwhelmingly circumstantial, and he simply disregards several explicit expressions of disapproval on Jolles's part despite citing them in his footnotes – for example, 'a real failure as a book, but don't you find that there is something to it?' Jolles to Huizinga, 12 January 1920, in Huizinga, *Briefwisseling*, vol. 1, p. 285. 'The book is causing quite a stir here [in Germany] and it is a peculiar symptom of the German mood at present. I should like to write a short piece about it . . . What is happening here is psychologically and culturally very remarkable, but it is anything but pleasant.' Jolles to Huizinga, 10 November 1919, in ibid., p. 273. This somewhat weakens Bodar's argument that Jolles and Huizinga 'always had a fundamentally different view of Spengler' (Bodar, 'Vorm en Geestelijke Occupatie', p. 267), without entirely confuting it.

24 Jolles, *Simple Forms*, p. 12.

25 Georg Simmel, 'The Concept and Tragedy of Culture', in David Frisby and Mike Featherstone, eds, *Simmel on Culture: Selected Writings* (London: Sage, 1997), p 55. See also Freyer, *Theory of Objective Mind*, pp. 17–18, 34.

26 It should be noted that Jolles displayed no clear signs of antisemitism in his

Jolles makes no secret of the romantic origins of his conception of simple forms as pre-literary structures arising autonomously within language itself, 'so to speak without the aid of a poet.'[27] In the Introduction to *Simple Forms*, he claims Johann Gottfried Herder, Johann Georg Hamann and Jacob Grimm, three main progenitors of German romantic linguistic theory, as ancestors of his own method of interpreting literary structure;[28] in the chapter on fairy tales, he maps the difference between simple forms and their literary actualizations directly onto Jacob Grimm's distinction between given tales as spontaneous creations of the folk soul and their actualizations as products of individual tale-tellers or poets.[29] There may also be an unspoken debt to Wilhelm von Humboldt's vision of language as humans' way of giving form to their world, and as a collective, autonomous ('objective') realm exercising constraints on human subjectivity.[30] This genealogy does not necessarily indicate *völkisch* sympathies,

---

letters or writings before October 1932. By January 1934, however, his strengthened allegiance to the regime would lead to a permanent break with his favourite daughter Jeltje, whose husband was Jewish. Before this – in October and November, 1932– we see three long letters to Jeltje on matters of race, *Volk*, religion, and 'das Judenproblem'. These deploy such an overkill of erudition to critique the dilettantism of Nazi racial theories – while at the same time accepting the differences they asserted, and ignoring their gravity for his daughter and her family – that one suspects an attempt to save intellectual face in a quickening descent into ideological compliance (Thys, *Gebildeter Vagant*, pp. 809–14). Shortly before their break, Jolles insists in a letter to Jeltje that his and his second family's commitment to National Socialism has little to do with antisemitism: 'For us the Third Reich means something completely different – antisemitism plays a minor role for us, and my personal attitude towards the few Jewish families that I know . . . hasn't changed' (ibid., p. 870). That 'minor role' is not quite what one could wish for – and other documents (such as a 1937 report to a dean at Leipzig describing the work of 'the Jews Gundolf and Strich' as 'immensely overrated'– ibid., p. 878) suggest that he could be antisemitic enough when the occasion called for it. See also Hinskens, 'André Jolles', p. 12.

27   Jolles, *Simple Forms*, p. 8.
28   Ibid., p. 8.
29   Ibid., p. 221–6.
30   On Jolles and Humboldt, see Silvia Contarini, 'Introduzione', in André Jolles, *I Travestimenti della letteratura: Saggi critici e teorici (1897-1932)* (Turin: Mondadori, 2003), p. xiii; Bausinger, 'Einfache Formen'; Michaela Weiß, 'Einleitung', in Weiß and Bayer, *Einfache Form und kleine Literatur(en)*, p. 8; Mölk, 'Bemerkungen zur Genese von André Jolles' Konzept der einfachen Form', pp. 32–5. On this aspect of Humboldt, see Hans Aarsleff, 'Wilhelm von Humboldt and the French *Idéologues*', in his *From Locke to Saussure: Essays on the Study of Language and Intellectual History* (Minneapolis: University of Minnesota Press, 1982), pp. 335–55, esp. pp. 343–5. See also Hans Aarsleff, 'Introduction', in Wilhelm von Humboldt, *On Language: The*

but it does lend substance to the idea that his theory is compromised by an understanding of 'language itself' as an agent of culture. 'In Jolles's meta-physics', Jurij Striedter observes, 'language is a being [*Wesen*]; for the [Russian] Formalists it is an array of instruments of a functional system . . . For Jolles, language is at work; for the Formalists, one works with language.'[31] This distinction reflects the ontological difference between Jolles's essentially Platonic conception of the morphological *Gestalt*[32] and the Formalists' concept of structure: 'Unlike the structure, the *Gestalt* is a real quality of the object independently of the knowing subject, an abso-lute, ideal essentiality that may certainly be combined with contingent factors in the historically concrete work, but which nonetheless consti-tutes its true essence.'[33] As Klaus Beekman remarks, 'giving essential defi-nitions belongs to an old-fashioned form of scholarship': the idea that 'the phenomena to be analysed have an essential character that it is the inves-tigator's task to establish' is problematic, thanks not least to the achieve-ments of post-Saussurean linguistics and structuralism.[34] Yet as Robert Scholes notes, although 'the Platonic thrust [of Jolles's method] is inescap-able . . . the simple forms themselves are not attributed by Jolles to any heaven of ideas. The forms are in the mind of man, of verbal man, that is, and emerge as his various ways of charging the world with meaning and value. They are necessary and ubiquitous forms of mental activity.'[35] It may thus be more accurate to call Jolles's method not metaphysical, but anthro-pological. With Jauss one could add that the notion that simple forms 'occur within language itself' describes 'a condition with which the philos-ophy of language and the sociology of knowledge are thoroughly familiar: that attitudes toward reality have the character of a preunderstanding

---

Diversity of Human Language-Structure and its Influence on the Mental Development of Mankind, transl. Peter Heath (Cambridge: Cambridge University Press, 1988), pp. vii–lxv, esp. pp. xxix–xxxi.

31 Striedter, *Literary Structure, Evolution and Value*, p. 54; Beekman, '"Enkelvoudige vormen" en hun nawerking', pp. 334–5.

32 Hempfer, *Gattungstheorie*, p. 82; Scholes, *Structuralism in Literature*, p. 43.

33 'The *Gestalten* are, in contrast to the structures . . . a reality of the object independent of the knowing subject – absolute, ideal entities that may well be bound up with contingent factors in the historically concrete work, but which are what constitute its true essence.' Hempfer, *Gattungstheorie*, p. 82.

34 Beekman, '"Enkelvoudige vormen" en hun nawerking', p. 340; Weiß, 'Einleitung', p. 8.

35 Scholes, *Structuralism in Literature*, p. 43.

resulting from prior experience taken in with the learning of one's native language, and that therefore they do not spring primarily from conscious selections'.[36] One could also simply observe that such conscious selections as human subjects make are predetermined, to a degree, by the linguistic and cultural forms – the 'objective culture' – available to them.

Regarding the theory's broader anthropological claims, it is certainly open to question what forms of mental activity are humanly 'necessary', whether 'forms of mental activity' are definable as such, and how universal the ones Jolles identifies may in fact be within Western culture or in world history generally.[37] Yet, to the extent that the book's descriptions of such activity ring true for a given culture, they may claim heuristic value. For Jauss, who understands 'the framework of traditional and non-canonical genres not as a logical classification, but as the literary system of a particular historical situation',[38] 'the great merit of the theory of simple forms is that it allows for the explanation of the implicit horizon of experience of such attitudes toward reality', and that it thus permits us to extrapolate from given historical constellations of the simple forms to 'particular styles of lived experience', or 'cognitive styles' that may characterize the worlds within which these constellations obtain.[39] By understanding the forms as answers to pressing cultural questions, the theory also allows us to use historically specific transformations of the forms as evidence for historical change in the cultures that pose those questions. Further, as Scholes remarks, there is some value in being reminded that literature, like any cultural product, originates in human needs, however difficult it may be to designate those needs or define their relationship to literature.[40]

---

36   Jauss, 'Alterity and Modernity of Medieval Literature', p. 213.

37   See for example Tzvetan Todorov, 'On Literary Genesis', transl. Ellen Burt, *Yale French Studies* 58 (1979), pp. 232–5.

38   Hans Robert Jauss, 'Theorie der Gattungen und Literatur des Mittelalters', in Hans Robert Jauss and Erich Köhler, eds, *Grundriss der romanischen Literaturen des Mittelalters. I: Généralités* (Heidelberg: Carl Winter, 1972), p. 118.

39   Jauss, 'Alterity and Modernity of Medieval Literature', p. 213. See also Petzoldt, *Dämonenfurcht und Göttervertrauen*, p. 75: 'If one regards Jolles's "simple forms" not as immutable categories but as basic forms of human attitudes toward reality, their heuristic value becomes visible.'

40   See Scholes, *Structuralism in Literature*, p. 50; also Ranke, 'Einfache Formen'.

The fact that Jolles's first recorded mention of Hitler occurs some three years after the publication of *Simple Forms* may suffice of itself to absolve his text of emphatic political implications.[41] One could add that his thinking on genre extends at least three decades back. As early as 1897, we find the inquiry into what he would later call 'simple forms' prefigured in a published lecture, 'Folklore and Art History' ('Folklore en Kunstwetenschap'). Here, in a text whose anthropological interest has been understood as a response to his friend Aby Warburg's travels of 1895–96 among the Hopi in the American Southwest,[42] Jolles already names six of the nine forms discussed in *Simple Forms* (myth, fairy tale, saga, legend, riddle, saying), defines the relationship of 'concept' to 'image' in art and literature in analogy to the relationship of question to answer that he will explore in the book's chapter on myth, and formulates a description *avant la lettre* of what he will later term 'verbal gestures'.[43] Meanwhile, the lecture's concern with the relationship between words and images and between art and literature raises the question of how much the method of *Simple Forms* may owe

---

41 Jolles's first recorded mention of Hitler (whose name he misspells 'Hittler'), in a letter of February 1933 about the elections in March, is both emphatic and noncommittal: 'Politics? – Yes, I'll vote Hitler again. If there is a party that claims that it can lead Germany, and a man who claims that he knows what he wants, then I for my part am prepared to give him a chance. This is very subjective; very sceptical – and it is happening in the conviction that my vote is worth very little.' The word 'again' suggests an earlier vote for Hitler, in the election of November 1932 (Thys, *Gebildeter Vagant*, p. 826). Jolles's remark in a letter to Huizinga of 22 June 1931 that his lectures on 'the concept of literary content and psychoanalysis' were currently much in vogue with the 'Hakenkreuzler' because he was 'throwing the last remains of Freud in the trash' – following as it did on the quip that his six-month-old daughter Eva Gertrud 'is so blond and "Germanic" that one could take her for a "timely antisemitic demonstration"' – is uncomfortable, to say the least, but hard to interpret definitively (Huizinga, *Briefwisseling*, vol. 2, p. 337).

42 'The reflections at the centre of the book of 1930 developed originally in contact with Warburgian intuitions regarding survivals, symbols and images, which Jolles transfers without difficulty to the tradition of [Wilhelm von] Humboldt's linguistic anthropology.' Contarini, 'Introduzione', pp. xvi–xviii, at p. xviii. See also Silvia Contarini, 'Tra folklore e scienza dell'arte; le forme del mito in André Jolles', in Marco Bertozzi, ed., *Aby Warburg e le metamorfosi degli antichi dei* (Modena: Franco Cosimo Panini, 2002), pp. 153–72, and Contarini, 'Specchio', pp. 331–2.

43 André Jolles, 'Folk-lore en Kunstwetenschap', *De Kroniek*, 1897 (11 July, 18 July, 25 July, 1 August, 8 August), pp. 252, 237, 229. See also Mölk, 'Bemerkungen zur Genese von André Jolles' Konzept der einfachen Form'.

to the discipline of art history, and to interactions with Warburg in particular. Silvia Contarini has traced the origins of Jolles's project of a morphology of late medieval and Renaissance genres to essays of the early 1920s on Boccaccio and the novella whose methodological centre harks back in turn to discussions with Warburg, around 1900, of Boccaccio, Ghirlandaio, Giotto and Botticelli, and especially to the fictitious correspondence between the two men on the recurrence of the 'nymph' type in Renaissance art.[44] This exchange, long recognized as the original seedbed of Warburg's signature concept, the 'pathos formula', left clear traces in Jolles's thinking as well. According to Warburg's biographer E. H. Gombrich, the impetus for the exchange was likely an observation by Hippolyte Taine comparing the posture of two female figures in Ghirlandaio's *Birth of St John the Baptist*, in the Tuornabuoni chapel of Santa Maria Novella in Florence. Taine had noted a difference in style between what he called 'a middle-aged duchess' (probably Giovanna degli Albizzi) – a 'somewhat bourgeois' figure type, 'dry [and] lacking in grandeur' – and, beside her, erotically energized, 'the servant girl bringing fruit, wearing the robe of a statue, with the *élan*, the *allégresse*, the force of an ancient nymph'.[45] In their correspondence, Warburg and Jolles elaborate on this perception of difference, Jolles remarking upon the servant-girl's 'extremely animated way of walking', on the length of her stride, on a special quality of her relationship to the floor, and suggesting an origin of her type in classical or pre-classical antiquity and its proliferation in Renaissance art, Warburg interpreting these qualities within the context of Renaissance social pretensions and networks of patronage.[46] Over the next few years, Warburg would come to understand the recurrence of the 'nymph' type in Renaissance art (Ghirlandaio, Botticelli, Filippo Lippi, Baccio Baldini) as the renewal of an ancient trope to serve present purposes, as an acceptably classical visual 'formula' for smuggling the

---

44   Silvia Contarini, 'Gesti verbali: Jolles lettore di *Decamerone* VI: 9', Antonio Ferracin and Matteo Venier, eds, *Giovanni Boccaccio: tradizione, interpretatione e fortuna. In ricordo di Vittore Branca* (Udine: Forum, 2014), p. 230.

45   Gombrich, *Aby Warburg*, p. 106, citing Hippolyte Taine, *Voyage en Italie*; Jean Cadogan, *Domenico Ghirlandaio: Artist and Artisan* (New Haven: Yale University Press, 2000), p. 243.

46   Gombrich, *Aby Warburg*, pp. 105–27; Thys, *Gebildeter Vagant*, pp. 218–24.

pathos of a new ethos of worldly aspiration and pleasure into an older institutional context: 'The lively gesture; antiquity has permitted it.'[47] In a lecture of 1904, Jolles uses a similar model to distinguish successive phases of style in Renaissance music, sculpture and painting, arguing that secular melody originates from variations on a liturgical musical figure, the neuma; secular sculpture from the carved ornament on the capitals of Romanesque church columns; and certain gestures of mourning in Giotto's *Lamentation of Christ* in the Scrovegni Chapel in Padova (c. 1305) from an 'ancient gesture' or 'hieroglyph' of pain (*antike Schmerzgebärde, Hieroglyphe des Schmerzes*) transmitted through the relief sculptures of Nicola Pisano's pulpit of 1260 for the Duomo in Pisa.[48] In a Warburgian vein, he asserts that 'Pisano adopts a motif that he knew from his medieval predecessors, but breathes new life into it by falling back on an ancient model.'[49]

In 1921, Jolles applied a similar logic in an essay on Boccaccio's *Decameron* (VI, 9), to an anecdote in which Guido Cavalcanti, a leading light of Renaissance science and poetry, 'by a quip meetly rebukes certain Florentine gentlemen who had taken him at a disadvantage'. Cornered amidst ancient marble tombs near the baptistery of San Giovanni by a group of noblemen bent on affronting him for having flouted their company and for being rumoured an Epicurean, Cavalcanti escapes with what Jolles will eventually call a 'verbal gesture' (*Sprachgebärde*).[50]

'Guido', they began, 'you spurn our company; but supposing you find that God doesn't exist, what good will it do you?'

Finding himself surrounded, Guido promptly replied:

'Gentlemen, in your own house you may say whatever you like to me.'

Then, placing a hand on one of the tombstones, which were very tall, he vaulted over the top of it, being very light and nimble, and landed on the other side, whence, having escaped from their clutches, he proceeded on his way.

---

47   Warburg cited in Gombrich, *Aby Warburg*, p. 122.
48   André Jolles, *Zur Deutung des Begriffes Naturwahrheit in der bildenden Kunst* (Freiburg im Breisgau: Troemer, 1905), pp. 26–7, 32–43.
49   Ibid., p. 36.
50   Jolles, *Simple Forms*, p. 35.

Betto and his companions were left staring at one another, then they began to declare that he was out of his mind, and that his remark was meaningless, because neither they themselves nor any of the other citizens, Guido included, owned the ground on which their horses were standing. But Messer Betto turned to them, and said:

'You're the ones who are out of your minds, if you can't see what he meant. In a few words he has neatly paid us the most backhanded compliment I ever heard, because when you come to consider it, these tombs are the houses of the dead, this being the place where the dead are laid to rest and where they take up their abode. By describing it as our house, he wanted to show us that, by comparison with himself and other men of learning, all men who are as uncouth and unlettered as ourselves are worse off than the dead. So that, being in a graveyard, we are in our own house.'

Now that Guido's meaning had been pointed out to them, they all felt suitably abashed, and they never taunted him again. And from that day forth, they looked upon Messer Betto as a paragon of shrewdness and intelligence.[51]

Like the Warburgian *Pathosformel*, the 'verbal gesture' of Guido's leap enables a modern mind to defend itself against reprimand by an older world whose codes it is wilfully violating. Jolles interprets this anecdote not only as an account of 'the first and the oldest war-cry of the generation that felt it had been reborn, [as] the earliest proof of a self-conscious Rinascimento, of a new life' – with Cavalcanti, 'a man aware that he has put one era behind him and that another has begun', informing the Florentine cavaliers that their courtly code of manners is effectively dead – but also as a first instance of a new literary form, the *facezia* or witticism, which Jolles defines as 'an anecdote in which one or another utterance is preserved of a *homo facetus*', of a man versed in the art of giving a cutting answer. As in the visual arts, 'the new form reveals itself simultaneously with the new content';[52] like

---

51 Giovanni Boccaccio, *The Decameron*, transl. and with an introduction and notes by G. H. McWilliam, 2nd edn (Harmondsworth: Penguin, 2003), p. 468.

52 André Jolles, 'De Facetie van Guido Cavalcanti', in his *Bezieling en Vorm: Essays over Letterkunde* (Haarlem: Tjeenk Willink, 1923), pp. 3, 5, 12, 14.

melody, secular sculpture and the derivative gestural innovations of Giotto, both the *facezia* and the novella come into their own as forms when Renaissance culture requires them to express the new values of cleverness, humanism, individual initiative, physical pleasure.

Like Ghirlandaio's nymph and his bourgeois matron for Warburg, characters in literature function for Jolles distinctively and meaningfully within their forms. As he observes in his chapter on fairy tales, '[I]f one sets a fairy tale princess next to a princess from a novella, one senses the difference'.[53] Likewise, the Faust of tragedy differs, as I have noted, from the Faust of legend. I would suggest that if one sets Marlowe's or Goethe's Mephistopheles next to the Vice of the English moralities on which he is based, one also senses the difference. One figure is moral – the Vice; the other, Marlowe's Mephistopheles, is psychological, and no longer categorically evil.[54] In a sense, once the Devil slips from his sources in legend (the *Faustbuch*) and allegory (the moralities) into tragedy (Marlowe, Goethe), he ceases to be what the Middle Ages knew as the Devil: he has become an acceptably traditional formula for smuggling the pathos of a new ethos of worldly aspiration and pleasure into an older institutional context.

This brings us to a practical limitation of Jolles's theory. The book states explicitly that the simple forms never appear in the world *as texts* – that, for example, the simple form 'legend' is only ever concrete as the literary 'art form' of the *vita*, as the life of a given saint: 'What we call the vita of Saint George ... is the realization of a possibility given and contained in the legend. Using Scholastic terminology, we could say that what is present in legend *potentialiter* (potentially) is given *actualiter* (actually) in the vita.'[55] How are we then to understand the relationship of the simple forms to the 'literary' forms that develop out of them? How can we speak of the difference of legend from tragedy, when 'legend' is a simple form and 'tragedy' is not, or of the relationship of the novella to, say, the fairy tale – which some critics protest is too complex a genre to

---

53 Jolles, *Simple Forms,* p. 190.

54 Cf. Douglas Cole, '*Doctor Faustus*: Tragedy in the Allegorical Tradition,' *Christopher Marlowe and the Renaissance of Tragedy* (Westport, CT: Greenwood Press, 1995), pp. 121–47.

55 Jolles, *Simple Forms,* p. 36.

be called a 'simple form'?[56] Jolles explores such questions only in passing, most notably in the chapters on 'fairy tale' (related to tragedy) and 'case' (a chapter derived from earlier work on Boccaccio and the novella). In his last chapter, 'Perspectives', he expresses the aim of writing another book to address the *Kunstformen* ('forms of art', 'literary forms'), a project that never came to fruition. We are left to extrapolate. The relationship might perhaps be grasped in analogy to Ferdinand de Saussure's distinction between *langue* and *parole*, where language (*langue*) is understood as the conventional system of abstract principles that makes individual acts of speech (*parole*) possible.[57] Extending Saussure to the semiotic study of complex texts, Roman Jakobson construed an analogous difference between 'code' and 'message', and A. J. Greimas a difference between 'system' and 'process', while Claude Lévi-Strauss found in myth a 'third level', an antecedent pattern of meaning, beyond *langue* and *parole*.[58] This – in addition to Propp – is the sort of work of which Jolles's is often considered a somewhat inadequate forerunner or outlier.[59] Yet the comparison may be invidious, or at least misleading.

---

56   See Bausinger, *Formen der 'Volkspoesie'*, pp. 122–3.

57   Ferdinand de Saussure, *Course in General Linguistics*, ed. Charles Bally and Albert Sechehaye, with the collaboration of Albert Riedlinger, transl. Roy Harris (La Salle, IL: Open Court, 1986), pp. 18–20 [*Cours de linguistique générale (CLG)* 36–9]. Indeed, both Jolles and Saussure use a chess metaphor to make the distinction, although the metaphor may be inadequate in both cases. Saussure states that 'a state of the board in chess corresponds exactly to a state of the language. The value of the chess pieces depends on their position upon the chess board, just as in the language each term has its value through its contrast with all the other terms ... A language is a system in which all the elements fit together, and in which the value of any one element depends on the simultaneous coexistence of all the others ... Signs thus function not according to their intrinsic value but in virtue of their relative position.' Saussure, *Course in General Linguistics*, pp. 88, 113, 116 [*CLG* 125–6, 159, 164]. For Jolles, in any given 'actualization' of a form, 'a form is doubly present, one mode relating to the other like a chess problem to its solution. The problem contains and presents a possibility; the solution realizes this possibility with a specific event' (*Simple Forms*, p. 36). For a critique of Saussure's use of the chess metaphor, see Fredric Jameson, *The Prison-House of Language: A Critical Account of Structuralism and Russian Formalism* (Princeton: Princeton University Press, 1972), pp. 21–2.

58   John Phillips and Chrissie Tan, 'Langue and Parole', in *The Literary Encyclopedia*, first published 8 February 2005, available at litencyc.com; Claude Lévi-Strauss, 'The Structural Study of Myth', in his *Structural Anthropology*, transl. Claire Jacobson and Brooke Grundfest Schoepf (New York: Basic Books, 1963), pp. 206–31. Petzoldt relates Jolles's approach to Jakobson's mapping the difference between 'folklore' and 'literature' onto that between 'langue' and 'parole' (*Dämonenfurcht und Göttervertrauen*, p. 72).

59   See, for example, Striedter, *Literary Structure, Evolution and Value*, pp.

On the one hand, the art-historical provenance of Jolles's conception of literary forms may help explain why his theory does not always
sit well with scholars of literature, or within a historiography of literary
criticism that centrally includes Saussure and his followers; on the
other, it can be tempting to overlook what a theory may offer by
concentrating on its defects.

> It is precisely the implicit relationship between Warburg's intuitions and
> the study of the *Simple Forms* – a context foreign to the horizons of struc-
> turalism, to which [Jolles's] book is often anachronistically compared,
> evoking instead a subterranean dialogue with the psychology of art of the
> turn of the twentieth century – that accounts for the difficulty modern
> exegetes have in taking formulas like that of the 'verbal gesture' literally.[60]

Beyond the connection to Warburg, Jolles's thinking on literary form may
also be modelled upon the treatment of the classical orders of Greek architecture in his 1906 dissertation on Vitruvius;[61] in a book review of 1923, he
observes that the terms for period styles applied to the arts in general
(Byzantine, Romanesque, Gothic, Renaissance, Baroque, Rococo) were all
applied initially to architectural forms and then adapted to the other arts.[62]
In his habilitation thesis of 1908 on Egyptian–Mycenean ornamental
vases,[63] one senses an unspoken debt to the Viennese art historian Alois
Riegl, whose arguments regarding ancient vegetal ornament, sculpture

54–5; Hempfer, *Gattungstheorie*, pp. 80–2; Beekman, '"Enkelvoudige vormen" en
hun nawerking', pp. 334–7. On Jolles and Propp, see also Beekman, 'Over het klassificeren van genreconcepten'.

60   Contarini, 'Gesti Verbali', p. 235.

61   André Jolles, *Vitruvs Aesthetik* (Freiburg im Breisgau: C. A. Wagner, 1906).
See also Bodar, 'Schoonheidsleer van André Jolles', pp. 42–4.

62   André Jolles, 'Kunsthistorische Methoden. Dr A. Pit, *Denken en Beelden*
(Amsterdam, Encyclopaedie van de Wereldbibliotheek, 1922).' *De Gids* 87: 1 (1923),
p. 312. See also André Jolles, 'De *Decamerone* van Boccaccio', in *Bezieling en Vorm*:
'Although literature is reborn ever anew in each single writer and for every people,
still it includes a series of forms that are passed down from person to person and
from people to people, and Antiquity has contributed by far the most to this treasure.
If the Romanesque architect worked continually with ancient motifs and details, the
writers who were his contemporaries did no differently' (p. 75).

63   André Jolles, 'Die ägyptisch-mykenischen Prunkgefässe', *Jahrbuch des
Kaiserlich Deutschen Archäologischen Instituts* XXIII: 4 (1908), pp. 209–50.

and metalwork (*Problems of Style*, 1893; *Late Roman Art Industry*, 1901) also influenced Walter Benjamin's work on German baroque tragic drama (1928).[64] Indeed, Riegl's concept of the *Kunstwollen* – 'an artistic will or urge or intent informing different period styles'[65] – so much resembles both Jolles's concept of the *Geistesbeschäftigung* and Warburg's of the *Pathosformel* that one suspects a connection, despite the fact that Jolles nowhere mentions Riegl by name. All three concepts seek to designate the prime mover in a morphology of collective cultural development, and all three understand this *movens* as a function of what Simmel called 'objective mind': as an expression of human creative intellect working within and against given cultural constraints.[66] This permits us to situate Jolles's method within a transdisciplinary discourse on the historicity of forms and styles that characterized his historical moment, and to which the many cultural morphologies of the 1920s were a response.[67]

---

64 Georges Didi-Huberman, *Devant le temps: Histoire d'art et anachronisme des images* (Paris: Éditions de Minuit, 2000), pp. 90, 101–2; Andrea Pinotti, *Il Corpo dello Stile: Storia dell'arte come storia dell'estetica a partire da Semper, Riegl, Wölfflin* (Milan: Mimesis, 2001).

65 Margaret Iversen, *Alois Riegl: Art History and Theory* (Cambridge, MA: MIT Press, 1993), p. 6.

66 Silvia Contarini ('Una Forma artistica', 122-3) supposes the connection to Riegl (as well as one to Wilhelm Worringer), but does not prove it. Contarini, 'Una forma artistica: Jolles e la teoria della novella', in Gian Maria Anselmi, Giovanni Baffetti, Carlo Delcorno and Sebastiana Nobili, eds, *Boccaccio e i suoi lettori: una lunga ricezione* (Bologna: Il Mulino, 2013), pp. 109–27. See also Hans Sedlmayr, 'Einleitung' [Introduction], in Alois Riegl, *Gesammelte Aufsätze* (Augsburg: Filser, 1929), esp. p. xviii; Silvia Ferretti, *Cassirer, Panofsky and Warburg: Symbol, Art and History*, transl. Richard Pierce (New Haven: Yale University Press, 1989), p. 179; Ezio Raimondi, 'Warburg, Justi e la "prima sostanza"', in Marco Bertozzi, ed., *Aby Warburg e le metamorfosi degli antichi dei* (Modena: Franco Cosimo Panini, 2002), pp. 86–98.

67 For example, Spengler's morphology of history, Propp's and Jolles's of literature, and the photographer Karl Blossfeldt's of the 'Urformen der Kunst' (*Art Forms in Nature*, 1928). See also Walter Benjamin's 'Arcades Project' (1927–1940) and Warburg's 'Mnemosyne Atlas' (1924–29). On Blossfeldt and Benjamin, see Didi-Huberman, *Devant le temps*, pp. 128–55. On Warburg's work as a morphology, see Pinotti, *Memorie del Neutro: Morfologia dell'immagine in Aby Warburg* (Milan: Mimesis, 2001). As Jost Hermand has shown, the revolt of the *Geisteswissenschaften* against positivism and disciplinary specialization in the period 1900–30 produced a new methodological symbiosis between the study of art and the study of literature, of which Warburg's 'science of culture' (*Kulturwissenschaft*), Huizinga's 'cultural history' (*cultuurgeschiedenis*), and Jolles's disciplinary border-crossing are all good examples. Hermand remarks that art history tended to take a leading role, partly because the discipline was by its nature more international than the more nationally oriented study of literature,

Although Jolles's theory is necessarily bound to the time and milieu of its origin, it also transcends that milieu, as I hope to have shown. The last eighty-five years have certainly proved its usefulness to scholarship; the book has been in print continuously in German since 1929, and it continues to be cited in work in many languages. In a letter of 1980, the German philosopher Hans-Georg Gadamer, who in a report of 11 May 1945 had evaluated his colleague at Leipzig as an old party member and a staunch National Socialist, observed nonetheless: 'His book *Simple Forms* can be counted among the standard works of scholarship. There can be no doubt about that.'[68] With one of the book's first reviewers, Robert Petsch – who did not pull his punches – I feel I can add: 'We can raise certain objections to the selection, definition and grouping of the individual forms that Jolles investigates, but there is no section of the book that we have not read without great profit.'[69] It is my hope that readers of this English translation, by all accounts long overdue, will agree.

I would like to express my gratitude to Will Waters, Nancy Bradbury, and Eric Wirth and the *PMLA* editorial staff for checking various parts of the translation, to James Uden for help with Greek and Latin, to Silvia Beier, Silvia Contarini, Carlo Ginzburg, James Schmidt, Keith Vincent, and Claudia Wedepohl for their helpful comments on drafts of the introduction, to Geertjan de Vugt for rare Jolles material, to Emilie Bickerton, Mark Martin, Charles Peyton and Duncan Ranslem for able copy-editing and proofreading, and to Sebastian Budgen, Johannes Endres, Fredric Jameson, Wolfgang Mieder, Elizabeth Powers, Anthony Spalinger and Walter Thys for their encouragement. Part of the chapter on 'Legend' first appeared in André Jolles, 'Legend', transl. Peter J. Schwartz, *PMLA* 128, No. 3 (May 2013), pp. 728–43.

Peter J. Schwartz
Boston, 30 August 2015

---

and partly 'because here the question of form and style analysis simultaneously includes the problem of dating, which plays only a subordinate role in literary scholarship'. Jost Hermand, *Literaturwissenschaft und Kunstwissenschaft: Methodische Wechselbeziehungen seit 1900*, 2nd edn (Stuttgart: Metzler, 1971), esp. p. 12.

68 Evaluation of 11 June 1945, in Thys, *Gebildeter Vagant*, p. 911; letter of 1980 to Antoine Bodar, in Thys, 'Toelichting van de Vertaler', p. 12.

69 Robert Petsch, 'Die Lehre von den "Einfachen Formen"', *Deutsche Vierteljahrs schrift* 10 (1932), p. 337.

Introduction

I. THE THREE ORIENTATIONS OF LITERARY CRITICISM
– BEAUTY, MEANING, STRUCTURE

Literary criticism has a threefold orientation. Using a somewhat outdated terminology, we could say that its three basic tasks are aesthetic, historical and morphological. Or, to put the matter more plainly: literary criticism undertakes to interpret literary phenomena with regard to their *beauty*, *meaning* and *structure*.

Now, even if these three are meant to form a trinity, still the motto holds: march separately, strike together. In other words: even if these three approaches are best used in concert to grasp the literary phenomenon in its totality, still each operates according to its own method.

To judge from the history of literary criticism, it would also seem that each method has sometimes been inclined to usurp hegemony for itself.

One part of eighteenth-century literary criticism was primarily aesthetic in character; from Christian Wolff to Immanuel Kant and in all parts of Europe, it joined in the currents and countercurrents that shaped the 'doctrine of the Beautiful' during this era. If we disregard its general speculations concerning the nature of beauty and restrict ourselves to what was asserted about the invention, judgment and classification of the Beautiful, we can say that the aesthetic approach – or, since here a plural seems apposite, the aesthetic schools – gave us the science of genre criticism. With diligence and acuity, its proponents explored the aesthetic laws and effects of the lyric, epic, dramatic and didactic genres; within these main genres they attempted to differentiate and define the subgenres of elegy and ode, epic and novel, comedy and tragedy, didactic poem and epigram, and many others, again from an aesthetic perspective. There was no lack of critiques of their method. Some said they proceeded deductively: instead of beginning by studying works of art to arrive at insights into the nature of art, they had established their principles purely through speculation and then applied them to the facts afterward. Others reproached them with being too much men of the Enlightenment: they had failed to appreciate the irrational in art, viewing even 'poetic creativity' as a mode of thought and granting 'reason' the highest authority in matters of aesthetic judgment.

I shall not ask to what extent such reproaches identify real weaknesses of the method itself, nor to what degree they depend on a misunderstanding that the proponents of another approach, another method, seem unable to avoid. It will be more useful to note that, despite their reciprocal polemics, the eighteenth-century aesthetes made a remarkable attempt to adapt a tradition of art theory with roots in antiquity to the mentality of a new era, and that by making the effort to define certain genre concepts and describe the aesthetic significance of these genres, they helped the progress not only of literary criticism but also of literature.

For there is another thing we should not forget: in every one of its schools, the aesthetic literary criticism of the eighteenth century was firmly convinced that its theories could and should exert an active influence on life – in this case, on contemporary art. What was sought after by Gottsched and the Swiss, by the Scots and the English, by Marmontel and the Encyclopedists in France, and by Johann Adolf and Johann Elias Schlegel, Mendelssohn, Lessing, Sulzer and many others in Germany, each in his own way, was finally always a serviceable poetics, a binding system of poetic art, which – however arrived at – could in any case claim validity for developing a national canon of poetry in the present.

Besides this pragmatic aesthetics we find – also already in the eighteenth century – a hermeneutic type of literary criticism whose goal is to explain the *meaning* of works of art; its fundamental idea is the concept of *genius*, as is well known. The beginnings of this approach can be found in the Renaissance, but it does not fully flourish until the early romantics. It opposes an *ars poetica* to an *ars poetae*, or poetics to the poet. 'Poet' is the epitome of all genius; poetry means creation by genius. Genius is 'a natural inborn spiritual talent that surpasses the normal in every respect; it can neither be learned nor acquired'. In genius, inventive fantasy and original creative power converge in such a way and to such a degree that, for the activity of genius, only the term 'creation', in the deepest sense, seems adequate. Certainly, to finish an object begotten with intuitive creativity requires reflection, method and practice, but perfect natural ability remains the primary and essential condition. The work of art acquires its meaning through the act of the genius, just as the world acquires its meaning through the act of its Creator.

This is not the place to trace the development of the concept of genius. But because it is a matter of some significance in the history of literary-critical method, we will mention that although in Germany we are inclined to believe that this concept took definitive shape in the period known, correctly or not, as the *Sturm und Drang*, in fact England is where we can best observe its uniform and continuous development: that is, along a trajectory from Shaftesbury to Shelley. In the nineteenth century, moving from England through France, the concept of genius affected European thinking in general, and with it the practice of literary criticism – an influence that has continued into the twentieth century. Shelley's assertion that the poet is 'the happiest, the best, the wisest and the most illustrious of men' has survived many a statement on genius made by Goethe when he was young, ideas long outgrown by the older Goethe himself.

Be that as it may, if we are to draw a methodological conclusion from the notion of genius, then it is this: that the mission of literary criticism is to place these individuals, with their sublime, elemental ability and their matchless accomplishments – creators with their crea-tions – into an ordered *historical* series. It is well known that the liter-ary historians of the nineteenth century did in fact draw this conclu-sion. We need only open any handbook of literary history to see that what we have there is a history of poets and their poetry, a historical succession of poets' biographies, in which the poetic achievements are then also ordered historically.

This method escaped the danger of superficiality thanks to its close connection with the other historical and historico-cultural disciplines then evolving everywhere. At the same time, however, its basic thesis – that the poet is a genius, a creator solely responsible for a unique work of art – was weakened by this connection. Increasingly, the historical poet became a man among men – and precisely the question of man's responsibility for what he makes has been one of the most daunting problems of positivism. It is remarkable to witness the drama of an individualistic era robbing the individual of the essential elements of his individuality – a show that we can enjoy to its full extent in the notion of the 'poet as a man among men'. The curve that ascends from Shaftesbury through to the *Sturm und Drang* or to Shelley then descends by strange twists and turns from Shelley to Hippolyte Taine. We need not describe these flourishes in detail. Suffice it to say that the era strove to define works of literary art historically, sociologically and psychologically, but the path to such definition still passed through the maker of works of literary art. The poet was, as a man, a product of race, of milieu, of time and heredity, of economic and other circumstances; a thousand currents of the past and the present worked upon him, transformed him, undermined him, and thus the conditions of his artistic production were to be sought in the multiple contingencies of his situation as a human being. If we explain the man – so the logic went – if we regard him as a son of his parents, as a descendant of his ancestors, as a child of his time, brought forth by a milieu and subject to the influence of circumstances; if beyond that we analyse him psychologically and observe how, with his intricate and contingent constitution, he reacts to external events, then we have explained the genesis of his works of art. On such a logic, however, these works of art could appear little more than the expression, by an exceptional talent, of all the historical and cultural currents flowing through a particular individual.

Meanwhile, the conviction arose once again that a work of art, a great literary work, should represent something different from and spiritually greater than all this. 'Phenomenology of Spirit' was the call of a man whose voice was not that of one crying in the wilderness.[1]

---

1   The reference is to G. W. F. Hegel's *Phenomenology of Spirit* (*Phänomenologie des Geistes*, 1807), and to John the Baptist (quoting Isaiah 40:3): 'I am the voice of our crying out in the wilderness, "make straight the way of the Lord"' (John 1:23; also Mark 1:3). [Translator's note: This and all subsequent footnotes are my own, and are intended for clarification of contexts less familiar to today's English-speaking readers than to the book's original audience; there are no footnotes in the original text.]

The philosophy of Spirit, the study of the principles of intellectual life, of the nature of Spirit and its products, of intellectual creation, of spiritual values and purposes, also made itself felt in the way people thought about literary works. An effort was made to interpret individual poetic works sympathetically, as part of a spiritual process, while literary art was wholly included in the history of Spirit. However, this method as well led not to the separate study of the literary work and of its creator, but to a peculiar transposition: the writer's life and character were no longer adduced to explain his achievements, but rather they were deduced from, and explained by, the work's intellectual significance. In a certain sense, this was the opposite pole to everything that had been implied in the concept of genius, but this pole was reached in a way that did not require any great methodological change. Whether the method of explanation begins with the writer and his work or with the work and its writer: either way, it regards this matching dyad as the 'historical' object of its research. It also distinguishes itself from a pragmatic aesthetics by remaining 'purely scholarly' from beginning to end – in so far as it manages to avoid degenerating into dilettantism. Unlike the aestheticians of the eighteenth century, its proponents – for all their differences of opinion – never believed that they could exert any influence on the progress of living literary art; nor did they ever attempt to do so.

Slowly, alongside these two approaches, the third became conscious of its mission and set out to conquer a method for itself.

'The Germans have a word for the complex of existence presented by a physical organism: *Gestalt* [structured form]. With this expression they exclude what is changeable and assume that an interrelated whole is identified, defined, and fixed in character.'[2]

We can posit this sentence from Goethe's writings on morphology as a foundation for morphology's mission within the field of literary as well as biological science. For the sum of all literary phenomena, too, it can be said that the *Gestalt* to be produced, the 'typically definite

---

2 Johann Wolfgang von Goethe, 'The Purpose Set Forth (from *On Morphology)*', *Scientific Studies*, ed. and transl. Douglas Miller (New York: Suhrkamp, 1988), p. 63.

morphological manifestation of things', is 'the effective power in all that occurs' (G. Simmel).[3]

By likewise excluding everything that is temporally contingent or individually mutable in the realm of literature, understood in the broadest sense, we can isolate and define this structure and recognize its fixed character. With each individual work of literary art, we can ask to what extent the forces that limit form and establish structure have produced a recognizable and distinct entity, to what degree a structure has become realized in a definitive manner. With respect to the totality of all literary art, we raise the question: To what extent might the totality of all known and definable forms constitute a unified, fundamentally ordered, internally coherent and structured whole – a system?

The mission of this approach is determination of forms, interpretation of *Gestalt*.

The aim of the following chapters is to apply this approach experimentally to a particular range of literary phenomena.

II. LANGUAGE AND LITERATURE

We have already seen that, in their analyses, both the aesthetic and the hermeneutic methods proceeded principally from the completed literary work of art; that they usually recognized 'poetry' only where it had achieved a singular and definitive end in the 'poem' or *poema*, the made thing; or that – to repeat – they regarded their proper object of study as poets and poetry, or poetry and poets.

Of course! Who would hold it against a 'doctrine of the Beautiful' that it grasps beauty where it is present in a most highly developed state? And how is one supposed to influence the life of literature if one does not understand it as 'art'? With a 'historical' approach, which always regards literary products in relation to their producers, this point of departure is a given.

If however we mean to recognize and explain the structure of a literary phenomenon, we must proceed in a different manner. If it is

---

3   Georg Simmel, *Goethe*, 5th ed. (Leipzig: Klinkhardt & Biermann, 1923), p. 126.

our goal 'to exclude what is mutable', we cannot begin with the completed individual work of literary art; instead, we must end with it. We must grasp 'poetry' not in its final literary state, but rather where it begins: that is, in *language*.

Were we to elaborate the history of a method that interprets structure, we would see that the eighteenth century already gave thought to the project of building a science of literature commencing with language. We already find the beginnings of such an approach in Hamann's oft-quoted sentence from the *Aesthetica in nuce*, 'Poetry is the mother tongue of the human race.'[4] No doubt we could also include the great double project of Herder's early years: the famous essay in which he investigates the origins of language as such, and his collection of *Old Folk Songs*,[5] in which he gives examples of a language, still close to its origins, that he sees as a 'collection of elements of poetry' or 'a vocabulary of the soul which is simultaneously a mythology and a wonderful epic of the actions and speakings of all beings.'[6] Finally, we find something similar in Jacob Grimm's concept of 'natural poetry' (*Naturpoesie*) – about which more later.

Yet at the time this did not issue in any stringent classification of forms. If we would continue the work then begun in a consistent fashion, we must use every resource of linguistic and literary study to discern the path that leads from language to literature, or – put more precisely, and in the idiom of the theory of objective spirit – to observe when, where and how language can and does become a *construct* without at the same time ceasing to be a *sign*.

Methodologically, this poses a series of problems.

From the units and structures of language, as given in grammar, syntax and semantics, we must ascend systematically, via the disciplines of stylistics, rhetoric and poetics, to the highest works of literary art,

---

4 Johann Georg Hamann, 'Aesthetica in nuce: A Rhapsody in Cabalistic Prose' (1760), transl. Joyce P. Crick, with modifications by H. B. Nisbet, in Timothy J. Chamberlain, ed., *Eighteenth Century German Criticism* (New York: Continuum, 1992), p. 81.

5 Johann Gottfried Herder, *Abhandlung über den Ursprung der Sprache* (Treatise on the Origins of Language, 1772); *Alte Volkslieder* (Old Folk Songs, 1775), with subsequently expanded editions under different titles (1778, 1779, 1807).

6 Johann Gottfried Herder, 'Treatise on the Origins of Language,' *Philosophical Writings*, transl. and ed. Michael N. Forster (Cambridge: Cambridge University Press, 2002), p. 103.

using comparisons to observe how a given phenomenon may repeat itself on another level in an amplified way, and how the same structuring (*gestaltbildende*) and form-delimiting force, increasing each time, dominates the whole system. For example, we might start with linguistic aspects of syntactic form to find the path to artistic composition, or derive the sense of a trope from the meaning of a word.

We might in this way come to understand the force that consolidates itself by ever-ascending steps within the great domain of language and literature until it appears to us in a final, finished state as a definite individual unity. Yet it behoves us to attend as well to those forms that have also emerged from language but which seem not to have become complete in this way, forms consolidated over time into what we might call a different aggregate state – forms explained not by stylistics, nor by rhetoric, nor by poetics, perhaps indeed not even as a matter of 'writing'; forms which, even though they are artistic, still do not become a work of art – in short, the forms we call legend, *Sage*, myth, riddle, proverb, case, *memorabile*, fairy tale or joke.

If, without neglecting the first problem, we begin with the second, it is because neither the aesthetic nor the historical approach to literature has ever paid these forms much attention. To be sure, literary historians did have a sense that these forms might somehow be present in works of literary art – that, for example, one cannot speak of the *Nibelungenlied* without also discussing the Nibelung saga – yet its interpretive method failed to plumb their significance. Their study was left to ethnography or to other not entirely literary disciplines.

We thus have some catching up to do. If only to fill in the gap, this book – the first chapter of *our* approach to literary criticism – will attend to these forms. They are those that arise, so to speak, within language itself, developing themselves in language, without the aid of a poet.

III. LANGUAGE AS LABOUR: PRODUCING, CREATING, INTERPRETING

How can we understand *language* as *labour*?

Right away the image appears of a human community of labour and of the people within it who perform the labour in their several ways: farmer, artisan, priest – the producer, the creator, the interpreter.

Producing, creating, interpreting are the activities that weld a community together as a work community.

I need hardly note that when we say 'farmer, artisan, priest', we have no ethnological theory whatsoever in mind, nor any classification of forms of economic life; nor do we intend to arrange these three figures as developmental stages in some historico-cultural sequence. What we would express with them is the division of labour visible as labour in the *world* and as labour in *language*.

Let us observe them in their activity.

The *farmer* produces: his labour consists of ordering things given in nature so as to organize them around man as their focal point. Nature, that which abides in itself, is taken up into the life of man – and since life means renewal, so too is nature renewed in this life, but such that the natural processes are allowed to continue unhindered. The farmer's production transforms generative nature into culture. He scatters the seed in the ordered furrows and there grows a field of grain; he plants the seedlings of the wood in a tree nursery and a grove arises; he brings the steer to the cow and the stud to the mare and calves and foals grow. As he cultivates, uncultured nature orders itself around him. There is more to the farm than the cowshed, crop field, tree grove, pasture, fruit or vegetable garden. The animals gather around the farmer. Not only the dog, which may play a role in the work of cultivation, but also the cat. The swallow makes its nest under the farmer's overhanging roof gable, the stork nests on its ridge; the spider lives in the attic. The seeds of plants are blown through the air – not only medicinal and ornamental herbs, but also ones that seem to attach themselves to man without aim or use and which follow him everywhere he goes, like chicory and plantain. Even things he cannot use: he is accompanied by parasites, weeds and vermin that take advantage of the newly created conditions, subject themselves in a sense to his cultivation, move from the sphere of nature to that of human life.

What in nature was locally bound becomes mobile. Trees and bushes wander from one part of the world to another – and what we call landscape is ultimately just nature that has ordered itself, centred itself, around the human producer.

The *artisan* creates – his labour consists in ordering nature's givens in such a way that they cease to be natural. He is constantly interrupting and destroying natural processes. What he renews becomes truly new. He even seizes hold of what man has produced. The grains of cereal are no longer used to produce new grain; they are pounded, ground, pulverized, moistened, heated, and from this unfertile material, bread is made. The trunks that have grown in the tree nursery are chopped down, cut, sawn into beams, planks, rafters – and a house comes into being, or a wagon. But he goes beyond what has been produced: he takes the large stones and piles them to make a wall; the small ones he strikes together until they give sparks and a fire burns. Bones and the skeletons of fish become daggers and arrows or hairpins; a cow's horn becomes a horn for sounding or drinking from; sheepgut becomes a bowstring or the string of a musical instrument. Plants and metals are mashed to yield pigment; food is fermented and becomes an intoxicating beverage. He does not stop at what is objectively given in nature; he also takes hold of nature's invisible powers, analyses them, rearranges them, puts them to use: water and air are made to yield their force, become motion and light.

But how would all this work of production and creation be possible if the third type of labour – the work of *interpretation* – did not constantly steer them, if each kind of labour did not have a meaning that made it obligatory, and if it were not understanding this meaning that brought the work as such to completion? Or, to stick with our terminology: if the work that *orders* and the work that *reorders* were not accompanied by the work that *gives orders*: the work that prescribes, decrees, regulates? Only once meaning is assigned to the manner in which things are produced and created, and the objects produced and created are themselves given meaning, can we call a community of labour complete.

Thus does the *priest* join the farmer and the artisan. Only in so far as the priest gives meaning to their labour does it become possible for the farmer to incorporate nature, with its natural processes, into his life, or for the artisan to disrupt nature and natural process and bring forth new things from it – which he does by imputing sense to this work, from its very beginnings to its utmost and final consequences, understood in the broadest sense.

How do I combine beams and stones in such a way as to protect me and mine and my possessions against nature – to isolate all of this from nature so that it can become a structure, a dwelling, a house? Further: What is the meaning of a house, a home, that includes a family, the life of a family, family possessions, from the forefathers down to the grand-children? And then, further yet: What does that house mean in a broader sense when it is reflected in other types of home – in the house of the gods, in the house of the dead, in the temple, in the grave? Or if we would concentrate on details: What is the meaning of the swallow that makes its nest under the roof of the house? What is the meaning of the stork that lives on the roof ridge? What do they add? What do they contribute to the people who live in the house? What do the rose, the myrtle, the lily in the garden mean to us?

It is through the interpretive work of the priest that labour first becomes complete, becomes fully labour. We have for the concepts 'complete' (*vollständig*) and 'whole' (*ganz*) a word in Old High German whose meaning shifted somewhat in Middle High German, and which is still used in the same sense in Low German and Dutch: the word *heil*. The work of the priest cannot be described better than with this word *heil*, for it also indicates his activity in the largest sense. By inter-preting the world, he makes it *heil* – that is, complete, whole, healthy, *sanus*. But in so far as he makes the world *heil*, he acts as a mediator between the work community and another sphere: not only does he make this community whole (*heil*), he makes it holy (*heilig*). Anything that is to endure must be interpreted from its beginnings as holy. The first day of the new year is holy, as is a child's first day of school. Holy is the first furrow drawn by the plough through barren land – like 'whole', 'holy' and 'heal' (*heil, heilig, heilen*), so are the words *colere* (cultivate), *cultus* (cult) and *Kultur* (culture) interrelated. This first furrow signifies all the ones that will follow, in their totality: it means the coming harvest; it means the fecundity of what is to be produced. When a house is to be built, we set the foundation stone; this action gives meaning to and sanctifies all the actions to follow; the founda-tion stone condenses the entire significance of the house within itself. Just as it is laid, so shall the other stones be laid; just as it is solid, so shall the others be solid; upon this stone shall rest the house and every-thing that will occur in the house, from the tranquility of its inhabit-ants to the authority that resides in the *paterfamilias*. Every principle of order and disposition rests within this stone. Such actions are undertaken solemnly, with feasts and fasts; this imbues them with meaning as they are completed, and expresses their originary integrity. Everything that is active or objective in culture, everything in culture that adopts a *Gestalt* or takes on form, must be hallowed by interpretation so that it may become *heil*, and its holiness can be renewed at any moment through reference to this interpretation; every cultural activity is ultimately cult activity, every cultural object a cult object.

It is clear – although given the tendency of today's disciplines to misunderstand each other, I must repeat the point – that here we are not engaging in cultural history in an evolutionary sense. We cannot say: first man produced, then he created, then he interpreted. It would be pointless to search remote corners of the earth for a people that may have come to a halt in the production phase, in a rustic stage. There is no such thing; there cannot be. Of course, I am aware that human economies have passed through developmental stages; but here, while regarding labour in its individual forms, our aim is to understand it holistically – and in this sense, there is nothing that man has acquired through work in which we do not recognize him as farmer, artisan, priest.

This bears repeating, now that we find ourselves in a position to compare the spheres of these three cultural actors. The three spheres are concentric, their periphery broadening from instance to instance. We have already seen that what the artisan creates amplifies what was given with the farmer's production. Not only did he make bread from the grain grown in the field: he went far beyond what the farmer produced to involve in his labour everything that seemed accessible and useful to him in uncultivated nature. And with the priest the sphere becomes larger still – he does not content himself with giving meaning to what man has produced and created, but his work of interpretation extends to everything that is not, and cannot be, produced and created: he imputes meaning to the sun, the moon and the stars; his interpretations go beyond what can be seen and grasped, to the invisible and the ungraspable.

This is how we may regard these three figures before us – this is how we can envision them in their spatial definition, in their movement through space. The farmer belongs to his clod, he is located in the countryside – if he should leave it, he ceases to be a farmer. The artisan roams the world as a journeyman, and then he settles where the countryside ends, in a locus where everything has been reordered and removed from nature, and where the natural processes in life have been modified – he moves to the settlement, to the city. In a certain sense, the farmer remains alone with his family – if he associates with others, it is usually for reasons that have to do with artisanship; the artisan, meanwhile, joins up with other artisans in a guild, in a union. The priest, finally, is both steadfast and mobile – he does not wander the world, but instead seeks a point from which he can survey it; he is solitary in that he does not band together with others of his kind, but at the same time he constitutes the focal point of a crowd, of a community that gathers round him. And in the three expressions family, guild, community, we once again see our three figures clearly before us.

All the work that is done by the farmer, the artisan and the priest is recapitulated in language.

Everything that the farmer, the artisan and the priest have accomplished belongs to life, passes away with life, renews itself in life, or endures with life. Through the labour of language, however, it acquires a new stability in language itself.

This occurs in two ways. First, everything that is produced, created, interpreted, is named by language. Second, however – and here we go deeper– language itself is a producing, creating and interpreting entity; it is something in which ordering, reordering and prescribing occur in a very particular way.

In the 'Commentary' section of his *Essays in Sound Analysis*[7] Gunther Ipsen has shown what 'naming' means – how it endows the world with a kind of 'air' that envelops and penetrates everything, in which everything lies embedded; how humans breathe this air and inhale with it everything that surrounds them, how with the act of exhalation the air becomes resonant, and how these resonant tones make up the names of things.

In its work of naming, language is as much a constant as the inhalation and exhalation of breath; it is as omnipresent as the 'air' of which we have spoken.

---

7   Gunther Ipsen, *Schallanalytische Versuche: eine Einführung in die Schallanalyse* (Heidelberg: C. Winter, 1928).

However: *nomen est omen*! Something issues from language; it is a seed that can grow, and as such it is *productive*. We know this, and we sense it especially, naively and instinctively, in moments of fear when we may have used words to produce something we would rather not have. 'Unbidden', we say, or 'misspoken', and we try through some action to limit the productive power of words. We can call it superstition, but we need to be clear about the fact that there is something to this so-called superstition – a knowledge that words can become realities. If we investigate the etymology of words like *loben, geloben, glauben, erlauben* ('praise', 'plight', 'believe', 'allow'), and all the other words derived from the Indo-European root **leubh*, we sense everywhere how they suggest the possibility of appropriating or producing something. To promise (*versprechen*) is much more than to announce a binding intention. It means: to speak (*sprechen*) in such a way that something will come about – just as in certain parts of Germany one can call up or summon a ghost (*einen Geist versprechen, heraufbeschwören*). In quite the same way, language is used to bind fire with water when both are spoken of together. Λόγος σὰϱξ ἐγένετο (*logos sarx egeneto*) – we know that a word can become flesh and live among us. In this context, what we often call magic – badly misapplying the term under the influence of an uncomprehending positivism – should be understood as the productive aspect of language. And again, productivity is here an *ordering of things* that does not hinder the natural course of events, but rather allows it to enter into and assimilate itself to the life of man.

Just as language produces, so too does it *create*; just as a word can become something real, so too can it engender something new, through a process of *rearrangement*. Language creates structure, in that language poetizes (*dichtet*) i.e. weaves into form – we use the German word *dichten* in its proper sense. What language has created is as solidly fixed as what the artisan creates in the sphere of life. We *know* Odysseus, Don Quixote, Mr Pickwick – we know these figures of language better than we know many people who live in our personal ambit. The pact that Faust made with the Devil has had its legal validity investigated by noted jurists. These persons and facts may remind us so much of specific writers that we are disinclined to consider them creations by language. But I would recall Serenissimus,[8] who cannot be connected with any writer in particular, and point to what happened to the burghers of Schilda[9] when they set about building their town hall – events more familiar to many, perhaps, than today's daily politics.

We tend to say that, where language operates poetically, literature arises. With this we have found the transition we sought. And we know that language, understood as a work of rearrangement, here leads directly to literature, even if this literature does not originate with a particular poet or is not fixed in a particular work of art. At the same time, we can see how something is seized upon by language or literature, and is changed and renewed; something that – to put it boldly – had been given in nature.

A living person who is widely visible in his time is in essence doubly present. We know one Mussolini from reports, stories, anecdotes – but we do not know to what extent he is the same as the 'real' Mussolini, Mussolini *in natura*. This second Mussolini is related to the literary Mussolini as grain is to bread: he has been pounded, ground, pulverized, moistened, heated – he is made poetic, created. He craves interpretation, for only interpretation can establish the relationship of Mussolini I to Mussolini II.

We have thus arrived at the third labour of language. In analogy to production and creation, we have talked of completion and poetic condensation by language. In this third case, the case of the interpretive labour of language, we can apply the words *knowing* and *thinking*.

Human beings are faced with a given manifold of phenomena; they discover similarities, they look for what the phenomena have in

---

8   A fictive character, the senile princeling of an imaginary principality, created by Otto Erich Hartleben (1864–1905) in the weekly journal *Die Jugend*. Jolles's observation is accurate only in so far as the literary figure became a generally recognized type.

9   The fictive foolish residents of the town of Schilda, characters in an anonymous comic novel first published in 1597 under the title *Das Lalenbuch. Wunderseltsame, abenteuerliche, unerhörte und bisher unbeschriebene Geschichten und Taten der Lalen zu Laleburg* (second edition, *Die Schiltbürger*, 1598). The closest English equivalent would be the 'wise men of Gotham.' In this story, the burghers of Schilda build a magnificent town hall, but the architect forgets to include windows in the design, and the building is pitch-black inside. They attempt to carry sunlight inside in buckets, potato sacks and mousetraps, but without success.

common. Let me present an example, which I have derived from Porzig's 'Etymological Studies' and Ipsen's 'Reflections on Linguistics'.[10]

A person observes the phases of a heavenly body that shows him a form completing itself by rounding itself out from a narrow crescent to a disc, and this completion to form becomes a standard for him when observing how time also fulfills itself. He carries within him a *feeling* that presses for completion, and an *ambition* to round out thought to a form. At the same time, he recognizes how he himself as a living being unfolds his own powers over the course of this life. But how, from what perspective, shall he apprehend what these various things have in common, these things that signify to him a world of development, unfolding, completion? This is where language begins its work; through interpretation, it comprehends all this in a sign; and this sign, mobile like the phenomena and yet still enclosing their shared identity entirely within itself, becomes the regulatory centre from which that unfolding proceeds and to which it returns. We call such a sign a *root*.

We shall see later that 'root' is a word that indicates a particular mental attitude, but which fails to do justice to the central position of the sign. Still, we do not want to change the terminology where this does not seem absolutely necessary; in any case, the word *root* shows us how deep within language the interpretive activity lies.

The root that underlies our example – with which we find ourselves in the sphere of Indo-European cognition and thought – is **men*. And from the perspective of this regulatory principle, the heavenly body must be called *mond* ('moon'), the derivative time segment *monat* ('month'), the feeling *minne* ('courtly love'), the mental ambition *meinen* ('meaning'), the living creature *mann* or *mensch* ('man', 'human being'). Were we to adduce other Indo-European languages besides the German, we would find many more examples, beginning with the Latin *mens* or the Greek μαίνομαι (*mainomai*), μάντις (*mantis*), and *maenad*.

---

10   Walter Porzig, 'Bedeutungsgeschichtliche Studien', *Indogermanische Forschungen* 42/1 (January 1924), pp. 221–74; Gunther Ipsen, 'Besinnung der Sprachwissenschaft (Karl Voßler und seine Schule)', *Indogermanisches Jahrbuch* 11 (1927), pp. 1–32.

We would then also see how this *men not only functions as a root word, but also takes formal hold of additional material and forces it into its sphere; how as a formative principle it endows very disparate things with meaning, objects both natural and instrumental: things *filled with power by being formed*, so that – to take one example – the meaning of the Latin word *semen*, which is etymologically distant from the words just mentioned, is extended by virtue of its *mn* ending to things that round themselves out like the moon, and which by becoming full also unfold their power.

Allow me to mention again the foundation stone, in which every action related to building and everything man understands by the word *house* is present and regulated, and we will understand how, beginning with what we have called *roots*, language not only indicates similarity so to speak radially, but also integrates the connotations of objects that manifest themselves disparately, such as when it assigns figures on the chessboard and troops on the battleground equally to a *field*.

IV. LITERARY FORMS

To some, this image of a world built up through production, creation, interpretation, in which we find the farmer, artisan and priest, and in which language recapitulates their labour, may seem too much a world of products of labour, a world of sown fields, ground cereals, baked bread, built houses, set foundation stones – in short, a world of objects, a world of particulars.

If this is so, then we need only think for a moment to see that the world does not generally appear to man in this way. Taken as a whole, in its blurry diversity, in its tumult and surge, to him it seems more a wilderness and a confusion. To understand the world, he must immerse himself in it, he must somehow reduce the endless number of its phenomena, he must intervene in it to set one thing apart from another. Humans in the world may remind us of the girl in the fairy tale who is placed before a chaotic heap of seeds of all kinds, and is then set the task of sorting them all out properly by the end of the night. We know how this story goes: friendly birds or insects come to her aid. The work is accomplished, and as the immeasurable pile is reduced to measurable smaller piles, what was in this pile comes into its own and becomes valuable. With like thus coming to like, what was but a confusing part of a greater confusion acquires its own characteristics, becomes itself. When the magician appears at sunrise, chaos has become cosmos.

The human being intervenes in the world's confusion; engaging with it, reducing, combining, he condenses what belongs together, sunders, divides, disperses, and collects in his little piles what is essential. The differences widen; ambiguities are excluded, or resolved and restored to clarity. Construing, constraining, he pushes through to the basic forms.

As we shall see, what is happening here is no fairy tale. That which lies massed in the world's confusion does not possess its own form a priori, as do the various seed types, or a pea, or a bean; instead, what is separated by differentiation acquires its proper form only as it converges in the process of analysis. And this is exactly the process we have to consider. Like comes to like, but in this case it does not form small piles of individual items, but rather a manifold whose parts interpenetrate, unite, become mutually intimate, and thus generate a structure [*eine Gestalt*], a form – a form that can be understood objectively as such; one that has, so to speak, its own *validity*, its own *concision* (*Bündigkeit*).

Where *language* has contributed to the generation of such a form, where it intervenes in such a form by a process of organization and rearrangement, where it reconfigures the form from within itself – there we can speak of *literary forms*.

CHAPTER 1

Legend

As the first of these forms I have chosen the *legend*, for in a particular era of Western culture we see it before us as a self-contained whole; I mean the Christian legend, as it evolved in the Catholic Church beginning in the first centuries of the Christian era and as it survives to the present day. At this point we will not survey the full range of shapes that legend can take, or its general character, but will focus instead on a fully developed individuation of the form.

It is useful to be able to grasp a form at a point where it has really come into its own, where it is really itself – which means, in our case, that we will explore legend at a time and in a place where it was read with a certain exclusiveness, where its importance cannot be discounted, and where it was one of the cardinal points on man's compass – perhaps in fact the only one by which people could orient themselves.

Of course, this also has its dangers; we cannot simply accept the medieval legend as a paradigm, and we must take care not to extrapolate concepts so quickly from the picture we gain from it that we think that we have grasped legend in the full range of its possibilities. It is difficult to make comparisons if we identify ourselves too closely with a particular manifestation of the phenomenon. To be sure, in this case the danger is not very great, for there is much in our own modern life that divides us from Catholic legend, and our perspective on it is thus somewhat distant.

Let us begin by considering the world of medieval legend superficially, as it is presented in the sources.

Summaries of stories with testimony about the lives and deeds of the saints have been available, in large and small collections, since the first centuries of the Christian era. We find *Acta Martyrum* and *Acta Sanctorum* throughout the Middle Ages, and not just as books that people read but also as ones that had a substantial effect on literature and the visual arts. In this regard the *Legendae Sanctorum* or *Legenda Aurea* of the bishop Jacobus de Voragine, where we encounter the word *legend* for the first time – a collection compiled in the middle of the thirteenth century and for centuries the prototype of a certain kind of artful construction of legends, as well as a source of great influence on the Italian novella – is of particular importance.

The first large collection proper of the *vitae* of all the saints recognized by the Catholic Church dates from the seventeenth century, an era significant in other ways for the definition of the saint. The collection was begun by a Jesuit, Father Heribert Rosweyde, of Flanders, and was continued after his death by a member of the same order, whose name the collection bears: Jean Bolland. It is generally called the *Acta Sanctorum,* and its compilers the Bollandists. Even today this work has not reached completion. Strictly speaking, it can never be finished, for the number of saints is in no way historically limited: more can always be added – and they *are* added. Because the veneration of the saints is connected with the daily rites of the Catholic Church, the *vitae* and *acta* are ordered according to the days of the Christian year. The two volumes prepared by Bolland for the month of January appeared in 1643. By 1902 the edition comprised sixty-three volumes. Several more have been added since then; the undertaking is now managed by a commission that since 1882 has published a journal as well, the *Analecta Bollandiana*. Today the anthology includes roughly 25,000 saints' lives, though one must keep in mind that on many occasions multiple *vitae* have survived of the same saint, all of them edited by the Bollandists.

We have thus collated sufficient material: first the lives collected in the Middle Ages, an era whose world view – to put it provisionally – contained the saint and his legends within itself; and then an incipient scholarly consciousness, of course still working within the Church, which undertook to compile them in their totality and in all their diversity.

Here *Heiliger* ('saint') and the adjective *heilig* ('holy') exist in their own world, a realm in which these words have a narrower meaning than we normally attribute to them; one more narrow, too, than the meaning we gave the words *heil* ('whole') and *heilig* in our introduction.

II. THE PROCESS OF CANONIZATION

What is the saint, what are the saints, whose lives are portrayed in a special way in the sources mentioned? Although they can be viewed as individuals, together they form a community by virtue of an inner fellowship and because collectively they represent the liturgical year.

The saint is thus bound to the institution of the church, and because the question, What is a saint? can be answered only in relation to this bond, it turns into a broader, more profound, and methodologically primary question: How does one become a saint? The question thus stems not from the person but from the institution by which the saint is recognized.

This recognition is accomplished in a historically developed and established form – the form of canonization standardized by Pope Urban VIII (1623–37, the same era in which the *Acta Sanctorum* originated).

Canonisatio means the declaration as a saint of one who is blessed (*beatus*); *canonisare* means 'to enter into the register (canon) of saints', and to assign to the saint the appropriate cult, including mention in the prayer the priest pronounces when consecrating the elements of the Eucharist.

Let us review the process of sanctification, as it has been followed since Urban VIII.

It occurs through the Congregatio Rituum, in which several cardinals and other dignitaries of the church have seats, and it is undertaken on the initiative of people convinced of the sanctity of the person in question, usually with the mediation of the local clergy. As a rule, a fairly long time (fifty years) must elapse between the death of the candidate for sainthood and the opening of the proceedings. The process takes the form of a trial – a court trial. It must be proved by witnesses that the person (who as soon as the trial opens is called *servus Dei*) demonstrated heroic virtues, first, and, second, performed miracles. The investigation begins under the jurisdiction of the bishop of the place where the *servus Dei* lived and is then reviewed by the Congregatio Rituum. If the examination is passed, the case can move on to the phase of beatification.

Once the beatification is achieved, the case moves on to a higher court – but for this to happen, new miracles must occur. These are verified once again; the process is reinitiated, witnesses are interrogated, objections presented, until finally, when all this has been carried out, the pope declares, ex cathedra, the *beatus* to be *sanctus*: 'We decide and determine that [name] is a saint, and worthy of being inscribed in the Catalogue of the Saints, and we inscribe him in a catalogue of this kind, establishing that his festal day and offices should be celebrated faithfully and solemnly by the Universal Church.'[1]

It must be added that such virtues of the *beatus* as are subject to the procedural examination – the theological ones: *spes, fides, caritas*; and the moral ones: *justitia, prudentia, fortitudo, temperantia*[2] – correspond to Scholastic classifications and Scholastic definitions. The concept of the miracle – the second main point at issue in the process – also follows the Scholastic definition: 'Things which are done by God, beyond causes known to us, are called miracles.'[3]

The treatises that discuss the *beatificatio* and *canonisatio* place special emphasis on the trial form of the proceedings. The grounds for beatification and canonization, it is asserted, must be handled just as strictly as evidence is in a criminal trial; the facts must be proved as exactly as they are when a crime is to be punished. There is even the equivalent of a public prosecutor at the Congregatio Rituum; he is called – not officially, to be sure, but routinely – *advocatus diaboli*, the Devil's Advocate.

This, then, is the procedure by which saints have been recognized since the time of Urban VIII. Were there no saints before then? On the contrary: what we see happening in the seventeenth century under the influence of the Counter-Reformation, the Council of Trent and the Jesuits is but a final, firm and possibly superficial regulation of a process that had been taking place in the Christian church, internally and of its

---

1 'Kanonisation', in *Real-Enzyklopädie für protestantische Theologie und Kirche*, 3rd ed., J. J. Herzog and Albert Hauck, eds, 22 vols (Leipzig: J. C. Hinrichs'sche Buchhandlung, 1896–1909), vol. 10, p. 18. Jolles seems to have drawn much of his description of the process of canonization from this article.

2 *spes* – hope; *fides* – faith; *caritas* – charity; *justitia* – justice; *prudentia* – wisdom; *fortitudo* – bravery; *temperantia* – temperance.

3 Aquinas, *Summa Theologica* 1.105.7

own accord, up to the time of the Reformation. The precise, juristically organized trial form is the consummation of a cultural process. What the ecclesiastical authority here decrees by the power of its office is the formula of a form, and this formula is composed in such a way that we still recognize the form in it and can derive the form from it.

First we can derive from the formula, once again, certain outward characteristics of the form.

III. ACTIVE VIRTUE AND PUNISHABLE WRONG
- OBJECTIFICATION – MIRACLES – RELICS

In a small, geographically limited area, there lives a person who attracts attention on account of his uncommon behaviour. His way of life, his manner of living, are different from those of other people; he is more virtuous than others, and his virtue also differs qualitatively. The meaning of this is made clear by the fact that the valuation of a saint occurs in and through the trial form, and here we begin to understand the significance of the trial form, the comparison with criminal law.

A person can be much more wicked than his neighbour, and yet there will be no occasion for criminal law to be concerned with this person and his wickedness. Not until this wickedness is revealed in an act, is translated into action – let us say, *becomes active* – does he become punishable through and in this act: we call the act a *crime,* and define crime in the broader sense as a punishable wrong. In the crime, the criminal differentiates himself *qualitatively* from all other wicked people. It is the crime that is punished, and if we punish the criminal, it is because our justice system identifies him, as an individual, with his *crimen.*

Accordingly, the criminal trial investigates not whether the defendant is wicked but whether a crime occurred.

If we reverse the issue, we have the process of canonization. But then we encounter the difficulty that we do not possess a word that expresses the opposite of crime, and also that we cannot change the definition *punishable wrong* into its opposite. We must be satisfied with the expression *active virtue,* or *activated virtue.* And we will define the conduct of the person, described above, whose virtue differs qualitatively from that of others as active virtue.

Now, in our penal law we have the fundamental provision *nullum crimen sine lege* ('no crime without a law'): the written law is the norm of the act to be punished, just as in the corollary *nulla poena sine lege* ('no punishment without a law') the law becomes the norm of the punishment.[4] There can be no such law in the ecclesiastical reversal of the form, and thus another norm must be sought, in a twofold manner.

First, the process of canonization, like the criminal trial, relies on witnesses. However, whereas in the criminal trial the witnesses are expected to testify solely to the facts of the case, leaving it up to the bench – however constituted – to establish whether a crime was committed, in the process of canonization the witnesses, who are in a sense also experts, must declare to what degree they believe that the *servus Dei* can stand as an instance of active virtue.

Second – and much more important – a higher norm is applied. The active instantiation of virtue is confirmed from on high – confirmed by the *miracle*, 'quod a deo fit praeter causas nobis notas' ('which God does outside causes known to us').[5] And once again it is the witnesses who must not only testify to the facts of the case but also voice their conviction that miracles really happened. In the end, of course, it is up to the ecclesiastical judges to decide whether miraculous power – sanctity – is present.

We have thus examined the first phase of the saint's trial, up to *beatification*. As we have noted, a good number of years must pass between the death of the *servus Dei* and his beatification, and often many more yet before the case of the *beatus* is again taken up, by a second authority, in a canonization trial. During this time, divine confirmation must again become manifest in a miracle, independently of the *beatus* as an individual.

How and where do these posthumous miracles happen, to which local witnesses must again testify? At his grave, in the place where he

---

4 *Strafgesetzbuch* [StGb] *für das Deutsche Reich vom 15. Mai 1871, nach der Novelle vom 26. Februar 1876, nebst Einführungs- und Abänderungsgesetz*, ed. Karl Lueder (Erlangen: Deichert, 1876), §2, 'Einleitende Bestimmungen', p. 4.

5 Aquinas, *Summa Theologica* 1.105.7

lived, through clothing he wore, through objects he touched or that touched him, through his blood, through parts of his body.

And what do they mean? It was once said, with a certain naivety, that 'a truly Catholic people values dead saints more highly than living ones'. Many a tale from the Middle Ages confirms this statement. We read in the *vita* of the Italian saint Romuald by Petrus Damianus that the inhabitants of Catalonia, where he was living, sought to keep Romuald – whom they regarded during his lifetime as a saint – in their country. When that failed, they sent out assassins to kill him so that if they could not retain him alive, they could at least keep him as a corpse: 'pro patrocinio terrae' ('as a protection for the land'). This story and similar ones show what is meant by posthumous miracles.

Active virtue must be perfected. It is conceivable only when detached not simply from the living person but altogether from life. Only after active virtue has gained autonomy through the death of the person does it really stand by itself, acquire a force of its own. Active virtue has become objectified.

Our penal code has a statutory period of limitation: after a certain time, the criminal can no longer be punished for his crime. The crime has lapsed. Here again we see how our penal legislation is predicated on identifying the criminal with the crime. There have been times, however, when the body of a murderer who had managed to avoid punishment during his lifetime was exhumed and hung on the gallows or bound to the wheel: the crime lived on and could be punished, had to be punished, even if the criminal was no longer living. This is how we have to imagine the virtue of the saint after his death. It endures – only now does it really come fully to life, only now is it really confirmed, not in the individual but in and of itself. We can contrast the statutory period of limitation of our penal code with the *eternalization* involved in the canonization process.

After the confirmation period, in which active virtue begins to live its own life and during which the *servus Dei* and his active virtue became separate from each other, the latter is joined again to its personal vehicle by a new authority, and in a different manner. This reunion is what is meant by the process of canonization, by *sanctification*. The *servus Dei* has become *venerabilis*, *beatus*; he is now in the beyond, among the blessed. There his virtue – now independent, objectified – returns to him. *Beatus* and active virtue take on a new quality: he becomes *sanctus*, and his festival and his cult are celebrated in the entire church, 'faithfully and solemnly'; he has acquired his divine personality. What was once his *virtue* is, however – now that he has rejoined it – his *power*. Recall that *virtus*, which to the Romans already meant 'virtue' and 'strength', or 'power', can mean *miraculum* in medieval Latin, and that the German word for virtue (*Tugend*) is related to *taugen*, meaning 'to be good for something'. If at first the miracle worked as a confirmation of virtue, now it is a sign of power. If in the beginning the miracle happened through God so as to indicate the saint, now it occurs through the saint, so to speak on God's behalf and with his consent, on behalf of another person or thing. One can place oneself or another under the protection of the saint, one can call on him, one can ask him to perform miracles.

Now, this power is also revealed in another place, one detached from the person of the saint, if not entirely independent of it.

The posthumous miracle is attached to an object – garment, grave, instrument of martyrdom – that testifies to the sanctity of the *servus Dei*, just as the miracle did. This object is indispensable when his person is dead but his active virtue is living. The object – which we, of course, call a *relic* – has to represent him in his absence. How else can one know whose virtue is being confirmed in a given context by a miracle? How else can one understand that God's incomprehensible acts have something to do with this person specifically? Now, just as the relic stands in for the *servus Dei* in his absence as a vehicle for the miracle, so too can it stand in for him once he enters heaven as a *sanctus*. It can absorb everything that is connected with the saint and his saintliness and then emit it; in a certain sense, it can itself be holy and become a vehicle of power.

Let us summarize these connections once again clearly:

The meaning this saint acquired as a person, after having been perceived, in a human context, as a doer of virtuous acts, and having had his virtue confirmed by miracles,

having then had the efficacy of his virtue experienced and confirmed again after his death, independently of his person,

having then been reunified with his virtue and endowed with power in a newly formed divine shape:

all this can also be construed as a property of an object – this is what a relic can mean in and of itself.

IV. MENTAL DISPOSITION OF THE LEGEND – *IMITATIO* AND *IMITABILE*

Having surveyed how the saint becomes a saint, both in the formulas of the canonization process and in the forms achieved on Earth and in heaven, we are faced once again with the question: What does this all mean? What drives people to see others in this way? What train of thought, what way of life, what mental disposition [*Geistesbeschäftigung*] gives birth to this world of forms, in which people become saints and objects relics, and in which we speak of miracles – the world form posited by the canonization process as a hierarchical parallel to a mode of life conduct?

What is especially striking in the way a saint is – so to speak – realized is that he himself participates so little in the process. Not that he is passive as a personality – not at all! Sometimes he is prophesied to his mother before his birth; she sees a shining light or a similar vision. And as soon as he enters into life, his entire being is centred on action. There are saints who in the cradle already join hands in prayer. As a boy, as a girl, they stand out from other children their age by virtue of their piety, their good works. And their active strength is later constantly manifest; they are continuously in action. There are courageous saints, who confront temptations, satanic enemies, the Devil, or a heathen tyrant. There are industrious saints, who write countless godly books or who travel continuously from land to land, preaching to convert the heathen. There are saints who joyfully bear the tortures imposed on them and heroically desire worse. They are active, certainly, and yet they do not participate in the process of sanctification that begins in their lifetime and is completed in the procedure carried out by the Congregatio Rituum. We could say that, although they are the principals in both trials, that of life and that of canonization, they are still tried in absentia in both.

To be more precise, we have the sense not that the saint exists in himself and for his own sake, but that he is created by the community and is there for the sake of the community, first in the small circle where his deeds are observed, later for the *ecclesia universalis*, and even when he is walking among the blessed in heaven or standing above the altar, adorned with his attributes.

But what does he mean to the community?

Good and evil can perhaps always be judged, but they are not measurable until they have acquired form – that of active virtue in the saint and of punishable wrong in the criminal. Not until we have seen them in this way in persons can we detach them, in their measurable autonomy, from their vehicles: saints and criminals are thus *persons in whom good and evil instantiate themselves in a particular way*.

This is the reason the community does not ask how the saint feels when he is being pious, when he acts, when he suffers. To the community he is in this sense not a man like other men; rather, he is a means of seeing virtue objectified, objectified to the highest degree, to the point of becoming divine power. This is why the saint is absent from his own trial, why we have witnesses and yet more witnesses voicing their conviction, as representatives of the community, that the objectification occurred, that it was confirmed by miracles – witnesses whose conviction is then certified as correct by the ecclesiastical authorities.

What is gained by virtue's becoming measurable, palpable, in this way? How exactly is virtue objectified in the saint?

Here we arrive at what will show us the *mental disposition* that forms the saint. We can do good and evil without knowing precisely how we are to be evaluated, how we are to be judged in so doing. Not until virtue has become measurable, tangible, palpable, not until it stands before us, unconditionally and without qualification, in the saint, do we have a reliable standard. For us the saint brings to consciousness what we would like to do, to experience, and to be, on the road to virtue. He himself is this road to virtue; we can follow the saint.

To characterize the mental disposition that gives rise to what I am calling a form – in this case, the form *legend* – I find myself obliged to introduce code words: words that do not fully 'signify' but that 'suggest', words that only indicate a direction.

Since neither of the German words *folgen* ('follow') and *nachahmen* ('imitate') suffices to indicate this direction, I will resort to the Latin word *imitatio*, commonly used in the Middle Ages.

Etymologically, *imitor* is connected with *aemulus* = *nacheifernd* ('emulating') (*aemulor*, to seek to equal) and with *imago* = *Abbild* ('image, likeness, copy'). Alongside the etymology, however, we have the concept *Eindeutung* ('a sharing of the sense of an experience in empathy'). Thus did the Middle Ages bring *imitari* into connection with *immutare*: to be transformed in such a way that one enters into something else.

The saint, in whom as a person virtue is instantiated, is a figure in whom his immediate and extended environment experiences *imitatio*. He represents in actuality that which we can seek to emulate, and at the same time he provides proof that, insofar as we imitate him, the activity of virtue is actually happening. Being at the highest stage of virtue, he is unattainable; yet in his objectivity he remains at the same time within our reach. He is a shape in whom we perceive, experience and recognize something that appears to us universally worthy of being striven for and who at the same time allows us to visualize the possibility of practice – in short, he is, in the formal sense, an *imitabile*.

From the saint, whose development we have surveyed so precisely, our eye turns to the world that formed him in his specificity. We look around in the Middle Ages and find the same pattern everywhere. On a steep rise there stands a church, and the path leading to it is divided into fourteen stations. Each station signifies a particular stage in the Passion of Christ. The pious man follows this road, and at each of these stations he experiences the scorn, the scourging, the bearing of the cross. He experiences them not only as a reminder of things that happened – he experiences them literally, he enters into them, he participates in the Passion; he too is scorned, scourged; he helps to carry the cross. To the degree humanly possible, he enters into a union with the inimitable; he becomes an *aemulus Christi*; in the church up above, which is in turn an *imago Christi*, he is taken up into Christ. A pilgrimage to a site where a saint lies buried or is represented by a relic is nothing other than an actual repetition of the path to sanctity – naturally, to the degree this is possible for a non-saint. If at the end of the journey the saint should grant what the pilgrim has travelled to him in the hope of obtaining – for example, being cured of a disease – this happens because the pilgrim has, in a limited sense, become the saint.

The Crusades also have this sense of a pilgrimage. They undoubtedly have some connection to the great Germanic displacements of peoples by which the Occident was formed; they are as much migrations as the later voyages of discovery. But they differ from both the earlier and the later migrations by virtue of their imitative character, which reveals itself both in their aim and in their means. Whether directed towards the East, towards Spain, or towards Palestine, they stand in the sign of the imitation of Christ: 'and he who does not take his cross and follow me is not worthy of me' is the motto. The knights sew the cross on their shoulders and in the grand, martial style make a pilgrimage whose final goal is the greatest relic of all – the grave of Christ, which in turn signifies Christ himself.

We can understand the highest actions and persons of Christianity in this manner, without exhausting their religious significance: the Eucharist, Mary, and Jesus himself. Certainly, Jesus means more besides this, but he is also the 'highest saint', whose *aemuli* are the other saints. And the events in the life of Jesus can in turn be understood imitatively, if one comprehends this life, as the Gospel of Matthew does, as the fulfilment of an earlier one – if one says, 'Then was fulfilled what had been spoken by the prophet Jeremiah, saying . . .', or if one regards these events in the New Testament as repetitions of events in the Old Testament, seeing, for example, the sacrifice on the cross as prefigured by Abraham's sacrifice.

We would come face to face with a large piece of the world of the Middle Ages if we were to demonstrate in detail how deeply the mental disposition of *imitatio* is embedded in the life of medieval humanity – this disposition of *aemuli*, of *imagines*, that is in no way restricted to religious life. And in each case, what happens is that one person, one thing, one action becomes the vessel of another, which completes itself therein and becomes an object in its own right. In this objectivity it provides others with the chance to enter into it and be comprehended in their turn.

V. PERSON – OBJECT – LANGUAGE – *VITA* AND HISTORICAL LIFE DESCRIPTION

Now, this form that is realized in life is also realized in language. We have the *saint*, we have his *relic*, we have his *legend*: we have the *person*, we have the *thing*, we have *language*. This mental disposition, this world of *imitatio*, is fulfilled in all three.

In the Christian Occident, the legend has a closed form, thanks to the care with which the ecclesiastical authorities observed and interpreted the entire process hierarchically. It recounts the life of the saint, or – to speak broadly – his history: it is a *vita*.

As a verbal form, however, this *vita* must proceed so that it corresponds in every way to events in the life – that is, so that in it this life is fulfilled once again. It is not enough to record events and actions; the *vita* must permit them to achieve the form in which they can be properly *realized*. For readers or listeners, the *vita* must represent precisely what the life of the saint represents; it must itself be an *imitabile*. This is why, in this *vita*, the life of a man looks different from how it looks in what we call a 'historical' biography. In such a biography – and we shall have to say later what we mean by 'historical' in relation to questions of form – we tend to understand the life of a man as a continuum, as a movement that runs from a beginning to an end, and in which everything that follows has a relation to things that precede it. If the saint's *vita* were to follow that pattern, it would not achieve what it sets out to do. Its task is to realize the process by which virtue becomes active, and to show how the activity of virtue is confirmed by a miracle. Here the overall context of human life is unimportant; important are only the moments in which the Good is instantiated.

The *vita*, the legend in general, decomposes the 'historical' into its component parts; it fills these components with the value of imitability and rebuilds them in a sequence determined by its logic. The legend is completely unfamiliar with the historical in this sense; it knows and recognizes only virtue and miracles. Where the saint is not a means of seeing virtue instantiated, where he cannot be valued as an *imitabile*, there he is not a saint, and there the verbal form that represents him as a saint simply cannot grasp him. We possess examples of saints writing their own lives – of course, not in the consciousness of their sanctity, but in a human fashion, autobiographically. Here we could mention the *Confessions* of Saint Augustine – or, more correctly, of the church father Augustine. These confessions do not in the least recall a legend; they do not belong in the *Acta Sanctorum*. On the other hand, we do have saints' lives from a time when the legend form was no longer fully alive, in which so to speak even the church made 'historical' demands on a *vita*. Here we can observe a struggle between two forms, and at the same time we perceive that as soon as the historical attitude makes any inroads into the genre, the possibility of *imitatio* ceases, and the form is broken to pieces. It is precisely the special character of historical biography that, in it, the person described remains himself, and although he can function as an example for us, yet he offers us no possibility of being completely absorbed in him. But if the biography proceeds in such a way that the historical personality is no longer completely self-contained, if the biography is constructed so that we are inclined to enter completely into it, then it becomes a legend.

We see something like this occurring nowadays with the figure of Frederick the Great.[6]

Language would not be language and verbal form not verbal form if what happens in life could not be fulfilled independently in the form. The verbal form thus is not only capable of representing the life of a saint in a commensurate way, but it also *makes* saints.

Having surveyed the process of sanctification in life and in verbal form, I would like to dig deeper and illustrate, with an example, how a form – *legend* – becomes, and is, language.

VI. AN EXAMPLE – THE VERBAL GESTURE – TRIPLE STRUCTURE – LEGEND-LIFE: POTENTIAL-ACTUAL FORM – SIMPLE FORM – ACTUALIZED SIMPLE FORM

We read in old acts of the martyrs roughly the following:

A man descends from a Christian family living in a western district of the Roman Empire at the end of the third century; he enlists in the Roman army, achieves distinction in war, and rises to the highest ranks of the military. The emperor resolves to persecute the Christians, those

---

6   Likely a reference to Gerhard Lamprecht's films from 1928 about Frederick the Great (*Der alte Fritz*, Parts 1 and 2).

around him agree with him, and only this man opposes him. The emperor, furious, has him taken prisoner and tortured on a wheel with sharp blades. A voice from heaven calls out to the tortured one: 'Fear not, I am with you', and a heavenly apparition in white garments reaches out its hand to him. Many people convert, including some of his fellow soldiers. He is tortured anew; new miracles occur. He is led into the temple of Apollo and is obliged to offer a sacrifice to the god. But he says, 'Will you accept sacrifices from me?' while making the sign of the cross. Thereupon a voice answers from the image of the god, 'There is no god apart from the god that you preach.' The martyr says, 'Then how dare you remain in my presence? Go and pray to the true god.' From the mouth of the idol there escapes a wild and heart-rending howl, and the images explode into pieces. The Christian is beaten and tortured again by the pagan priests, and finally beheaded by order of the emperor.

The above is clearly a report of active virtue, miracles, a saint. We shall set beside this report – which reproduces schematically what we find, with minor variations, in many acts of the martyrs – a short over-view of the contemporary events out of which it emerged and to which, in its fashion, it corresponds.

We find ourselves in the era of Diocletian's persecution of the Christians. Diocletian, who sees in the growing Christian community a threat to his extensive reorganization of the Roman Empire, decides in 303, pressed by those around him, to issue severe decrees criminal-ising the adherents of Christianity. Christians, however, are to be found in all circles, even among the highest officials of the army and the court; we know that the *praepositus cubiculi* Dorotheus and his comrade Gorgonius were executed. It goes without saying that the more courageous among the Christians oppose the emperor. The church historian Eusebius tells how in Nicomedia, where the persecu-tion began, a higher official, whose name he withholds, tore down the posted edict while deriding it. In all parts of the empire there follow arrests, torture, executions; these continue under Diocletian's succes-sors, Galerius and Maximinus Daia. Churches are burned to the ground, church property confiscated. Thousands break away from the church, though many remain faithful. But even before the death of Diocletian, who abdicates in 305, Constantine intervenes. In 313 comes the toleration edict of Milan; by 325 the first council of Nicea is underway. Christianity has won, and the Roman state religions are disappearing.

Let us observe further in what special way our report emerged from these events, in what special way it corresponds to these events, to these proceedings, to these facts, so that we can gather that what we have named with the neutral word *report* must in reality be called a *legend*.

The complex phenomenon of the persecution, imprisonment and torture of Christians is summarily characterized and expressed, reduced to a common denominator. It is called *a wheel with sharp blades*. The contrast, running through all social circles and levels of rank, between the variety of the Roman state religions and the unitary new religion is captured by the phrase *the martyr is led into the temple with many idols*. The resistance of the Christians becomes *he speaks to the false gods; they answer and submit to him*. The uselessness of the persecutions and the victory of Christianity are expressed as *the idols explode*. When the Christian survives the persecution and the torture, this becomes *a heavenly voice calls to him* or *a heavenly apparition in white garments reaches out its hand to him* . . .

It is as if the variety and multiplicity of the events condensed and formed themselves, as if events of the same kind were whirled up together and then rearranged in the vortex so that they issued in a concept, described a concept. When one says *a wheel with sharp blades* – well, it is not entirely clear how one might torture a person with that, but it is impossible to express the concept of all mental and physical tortures put together better than with the phrase *a wheel with sharp blades*. How much is implied in a *god that explodes*!

But what happens in this process of recomposition? What divides that which has occurred into units that are somehow not further divisible, and imbues these units with meaning? What reaches selectively into the vortex of events and binds these events to concepts? It is language; this *wheel with sharp blades*, this *god that explodes* are verbal formations, verbal images. A process occurs in which the two functions of language – pointing to something [*Auf-etwas-hinweisen*] and representing something [*Etwas-darstellen*] – are made into one. There occurs a sudden coincidence and a complete merging of intending [*meinen*] and signifying [*bedeuten*].

We thus see a repetition, at a second level, of a process that was first fulfilled when language itself took shape. Language jells with the event units into a first, rudimentary literary form. Something is born for a second time that will be born once again on a third level when, in a singular and unrepeatable process, the form congeals into an artwork, into an artist's creation, and thus reaches its definitive fulfilment.

Hence, where under the sway of a mental disposition the variety and multiplicity of being and of events condense and take form, where language lays hold of events in their ultimate, indivisible units and, in verbal formations, intends and signifies at the same time, we shall speak of the emergence of *simple form*.

It is not easy to name these creations, which we have called, up to now, 'event units' [*Einheiten des Geschehens*], and which are registered by language. Using a vague terminology, literary history tends, where it touches on these things without fully understanding them, to speak of *motifs*. But with this term literary historians tend also to mean given units of subject matter, or material already 'preformed' in some complex in the artwork. *Motif* is a dangerous word. *Motif* means, first of all, motive, determinant, something that catalyses something else. In this latter sense one could, in a pinch, use the word. Our creations certainly catalyse something, insofar as through them events become imaginable as a consequence of a mental disposition. But this is not their primary or most profound sense. This expression derives from the field of music, where *motif* signifies 'the final characteristic unit' of an artistic formation. Wilhelm Scherer was the first to use the term in this sense, in his *Poetics*.[7] But here we cannot accept this usage. Nietzsche defines the musical *motif* as 'the individual gesture of the musical affect'. Indeed, what we have called until now events grasped in concepts, charged units, are *individual gestures of language*.

In the following, we will use the term *individual verbal gesture*, or *verbal gesture* for short, in this sense.

In our example the individual verbal gestures are a wheel with sharp blades, a heavenly voice, an apparition in a white garment that helpfully extends its hand, gods that are spoken to and that submit to the sign of the cross, idols that explode, and so on.

---

7   Wilhelm Scherer, *Poetik* (Berlin: Weidmann, 1888), p. 212.

These verbal gestures, collected thus all together, produce not a particular saint but only some pious Christian in an era of persecution, a holy martyr in general – and so we see in a number of acts of the martyrs the same verbal gestures recurring in the same fashion. They are, however, stored up in such a way that at any moment they can be directed and bound in a determinate manner so that they achieve a present significance. In our case, what jumps out of the gestures (so to speak) into which the events of the era of Diocletian's persecution condensed is not *a holy martyr* but *Saint George*; that is to say, the gestures are organized in such a way that they become present in their totality in an individual person, that in their realization they create a particular saint.

This shows us that a form is doubly present, one mode relating to the other like a chess problem to its solution. The problem contains and presents a possibility; the solution realizes this possibility with a specific event. What we have called *legend* is at first nothing but a particular disposition of gestures in a field. What we call the *vita* of Saint George – exceptionally, we possess a particular term for the genre – is the realization of a possibility given and contained in the legend. Using Scholastic terminology, we could say that what is present in legend *potentialiter* (potentially) is given *actualiter* (actually) in the *vita*. We can clarify the relation of both modes in which we perceive the form by transposing them momentarily into life. From the perspective of a certain mental disposition, a legend *had* to arise from the way Diocletian acted against the Christians; at the point where this legend became connected with a suitable personality or of its own accord created such a personality, it became the *vita* of that particular person.

We will see with the other forms also how necessary it is to distinguish between these two modes. I call the first *simple form*, the second *actualized* or *present simple form*. And I will repeat once more that I am speaking of a *simple form* where verbal gestures – in which, on the one hand, life situations have condensed themselves in a particular way under the sway of a mental disposition, and which, on the other hand, are themselves also led by this disposition to generate, create and represent life situations – are stored up in such a way that they are able, at any moment, to take a particular direction and become meaningful in the present. In this case, where it has achieved a particular direction and has become meaningful in the present, it is an *actualized* or *present simple form*. Legend is simple form; a legend, or – as we could say – *the vita* of Saint George, is present simple form.

VII. EXPANDED EXAMPLE: SAINT GEORGE

Let us turn now to this particular individual saint, Saint George, about whose historical existence nothing is known.

As a consequence of the mental disposition that we have called *imitatio*, verbal gestures were condensed out of life events: each of the gestures was stored up in such a way that one could follow them, enter into them, and be assimilated by them. They were all arranged in such a way that they could be made present, actualized, by being joined with a personality. It does not matter whether they referred to a particular living person or whether a particular person was created by them. The fact is that the person who came into being meant and signified all people who had found themselves in such a situation, and that this person made it possible for one to follow him. He was an *imitabile*.

That is how the soldier as Christian, the Christian as soldier, the Christian knight Saint George came into being. Wherever the two concepts warrior and Christian, the duty of courage and the duty of faith, reveal themselves together in any manner, this saint is there; he stands before us, worthy of imitation, inimitable – in short, as a figure who corresponds perfectly to the need to imitate. Thus does he make his way from late antiquity into the West. Constantine is the first to build him a church. And when – not two hundred years after Diocletian's death – armed struggle and Catholicism enter into relation in France, the militant youth appears there. The Catholic Burgundian Clotilde prevails upon her husband, Clovis, a convert to Christianity, to introduce his cult. Saint George comes personally – that is to say, his relics are carried from the Orient to Paris; now he is there, and it is as if the churches of Palestine and Byzantium had come over with him.

Slowly, at the end of the millennium and the beginning of the new one, his shape changes. His tasks change too: he acquires new characteristics. The relationship of the duty of the soldier to the duty of a Christian has changed. The warrior – who, when it was a question of coming forward as a confessor, delivered himself, suffering, to the executioner – becomes a fighter who defends his belief, who physically attacks the enemies of his faith, who defeats them. Saint George is no longer a martyr; he becomes a dragon killer and the rescuer of the virgin.

To explain this fully, we would have to set beside the reports of the acts of the martyrs, which we outlined, the other literary tradition of Saint George. This tradition is widespread and extensive; Karl Krumbacher recently collated it in a posthumously published treatise, *Saint George in the Greek Tradition*.[8] Though the prospect is tempting, that would take us too far afield. We can only indicate the most important aspect of this remarkable phenomenon. The holy martyr, who emerged from events of the era of Diocletian as a *miles christianus* at the end of antiquity, must have already merged, at an early stage, with figures adapted, in their own way, from antiquity by a new era. The city of Lydda (in Judaea – Greek: Diospolis) was connected with Georgios at an early stage; it was said that, after his birth in Cappadocia, his mother had raised him in Lydda. On the coast, not far from Lydda, lies Joppe; and in Joppe, according to Greek tradition, the hero Perseus had killed a man-eating sea monster and freed the virgin Andromeda. Thus, our martyr appears to have absorbed (several elements in the tradition suggest this), along with much else, the character of Perseus, as it was reshaped in late antiquity. Saint George, who was realized anew in the era of persecution, was at the same time the continuation and the representative – *aemulus* and *imago* – of an older figure. As such, he was now no longer a steadfastly suffering hero but an actively liberating hero. For a long time in the West, he made no use (so to speak) of this actively liberating capacity. Not until the West needs him as a knight, as a Christian warrior, does he reveal his militant powers; the old figure of Perseus returns, represented by him, newly realized in him; he shows how this knightly virtue too becomes active in him: *he kills the dragon, he frees the virgin* – two verbal gestures

---

8   Karl Krumbacher, *Der Heilige Georg in der griechischen Überlieferung* (Munich: Verlag der Königlich Bayerischen Akademie der Wissenschaften, 1911).

condensed from the new events at the time of the Crusades, then just beginning.

This recasting begins soon after 1000; in the legend and in the *vita*, as presented by Jacobus de Voragine, it is already complete.

Now Saint George rides in advance of the Crusaders, carrying their banner. He appears to Richard the Lionheart, just as the ancient gods had appeared to the heroes in battle. He is the saviour of knights, the patron in the holy war; where soldiers march to battle, he is called upon, and he grants victory. No fewer than thirteen knightly orders place themselves in his charge, choosing him as their forerunner. The best known are doubtless the Bavarian Order of Saint George and the English Order of the Garter (Edward III, 1350). Thus does he become the national patron of militant Old England during the Hundred Years War, and the war cry is: England and Saint George!

All this together is what we will again call *legend*. It is a verbal, a literary process. Naming, producing, creating, interpreting, under the sway of a mental disposition language forms a shape that emerges from life and intervenes everywhere in life. It does not need a work of art for the purpose: the form did not condense anywhere into an image created by an artist in a singular, nonrepeatable process; we have no epic of Saint George. Yet he is there – we can make a picture of him, and when we see his image, in which the verbal gesture is now objectified as an attribute and he is represented with a wheel, dragon, banner and horse, we recognize him, and to us, to the degree that we need him, he is an *imitabile*, a person who concretely brings to consciousness what we would like to experience and what we must do in a particular life situation.

VIII. COUNTERFORM – THE UN-SAINT – ANTI-LEGEND

We have surveyed the development of the form that arises out of the mental disposition of *imitatio*, which we call legend, in the context in which it became completely itself and came to dominate the world. For the sake of completeness, we must now survey it in other places, where it is diluted and less clearly recognisable. Let us now consider legend as a more general phenomenon.

Before we proceed with this, I would like to do something like a countercheck.

When we discussed the process of canonization, we saw that active virtue is a concept that is dependent on and complemented by a counterconcept. The opposite of virtue is crime, and the way in which virtue was ascertained resembled the way in which a crime was ascertained.

Now, if in the mental disposition of *imitatio* the saint is a figure in whom virtue becomes measurable, tangible and palpable; who brings to consciousness for us what we would like to do, to experience, and to be on the way to virtue; and who enables us to follow virtue's example by presenting it to us as a practical standard, then in the same form there must also be figures in whom crime becomes measurable, tangible and palpable, and in whom evil, punishable wrong, is objectified in the same manner. Some figure must be able to be contrasted with those who are both worthy of being imitated and inimitable – a figure we should not follow under any circumstances, one that gives us a concrete awareness of what we should not imitate. The saint must be faced with an anti-saint, the legend with an anti-legend.

Do such anti-saintly antipodes exist? It is clear that the ordinary criminal will not suffice here; he is as little an anti-saint as the man who is virtuous in the usual sense is a saint. We must see him before us, like Saint George.

One could begin with the highest by pointing to the Antichrist; the Antichrist, however, belongs as a figure originally to a different form. He represents evil in a manner unlike the one we have thus far described – not as punishable wrong, not as that which is not to be imitated. Only in the period when Christ becomes the highest saint, the ultimate *imitabile*, does the Antichrist acquire traits of unsaintliness, which are, however, not very pronounced.

But other figures stand beside him.

Christ carries the cross and, exhausted, stops to rest before the door of a cobbler's shop. But the cobbler pushes him away: 'Go!' The Savior answers, 'From now on you shall walk without rest.' And it comes to pass. From then on, the cobbler wanders from land to land, without pause, without rest – even the rest of death, the *requies aeterna*, for which one asks God, is denied him. Wherever he goes, he presages trouble.

This is a counterpart to the legend, in every way.

Here a life situation – that many could accept the new doctrine but nonetheless reject it – is condensed into a verbal gesture. It becomes *the Savior, weary of bearing the cross, rests; the Jew says, Go!* The fact that punishable wrong has become active, that it is objectified in this Jewish cobbler, is confirmed – *quod a deo fit praeter causas nobis notas* – by a miracle. It would not have been a miracle had this man been compelled, like other sinners, like Judas himself, to atone for his wrong in hell; the miracle is that he does not die, that he continues to wander, living eternally, in the sight of all. Just as in the process of canonization, this miracle is confirmed by witnesses: he has been seen here, he has been there, this person spoke to him, that one has heard tell of him. Just as in the saint active virtue becomes beneficent power, so in the Wandering Jew does punishable wrong become a baneful power; naturally, not a power one calls on him for, and not a power that he can grant as the saint can, but nonetheless a power: wherever he appears, plague, war and calamity follow.

The attitude of scholars, of humanists – who, with a greedy thirst for and an overbearing pride in knowledge, attempted to fathom everything, even that which is unfathomable, and whom one suspects of having strayed from Christian humility and from submissiveness to God's decrees – is condensed into the shape of Doctor Faust and actualized with the verbal gesture *alliance, pact with the Devil.* The Devil is, of course, the representative of evil – he is evil itself – but he is not the one who gives us the objectification of punishable wrong; he is not the realization of that which is not to be imitated. On the contrary, in a certain sense we must admit that he is within his rights. After all, he is the Tempter, the Devil. But Faust is the anti-saint, the bringer of ill fortune, whose magic money is transformed into muck, who performs further inverted miracles, whom dozens of people have seen and have spoken to, and who in the end does not die as other people do but is taken instead by the Devil himself.

Thus, we could compile a calendar of the great anti-saints, among whom were counted, in an earlier age, Simon Magus and later Robert the Devil, Ahasverus, Faust, the Flying Dutchman, Don Juan, the count of Luxemburg. They too are there; they too stand before us as Saint George did before the Crusaders – only here the *imitatio* is transformed into its opposite. All of them are attested to; the counter-miracles are pinpointed geographically in every case.

And next to the great stand the small. Just as the saint first appears in a small circle, so also can the unsaintly appear and remain in a small circle. From a certain point onward, crime can be instantiated in a criminal as active wrong; it can be detached from him and then reconnected with him. Then he becomes condensed into a form, the verbal gesture lays hold of him, and the wrong that has become active in his person remains alive, even after as an individual he has completed his sentence or been executed. He is no longer there, and yet he *is* there: he walks about, he haunts, he brings trouble, he is geographically bound to the scene of his crime. People avoid these places – a regular reversal of the pilgrimage. He receives his relics, the stone where he murdered, the wheel on which he was broken, the instruments with which he was executed. His prison, his cell, are named after him, just as the church is named after the saint.

In the mental disposition of inverted *imitatio*, punishment itself is in many respects an inverted miracle. Gallows, wheel, and executioner's sword are confirmations that wrong has become active, that it has become objectified in someone unsaintly. This is why at an execution it is not the criminal that is primarily targeted but rather the crime, which here too is conceivable and was conceived as detached from the individual who committed it.

We have to keep this in mind to understand a series of cruel and more or less symbolic punishments or forfeits known to us from the Middle Ages, as well as the crowds that attended their execution. To our modern sensibility, these punishments or forfeits affect a person and are evaluated as actions performed by people against people. This is why we find them cruel. In the world of *imitatio*, neither the punished nor those punishing are 'people' in this sense. In the punished, wrong has become objectified as a crime – the fact that this has occurred is confirmed by the punishment, as we have said: by an inversion of the miracle. In a time as preoccupied as ours with the concept of the death penalty, this is perhaps worthy of mention.

There are only a few places where we cannot, even today, find traces of such local anti-saints, and wherever we find them they belong to legend; they are born of this mental disposition. From the perspective of this mental disposition, they make us conscious of what we should avoid doing, what we prefer not to experience, in a particular life situation.

The Catholic Church has not established any procedure that corresponds to the process of canonization either for the great anti-saints, or for the small ones. The un-sanctification was performed unofficially in the community by means of language, which normally led to legends and very seldom to *vitae*. And where there was a legend, it often transformed the characters so that they remained within the mental disposition of *imitatio* but were marked with a different valence.

The saint's life too knows such transformations. It is not rare for a saint to begin his life as an anti-saint; indeed, it is almost the surest sign that virtue has become active by God's grace that one who begins by murdering his father and mother or living in incest nonetheless ends his days, like Gregorius, as a saint. It may be that these are the saints who stand closest to ordinary mortals.

Where the *vita* of an anti-saint arises, it sometimes produces a similar transformation, if in a different sense – Rinaldo Rinaldini, Fra Diavolo, Schinderhannes, lose their noxious character and cease to represent a crime.

The same thing can happen when in a work of art such a figure achieves new fulfilment: when Goethe's Faust becomes Faust II.

This shows us that the simple form, where it is present, by this token forfeits something of its essential character. Methodologically – that is, when we define literary forms – this means it is best to grasp them not where they have become fixed in a certain direction but where they are wholly themselves: as simple forms.

IX. THE MENTAL DISPOSITION OF *IMITATIO* IN OTHER PLACES – PINDAR'S VICTORY ODES – EXPLANATORY LEGENDS

Unfortunately, this is not always possible. We know that in our own era the mental disposition from which legends arise is revealed in a manner completely distinct from that of the Middle Ages, that it is by no means a generally prevailing phenomenon, and that the world of legend comprises only a very small part of our own world. We can even specify the historical moment when legend lost its general validity: this moment coincides with the end of the Middle Ages. In all the phenomena that we have called reformations and the Reformation, legend has lost its force; another form has achieved mastery. In Luther's Schmalkald Articles, the saints are numbered among the 'anti-Christian abuses'; for Luther, the true Christian is a saint, and there is no class reserved for special heroes of virtue. This means that he does not imagine virtue instantiated as action in this way, he does not see it confirmed in miracles, and he does not recognize it as a power of individual divine personalities. And in Luther's position we have the position of the whole circle he represents. Christ's role as sole mediator and the certainty of the salvation gained from belief in Christ portend the vanishing of a world in which saints, miracles, and relics had their place.

This is not to say that the mental disposition of *imitatio* is thus completely abolished; but the emphasis is displaced elsewhere. What was normative becomes ancillary. That this is the case in Reformation circles as well is proved by the fact that the attitude of the Council of Trent differs with regard to the matter of saints, is more hesitant and more careful; it is for this very reason that – as we have seen – the procedure of *canonisatio* is at this juncture established formulaically. The reason for this is not to be sought in a fear of critique by the Reformation; in Catholicism as well, the mental disposition of *imitatio* has become less effective, and other forms have come to prevail. That *imitatio* and its opposite still have not ceased to be active can be seen in the steadfast devotion to the cults of the saints continuing in other Catholic circles, as well as in the development of numerous anti-legends, arising for the most part in Protestant circles.

In times when *imitatio* no longer dominates as it did in the Middle Ages, we are often compelled to push through to the simple forms via works of literary art – or, more often, by way of numerous and diluted realizations of them.

The time has not yet come for a complete account of legend in all eras. That is also not my goal here. I aim in what follows simply to make a few points regarding what legend is in antiquity and what it is in our own time.

The victory songs or epinikia of Pindar are all constructed according to a common scheme. They begin with a reference to the occasion – the victory won; then they make a transition to a story of gods or heroes, and end by coming back to the victory. As a rule, this interpolated story is called the *mythos*.

This is how the first Olympian Ode – to name the most famous example – begins, and this poem precedes all the others in the Pindaric canon as a kind of prototype. First it praises the Olympic games generally, and then it moves on to the real occasion, the victory of the horse Pherenikos, belonging to Hieron, King of Syracuse: the victory of Hieron. But then the poet suddenly begins to tell the story of the hero Pelops, the founder of Olympia, beloved of Poseidon. Before this story is narrated completely, Pindar interrupts himself and speaks of Tantalus, the father of Pelops, who did not honour the gods and who abused their gifts. He tells of how the gods punished Tantalus. After this he returns to Pelops and reports how Poseidon helped him in courting Hippodameia, how from the god he received a golden chariot and winged horses and with these won the victory and the bride. This brings Pindar back to the Olympic games and their meaning, which he then links with praise for the chariot victory of Hieron.

As we have noted, this is the structure of all epinikia. And there is more. In an essay entitled 'Literary Applications of the Instance', to which we shall return, Franz Dornseiff has said that all 'cult poems sung by choruses, be they paeans, dithyrambs, epinikia, hymns, partheneia, or prosodia', include this main narrative section; he goes so far as to call these cult poems 'a sort of blend of cantata and ballad.'[9]

What then, in this context, is the meaning of this figure Tantalus, enemy of the gods, and of this figure Pelops, helped by the gods? Are they not also characters who make us conscious of what we should do, or avoid doing, in a certain life situation, characters whom we might follow and who can absorb us, or vice versa? Is not something instantiated in them in such a way that it becomes power, and for which they

---

9   Franz Dornseiff, 'Literarische Verwendungen des Beispiels', *Vorträge der Bibliothek Warburg, Vorträge 1924–25,* ed. Fritz Saxl (Leipzig: Teubner, 1927), pp. 208–228.

then stand as a warrant? Does not the wagon victory of Pelops both intend and signify the wagon victory itself, and every subsequent wagon victory? And are not δίφρος χρύσεος and πτεροῖσιν ἀκάμαντες ἵπποι – *diphros chruseos* and *pteroisin akamantes hippoi*, the golden wagon and the horses untiring in their wings[10] – verbal gestures condensed from a particular mental disposition? Does not the figure of Pelops occupy the same place in the cult festival following victory that the saint occupies in the daily cult of Catholicism? Do we not have, in this main story section of the cult song, legend and anti-legend? If all this is the case, then we should no longer call this part 'mythos' or 'mythical tale'; we should set it within the world to which it belongs – the world of *imitatio*.

Dornseiff recognized that this 'main section' is not limited to Greek cult poems, that similar story units are to be found much further afield, in the cult poems of the Egyptians, Babylonians, Indians, Germans, and many primitive peoples.

When we hear in the second Merseburg Incantation, meant to heal a lame horse, first how Phol and Wotan are riding in the woods, then how the colt belonging to one of them sprains its foot and afterward various goddesses act along with Wotan to heal the horse through magic spells, and how with spells – this is the transition – any horse, belonging to any man, may be healed in the very same way, there can be no doubt that we are in the world of *imitatio*: here Phol and Wotan are saints, and their story is a legend. The same is true of the Egyptian doctor who, having a snakebite to heal, begins by telling the story of how the god Re was bitten by a snake. The Assyriologists are quite right to have called the beginnings of such incantations *explanatory legend* [*Begründungslegende*].

When Virgil begins his epic with the words 'I sing of arms and the man', then connects his Trojan hero with Roman events and closes his introduction with 'such an effort it was to found the Roman race',[11] we can still see legend shimmering through the developed literary form.

But – a history of legend remains to be written.

---

10   Pindar, *Olympian* 1.87.
11   Virgil, *Aeneid* 1.1 and 1.3.

X. LEGENDS IN OUR TIME

And how about legend in our own time?

Certainly the mental disposition of *imitatio* is no longer especially active with us; it is not very vibrant; where we see legend, it is usually a traditional remnant from other eras. But let us recall the Greek victory festival, and consider how we see the victors of our own era – I mean victors in sport. What do Rademacher and Peltzer mean to us? Nurmi, Suzanne Lenglen, Tilden, Tunney, Dempsey, Schmeling, Vierkötter, Ederle . . .?

Personally they mean nothing to us, but they do represent something that seems to us worth attaining and worthy of imitation. It is not virtue that is instantiated in these figures, but a force does become active in them in which we invest our own force, a force that absorbs us: they are *imitabile*. And this active force, too, becomes measurable, in a confirmation that we call a *record* – a curious word, which first entered usage in this sense in the 1880s. *Recordari* means to remember, and the English word 'record' means something that reminds us of something, or something that we recall. 'Records of the past' are what remain from the past, and are what recall the past for us. According to the Oxford English Dictionary, however, our word 'record' means 'a performance or occurrence remarkable among, or going beyond, others of the same kind' – a definition that tends in the same direction as the word 'miracle'.

A record in sport is not a miracle in the medieval sense, but it does mean a miracle in the sense of an achievement that was not there until now, something that seemed unattainable and impossible, and which attests to an active force. Naturally it is possible that a man fleeing a crazed bull could break all records for the hundred-metre dash, but even if he should happen to check his watch he still would not consider this a record, and the newspaper would not mention it. We speak of records only when active force has become a fact in the shape of a victor. Only the victor 'holds' the record. If 100 metres are run in x seconds, then theoretically nothing stands in the way of the possibility that someone will run them in x minus n seconds, but in the sporting sense this possibility is only recognized once a *victor* runs them in x minus n seconds: that is, when the miracle occurs.

The record can be transmuted into an object, into a prize awarded as soon as a new victor has broken the prior record. To the sports club to which the victor belongs, this object is a relic. Nor do we lack the warrant: the victor donates the prize to his club, to his country – it makes a difference where the record is held, and even a person who does not follow sports feels something when he hears that an Englishman has swum the Channel more quickly than a German.

The victor in sport does not possess a *vita* in the true sense, but the simple form of the legend may be found in the sports section of the newspaper, which is always kept sharply distinct from the rest of the paper. The verbal gesture often looks like slang or jargon – and yet, *knockout* is a verbal gesture.

We said at the outset that it is dangerous to identify ourselves too much with any particular instantiation of a form. And with such a clear picture of the saint's legend as it appears in the Catholic West, it can be difficult to comprehend that the same mental disposition might underlie the sports section of our newspaper. But discovering forms even where they have lost much of their force, where they lie partly buried, defining forms that no longer look entirely 'literary', is also an essential part of our task.

CHAPTER 2

Saga

Before I move on to the simple form of the saga, or, more correctly, the *Sage* (a German term normally rendered in English as 'local tradition' or 'local legend'), I shall insert a short preliminary remark on the meaning of the word.

Legenda, a neuter plural noun that means 'things to be read', becomes in the Middle Ages a feminine singular noun with the genitive ending -ae: *legenda*. It indicates an activity half ritual in nature: the life of the saint is ritually read aloud on certain occasions, as well as being seen generally as reading material for personal edification. We are now set to understand just how this reading is undertaken in the sense of *imitatio*. In its meaning of a sequence of multiple lives, the word received the supplementary sense of *legere* – to collect, to select. Beyond this, however, the word 'legend' also acquired the meaning of a story that is not historically authenticated, and this meaning adheres very strongly to the adjective 'legendary'; it virtually signifies something that is historically not true.

It is obvious what happens in this transfer of meaning. Everything that belongs to a particular mental disposition and to its corresponding form has validity only within this form. The world of a simple form is valid and concise [*bündig*] on its own terms; as soon as we remove something from this world and transpose it into another world, it loses this affiliation with its former sphere and becomes invalid.

Let us speak for a moment about the world of the history [*Historie*] – we will see in a moment which world we mean by this. In this world, everything that was significant within another form becomes insignificant, and thus from the perspective of history everything that belongs to the sphere of legend becomes incredible, doubtful, ultimately untrue.

We shall notice the same phenomenon with the forms myth and fairy tale: from the perspective of history, they also mean something unauthenticated, something untrue. And this applies in a special degree to the *Sage*.

According to Grimm's dictionary, *Sage* means: 1) in the linguistic sense, the ability to speak, the activity of speaking; 2) that which is said, in the general usage of utterance, communication, declaration, etc., and then, in specific usage, a statement in a court of law, a documentary testimonial, a prophecy, etc.

As a third definition, however, we find: an orally disseminated report of something, news of something. And here some distinctions enter in. *Sage* can a) refer to 'roughly' contemporaneous events – this is how the dictionary puts it; and the editor adds (the volume was edited in Moritz Heyne's seminar): '*Sage* is readily associated with notions of uncertainty, implausibility, also slanderousness, but it is also used without such modifications of the concept.' *Sage* can b) refer to past events, in which case it means: news or report of past events, and particularly of events that lie far back in the past, as transmitted from generation to generation. The dictionary adds: α) that in more archaic usage, the notion of non-historicity was not yet insolubly linked with the concept *Sage*. But then: β) 'with the growing power of critical method, the modern conception develops of *Sage* as a report of past events that lacks historical authentication'; and finally: 'the concept is subsequently extended to signify naive historical narrative and tradition transformed by the poetic powers of the folk mind in the course of its wanderings from generation to generation, a free creation of folk fantasy whose constructs have drawn on significant events, persons and places; ordinary usage makes no strict distinction between *Sage* and the concepts *myth* and *fairy tale*'.[1]

At this point we must note that what we have supplied in the last paragraph is not the meaning of the *word* '*Sage*', but a definition of the

---

1 *Deutsches Wörterbuch von Jacob und Wilhelm Grimm*, ed. Deutsche Akademie zu Berlin in collaboration with der Akademie der Wissenschaften in Göttingen, 16 vols (Leipzig: Hirzel, 1854–1961), vol. 14, pp. 1644–49.

concept 'Sage', and indeed the definition propounded by a specific school – one that sees the *Sage* exclusively in its relation to another concept, which it calls history [*Historie*]. This definition construes and delimits the notion of *Sage* from the perspective of history. It is very dangerous to confuse words and concepts, especially for the editors of a dictionary. Here, the consequence of the confusion is that it could seem to a foreigner consulting this article that in the German language the word *Sage* actually has a negative connotation, and that we use it to designate something that 'lacks historical authentication'. This is simply wrong. When we use the word *Sage*, we mean something positive – provided we do not use it in express contrast to history. It may be that we are using the word incorrectly – that is, not in conformity with its original meaning; it may also be that the concept we connect with it is somewhat indistinct; but still, for us it connotes a positive form. When I speak of the Burgundian *Sage*, I do not at all mean a representation of events in the Kingdom of Burgundy that lacks historical authentication, or a free creation of folk fantasy that draws on significant events in the Kingdom of Burgundy; rather, I mean precisely the construct known as the Burgundian *Sage*, an object which lies before me, tangible and definite, which is concise [*bündig*] in itself and possesses its own validity.

In any event, I would not have spent so much time on Heyne's slip if it did not so clearly confirm what we have already stated: that the form we have provisionally called 'history' acts as the enemy of *Sage*, threatens it, stalks it, slanders it and perverts the meaning of its words as they come out of its mouth. From the perspective of one mental disposition, everything that was positive in the other becomes negative, everything that was a truth becomes a lie. The tyranny of 'history' even manages to claim that the *Sage* really does not exist, and that it is best understood as a precursor to 'history' itself. Thus in popular usage the word *Sage* loses ever more of its meaning and finally finds itself thrown together – as in Grimm's dictionary – with words like myth and fairy tale, which are likewise understood, from the perspective of 'history', simply as 'non-historical'.

If we compare the German dictionary with the English, we get a different picture. English does not know the German word *Sage*, only 'saga'. The Oxford English Dictionary defines 'saga' as follows: '1. Any of the narrative compositions in prose that were written in Iceland or Norway during the Middle Ages. Then 1b, figurative sense: a narrative having the (real or supposed) characteristics of the Icelandic Sagas.'

The English word refers first of all to a literary genre of a particular country at a particular time. After this, we have: 2. 'in incorrect usage' (partly as the equivalent of the German cognate *Sage*): 'a story, popularly believed to be a matter of fact, which has been developed by gradual accretions in the course of ages, and has been handed down by oral tradition; historical or heroic legend, as distinguished both from authentic history and from intentional fiction.' Thus: a history that the people or folk believes to be true, one that developed and expanded over the centuries and was transmitted orally: a historical or heroic 'legend.' We note in passing that in English too the word 'legend' is used to designate something that is not 'true' – something which can be distinguished from authentic history on the one hand, and from deliberate fiction on the other.

The English paraphrase approximates the German paraphrase; but – again I shall stress it explicitly – this is *incorrect use*: an erroneous and inexact application of the word. And this incorrect use of 'saga' in English corresponds to the incorrect use of *Sage* in German.

From England we move on to the north. In the Norse language we actually have two words: one, *sagn*, which corresponds generally to what we have seen in the last part of Grimm's dictionary definition and to what the OED calls the *incorrect use* of the English word 'saga'; and the second, *saga*, meaning the Icelandic literary genre.

II. THE ICELANDIC *SÖGUR*

Thus we find ourselves on a similar path to the one that we followed in our discussion of legends. Just as we explored the latter beginning with their individuation within the world of medieval legend, we can now try to pinpoint the essence of the *Sage* as a form by taking a closer look at the Old Norse *saga* genre.

These are prose narratives written in the vernacular, available to us in manuscripts of the thirteenth through to the fifteenth centuries. All manner of data suggest that these prose narratives derive from oral tradition, and that their form was built up from oral tales.

First of all, these narratives differ stylistically and syntactically from other prose works written in the so-called scholarly style; they show no sign of influence from the Latin. Second, they refer explicitly to their own origins: the formula 'it is told' or the equivalent appears frequently. Third, they are not regarded as proper works of literary art, in that they are not attributed to any particular writer or poet: they represent an anonymous tradition. Finally, we have reports to the effect that tales were really told like this at ceremonial and other occasions even some centuries earlier.

Historical and internal evidence both allow us to establish how far back this tradition stretches. We reach back to the end of the first third of the tenth century, to the time when Iceland's settlement was completed. Thus we can say that the *sǫgur* manuscripts comprise a transcription of what had evolved through consolidated and self-contained oral tales beginning in 930 and proceeding throughout the tenth, the eleventh, and following centuries.

If we inspect these tales with regard to their subject matter, their content, we can distinguish three categories or groups.

A first group includes narratives about the Icelandic settlers – about their neighbours and contemporaries, their parentage, their relationships with one another, and about natural and supernatural things that happened to them. It is not at all the story of the occupation of Iceland by the Norwegians, but always the story of individual characters who, as individuals, also belong to a family. It is told where this family built a house, a farm; how the family holdings increased; how it came into contact with other families of the same district, quarrelled with them, competed with them, lived in feud or harmony; how many sons and daughters it counted, where the sons got their wives from, what families the daughters married into. Sometimes the family is understood in relation to one character, its head; sometimes it enters onto the scene as a whole.

These stories move along vigorously, rendering only action; when a house is built, the narrator tells only as much as is needed to represent the fact of house-building as an event – he does not show any inclination to linger upon the house itself. All concrete details are subordinated to the action; attributes are never used as embellishment to single out objects from the narration and render them definite. The same is true of the landscape. These prose narratives normally also make use of verses and poem sequences.

A second group does not cover family histories in a strict sense, but rather stories of kings. Yet these king stories are very far from what we call *historia politica*. The king acts just like a north-Germanic king: he is a Viking, he conquers, he fights; but everything we attach to the concept of the state is lacking. He fights as a person, as part of a family; on his other, royal level he stands no differently from the way the patriarch stands on his clod of peasant earth. In style and syntax this second group differs from the first only in that it has substantially different things to describe.

The historical boundary between these two groups cannot be pushed any farther back than the middle of the eleventh century. We find no later events in them. Their setting includes the island of Iceland, the coast of Norway, Greenland, the Faroe Islands, and those parts of the world where the Viking kings alighted in the course of their expeditions. They stop after the introduction of Christianity.

These two groups of tales are ultimately joined by a third – one that extends far beyond what we find in the first and the second. First of all, this group is temporally and geographically much less restricted; it includes and embraces materials that date to a time considerably before Iceland's settlement. It is familiar with heroes who are clearly not at home in Iceland, or even among the north-Germanic tribes. And ultimately these tales go beyond this, recounting things that – generally speaking – we include in genres that are neither temporally nor geographically determinate, genres that begin for us with 'long, long ago; far, far away'. But – and this is for us the important thing – they present this subject matter in such a way that it cannot be separated from the earlier material; in a sense, they tell these stories as if the characters were the same ones as in the stories of Icelandic settler families, as if the events they relate were comparable to the ones that occurred in these families. In their style and syntax they are also indistinguishable from the other groups.

We call the tales belonging to the first group *Íslendinga sǫgur* (*sǫgur* of the Icelanders); those that belong to the second are *fornaldar sǫgur* (*sǫgur* of the olden days).

It is obvious that literary historians would begin early on to arrange these groups in a historical sequence. And it is equally obvious that an era concerned with the history of *Stoffgeschichte* ('history of literary themes') and partial to evolutionary thinking would take the group that included the oldest material for the oldest group, and then construe a development from this group to the other, more recent one. Thus people believed that one could say that material already extant in Germanic or Irish culture in the early and earliest Middle Ages was being retold by the Icelanders in their *fornaldar sǫgur*, and that afterward the Icelanders told the histories of their kings and their settlers in the same fashion.

At this point Andreas Heusler intervened, and this intervention is an important moment in the history of the morphological method. In a paper presented to the Prussian Academy of Sciences in 1913, *The Beginnings of the Icelandic Saga*,[2] Heusler, with his strong sense of form, offered the proof – which to me seems irrefutable – that the form of the *Íslendinga sǫgur* had to have been the point of departure for the other groups, and he did more than just this: he also proved that approaching problems like this one with the methods of *Stoffgeschichte* must necessarily lead to errors; errors that – I am hardly exaggerating – could be compared with such as might arise if one were to maintain that the historical novels of Willibald Alexis must precede *Werther*, or that Scott's novels precede those of Fielding, since we find medieval themes in Alexis and Scott, whereas we have contemporary ones in *Werther* and *Tom Jones*.

Here, Heusler – who in his book *Song and Epic in Germanic Saga*[3] had already clarified a number of issues with regard to the burning question of how the epic art form relates to other forms such as the 'song' – attacks the problem more sharply, within a more restricted field. He demonstrates that the true saga form, as it developed in Iceland in a particular period, is precisely the form that we find in the family histories belonging to the first group; that this is where the form

---

2   Andreas Heusler, *Die Anfänge der isländischen Saga* (Berlin: Verlag der Königlichen Akademie der Wissenschaften, 1914).

3   Andreas Heusler, *Lied und Epos in germanischer Sagendichtung* (Dortmund: F.W. Ruhfus, 1905).

came into its own; that it was not until it had thus acquired its own concision [*Bündigkeit*] that it began to include other thematic material; and that, whether it became 'saga of the kings' or *fornaldar sǫgur*, it nonetheless preserved its first form and impressed the character of this form on the new material. As we have already noted, Heusler shows further that this form originated orally, and that in its oral transmission it had already established itself so broadly in Iceland and become so polished that it could pass into a written form that suited its character without much difficulty or change.

I stress all this the more because Heusler himself later went in other directions, ones that – although they do not fall back into the old *Stoffgeschichte* – are less attentive to the morphological method, and because lately many people have felt a pressing need to return to the early Heusler. De Boor writes in a review of Nibelung studies: 'Here, too, it seems necessary to abandon the overly restricted focus on German interests and to recognize that the saga has its own right to scholarly inquiry. Here, too, we are constantly dealing with an equation that includes two unknowns. It would be better to turn to the simpler equation and ask of the saga the question of form, which may be answered using existing resources.'[4]

III. THE MENTAL DISPOSITION OF THE *SAGE* – KEYWORDS: FAMILY, TRIBE, BLOOD RELATIONSHIP

For us, the goal is to understand as a whole, and in its full significance, the process that Heusler observed so precisely in this one place – Iceland in the tenth and eleventh centuries.

We begin by establishing the following: that what we see in the Icelandic manuscripts of the thirteenth through fifteenth centuries is as little a simple form per se as are the lives collected in the *Acta Sanctorum*. Here too we have what we have called the actualization of a simple form, or actual form. But beyond this, the stabilized oral tradition that was

---

4 Helmut de Boor, review of Heinrich Hempel, *Nibelungenstudien. I. Nibelungenlied, Thidrekssaga und Balladen* (Heidelberg: Winter, 1926), *Zeitschrift für deutsche Philologie* 52 (1927), p. 477.

fixed in written form in the manuscripts is still not a simple form – although it is unwritten, it too relates to the thing we are looking for much as the *vita* does to legend; it too is *actualized*, and therefore in a certain sense already a literary form. To push through to the simple form from which the actualized oral and written *sǫgur* evolved, we must once again seek the mental disposition in whose world the form has validity.

What do we have in the *Íslendinga sǫgur*? I already indicated this when I discussed the group in general terms; now I must go into detail: we have what is usually called family history. But is the phrase 'family history' not misleading? We have already established that the concept 'history' is inimical to a number of simple forms: we must employ the word 'history' with care. For someone whose ideas follow 'historical' lines of reasoning, it can seem as if these *sǫgur* actually presented a historical report about a family; to one who tries to understand them impartially and without prejudice, they look different. In effect, they do not recount the history of a family; instead, they show how history exists only as family history, how family makes history. But I would prefer to avoid the word 'history' entirely and say: the inner structure of the *Íslendinga sǫgur* is determined by the concept: *family*.

The relationship among themselves of the characters of the saga is in the very first place the relationship of father to son, of grandfather to grandson, of brother to brother, of brother to sister, of husband to wife. The bond of blood is what binds the characters among themselves; clan, descent and matters of ancestry are what establish the relationships. If the family comes into contact with outsiders, then these are understood and evaluated from the perspective of the clan; the foreigners constitute a family of their own, or they are individuals who can be accepted into the family or rejected by it. Everything implied by the noun 'underling' [*Untergebener*] is included in the family, belongs to its sphere of responsibility.

As Heusler established, the people of the *Íslendinga sǫgur* are not Norwegians who have emigrated and settled in Iceland, yet they are also not Icelanders; they are people who live on this hill, by that bay. They do not make up a kingdom, a nation, a state; their collectivity is like an algebraic sum in which the summands cannot be combined into a single number. Naturally, they have much in common, but 'common' here signifies only what each individual owns in his own right. Even in the place where they meet for discussion and to make certain resolutions in common, at the *thing*, the governing assembly, they come as the heads of families.

In the first instance, indeed nearly exclusively, their legislation regulates encroachments on the rights of a family, or family feuds; the execution of punishment is not assigned to a special authority, but is delegated to the affected family. One of the most severe punishments is *Ächtung* ('ostracism'), which here does not mean ejection from the organized state, but from all family associations. Whenever the *Ächtung* is not recognized by another family, and the latter shelters the ostracized party, from now on he belongs to this family. Ownership [*Besitz*] literally occurs where the family sits [*sitzt*]; it is what is passed on by inheritance within the family, what is left behind by the family.

In a *Sage* like that of the people of Vatnsdal (*Vatnsdaela saga*), we follow a clan through six or seven generations. But the narrative is built up in such a way that the fame and the power of the clan climax in one generation and that in this generation it is represented by one person in particular. Ingimund, the man who migrates from Norway to Iceland and takes ownership of the site, and after whom the *Sage* is named, represents this moment of brilliance. Seen with regard to the characters, the whole thing could be called the *Sage* of Ingimund, of Ingimund's ancestors, of Ingimund's progeny. The closer the previous and following generations come to this representative of the clan, in whom the clan appears at its most powerful, the more sharply the *Sage* delineates them. Besides Ingimund, it is his father Thorstein and Ingimund's three sons that are most clearly visible. His grandfather and his grandsons are implied in a sketchy fashion, while his great-grandsons disappear into the shadows. Between the fifth and sixth generations, the power of the clan shifts to a collateral line; the illegitimate son of a concubine joins the family and represents it. He is the one who adopts Christianity; with him, the family enters into a new phase of its existence, ending the phase that peaked in Ingimund. Reading this *Sage*, we sense on every page how concepts that we are accustomed to understand in relation to a people or folk, concepts like conquest, defeat, oppression, liberation, here have nothing to do with a folk; they always apply to a clan, a tribe, a family. National consciousness is here a matter of family solidarity; right and duty are dictated not by the needs of society or the *res publica* but by the welfare of the clan, by the requirements of kinship. Civic solidarity is here the bond of blood. Consanguinity, blood vengeance, blood feud, marriage, clanship, the collectivity of kin, heritage, inheritance, heredity here make up the foundation, the ground plan.

Thus we have moved from what we initially found in a temporally and geographically definable location, in an actualized form, to the general entity we sought. There is a mental disposition according to which the world is constructed as family, by which the world in its entirety is interpreted in consonance with the concept of the clan, the family tree, blood relationship. This mental disposition and its world can be recognized in places other than Iceland in the tenth and eleventh centuries; and this is the world we mean when we use the word *Sage*. It is this world and this world alone that we would designate with the term *Sage*.

I know that this use of the word *Sage* will encounter more difficulties than that of the word legend, as we have understood the form. We have seen that the usage we extracted from the dictionary definitions is different; anthologies and scholarly and non-scholarly accounts are ready to call many things *Sage* that we cannot count as such. What we find collected in Grimm's *German Sagas* or Dähnhardt's *Nature Sagas*[5] corresponds only in the smallest degree to what we will call *Sage*. But it is one of the tasks of morphology, and possibly not its least important, to counter a loosened and sloppy usage with its own definitions of and reflections on form. Thus when I speak of the *Sage* of a hero, I do not at all mean an oral tradition concerning a course of events that is not entirely known to me historically or that is not historically authenticated; nor do I mean a historical personality that has been reshaped by the poetic gifts of the folk mind. Instead, I mean the heroic representative of a particular clan, the hereditary carrier of the great qualities of his people.

---

5   Jacob Grimm and Wilhelm Grimm, eds, *Deutsche Sagen*, 2 vols (Berlin: Nicolaische Buchhandlung, 1816–1818); Oskar Dähnhardt, *Natursagen: Eine Sammlung naturdeutender Sagen, Märchen, Fabeln und Legenden*, 4 vols (Leipzig: Teubner, 1907–1912).

Sage is for us the simple form that has become actualized as saga, first orally and then in writing, and in such a definite way that it was able to reconfigure material that originally did not belong to it; the *Íslendinga sǫgur* is a particular individuation of the form. From this actualization we can derive a tangible sense of the form-giving mental disposition and its train of thought. We can indicate the mental disposition of *Sage* with the key words *family, clan, blood relationship*.

IV. COUNTEREXAMPLE – EXAMPLE – THE VERBAL GESTURE OF THE SAGA – MOBILITY – GREEK SAGA – ACTUALIZED AND SIMPLE FORM: SAGA AND *SAGE*

At this point I would like to look more closely at what we have called a *mental disposition* [*Geistesbeschäftigung*]. For the form *Sage* is not generated everywhere that family, family relations, family catastrophes converge in a set of events.

One example: by marrying Elizabeth of York, Henry Tudor combines the claims of the houses of Lancaster and York – which have been fighting each other for several decades as the 'red and the white rose' through civil war, assassinations, insurgency and betrayal – and ascends to the English throne. He has two daughters, Margaret and Mary, and a son, who becomes his successor. This successor, Henry VIII, marries six times. He divorces twice; twice he has his wives executed, one wife dies giving birth to his only son, the last wife survives him. This son, Edward VI, is ten years old when his father dies. Two dukes, one after the other, control the government; the last of these marries his own son to a granddaughter of the second daughter of Henry VII, and when King Edward dies at the age of sixteen he attempts to elevate this couple to the throne. The effort fails; those involved are executed. Instead, a daughter born of the first marriage of Henry VIII becomes queen, Bloody Mary. When she dies childless, her half-sister Elizabeth, with whom she has lived in enmity, becomes her successor. One of the most famous conflicts of the life of this queen is the quarrel with the granddaughter of her aunt Margaret, Mary Stuart, who – herself Queen of Scotland through her marriage to the Scottish king – married three times, once a French king, once a cousin, and once a third husband who had killed the second. Elizabeth has

Mary executed. When she dies childless, Mary's son becomes her successor.

Family relationships, family complications, of a kind that could not be more convoluted. Nonetheless, we would be letting the *Stoffgeschichte* we just said goodbye to back in through the window were we to assert that what happened with the House of Tudor in sixteenth-century England somehow actualized the form *Sage*. It was experienced as a saga neither by those involved nor by contemporaries. It is as little a *Sage* as the good daughter from the first marriage and the evil stepmother with her two arrogant daughters make the fairy tale 'Cinderella' a *Sage*.

Why not? Because neither Henry VIII nor Edward VI nor Mary nor Elizabeth consider themselves primarily as a descendant of Henry VII, as a member of the Tudor family or clan, because neither at the execution of Jane Grey nor at the execution of Mary Stuart is the feeling dominant that here a blood relation, a member of the clan, is being killed; because the distance between Mary the Catholic and Elizabeth the Protestant is seen not as a question of Catholicism and Protestantism being things that divide two sisters who should be bound by bonds of kinship, but instead the two women are understood as representatives of two religions at odds with one another. Because, finally, the English people does not observe all this, experience it, intervene in it and ally itself with one side or the other as participants in a family quarrel, but rather interprets this all from a political or a religious perspective. The mental disposition that we find realized in the form *Sage* is lacking.

Is it completely absent? Certainly not. That *the throne is heritable* is a verbal gesture; it shows the point where events have coalesced into form and become language within the mental disposition of clan and consanguinity. Yet although in this case the throne may be heritable, still it is not *the inheritance*. The throne does not belong to the House of Tudor; rather, the House of Tudor belongs to the throne. Here the throne is not an object that represents the prestige and honour of a family, a thing in which the might of a clan instantiates itself and which is charged from now on with the power of a family: this throne does not relate to the *Sage* form as the relic does to the legend form. This throne here means England, the kingdom of England, the state of England; and although the Tudor family rules England and its members have the hereditary right to rule England, in the eyes of the English, England is nonetheless not the family property of the Tudors, not their inheritance.

We see that the *Sage* form is harder to grasp than the legend form. Just as the German word *Sage* was attacked, diluted, baffled by a different mindset, so too was the form. In the English case, a state idea or a national consciousness suppresses a world built up according to the mental disposition 'family'.

Thus it is no coincidence that the *Íslendinga sǫgur* stops where Christianity, or more precisely the Christian church, begins. The Christian church binds its members to a community; it introduces another sort of relationship, the relationship of man to man; thus it even adopts the language of the *Sage*: it commandeers the verbal gesture of the *Sage*, it calls its priests 'father', its members 'brothers' and 'sisters', those living in its spiritual communities *fratres* – but with its analogy it destroys the true form of the *Sage*, which knows only blood and blood relationship. What was meaningful in the *Sage*, in the family – birth, marriage, death – the church carries over via a sacrament into a new mental disposition, and thus wrests it from the *Sage*.

To this example I shall add another.

In the second book of the Iliad (l. 100ff), the whole Greek people has gathered for an important assembly; resolutions of the greatest importance are to be made. It must be decided whether the operation against Troy is to be abandoned, or if it should be carried out. Now the highest commander stands up, Agamemnon – he who holds the sceptre or staff of rulership, the σκῆπτρον (skêptron). Hephaestos had formed it with art and given it to Zeus, son of Cronos. Zeus passed it on to Hermes, and Hermes gave it to Pelops, that fine charioteer; Pelops gave it to Atreus, marshal of fighting men, and Atreus, dying, passed it on to Thyestes rich in flocks. Thyestes gave it to Agamemnon, and with it many islands and the lordship over all Argos.

We have seen how Saint George stands upon the altar, identifiable by the wheel with which he was tortured, or by the horse and lance with which he fought the dragon; how what was a verbal gesture in his legend became an attribute in his heavenly form. Here in the Iliad, we see something similar: we see the ruler in a decisive moment, leaning upon an attribute. This sceptre is made by the gods and has passed among them from hand to hand. Then it came to men, to a clan, and within this clan it has again travelled from father to son, from brother to brother, from uncle to nephew. In this clan it means the power to rule, within and outside the clan. Agamemnon stands here as a ruler, because the gods have conferred rulership upon his family and because in this family he himself is the head, the carrier of the sceptre.

Agamemnon speaks to the other Greeks at this moment because his family has been done an injustice: his brother's wife has been abducted. The abductor's family did not approve of this act, but since it is family, the abductor remains kin, and as long as he is considered kin, the family bears responsibility for his deeds and shares his fate. Thus family stands against family, and between them is *raptio*, feud, revenge – the verbal gestures of the *Sage*.

Again, we cannot say that the entire text that we call the Iliad is nothing other than *Sage*. First of all, what we have here is the literary form epic, which has its own laws. Second, within this epic the mental disposition of *Sage* is slightly modified – here we already find something of the folk; meanwhile, the allies who originally attached themselves to families understood solely as families start to acquire a national tinge – there is in the Iliad already something of Greeks versus Trojans, of West against East; the Iliad even presages the opposition of Hellas and Asia. But the *Sage* still remains powerful, it preponderates, and in many places it decisively governs the sequence of thought. Here, at the place where we have grasped it, we see it become actualized in the simplest of ways: we see how, in the house of Pelops, under the Atreides, power passes by inheritance within the clan; we see how this power is connected with the sceptre that originated with the gods and is inherited from generation to generation among men. Here each character is the *inheritor*; in its objective meaning, every object can be the *inheritance*. Once more, these nine verses constitute for us the actualized form of a *Sage* per se – and in them we recognize the simple form as such.

If we were to trace through the Greek world in further detail what the Iliad so plainly presents us with – the saga of Atreus and the Atreides – we would find an extremely convoluted, often knotty tangle of *Sagen* that is actualized each time in a different way, but which in its countless guises contains nearly everything that *Sage* in general can encompass. Convinced though I am that this knot must someday be untangled, I cannot do so here. I will merely select some examples that will help us understand *Sage* better.

Thus we hear that the sons of Pelops – Atreus and Thyestes – murder an illegitimate, socially inferior son of their father's with help from their mother Hippodameia and throw his body into a well, and then how their father utters a curse on his clan that will remain in effect even unto the last generation. We see here the verbal gestures, the units into which *Sage* becomes condensed. These are on the one hand *illegitimate child*, bastard, the foreign body within the family that is descended from the father, that is consanguineous with but still does not belong to the family, that fractures the family; and on the other, a *curse*, something that instantiates hatred and repugnance against one's own clan, something that also exerts power in the family beyond the lifetime of individual persons, comparable with the miracles of the saint after his death, but here an inheritance that bequeaths itself.

We hear further that the brothers come into conflict between themselves – about power, about women, about property. We read in the Iliad (II. 106) of πολύαρνι Θυέστῃ (*poluarni thuestēi*), Thyestes rich in flocks. Later we read in an epitome that one of the brothers acquired a *golden lamb* with which rulership was connected. Now the other brother seduces his sister-in-law, and with her help he steals the lamb. *Adultery* encroaches upon the family.

Further: Atreus murders the sons of Thyestes in revenge, and serves them up as a meal to Thyestes, his brother, whom he has summoned back from his flight by means of a herald. After the ghastly meal the father is shown the hands and feet of his sons: *parricide*, escalated to a coercion to devour one's own blood. And finally Thyestes begets a son with his own daughter, a son who will later slay the son of Atreus with the help of his own wife. Incest in the family – an inextricable entanglement of the clan network.

The question of whether these last wild strokes represent a very early realization of *Sage* or a very late one need not bother us here. The point of these examples is simply to show the world of *Sage* in its most extreme expression.

Whence do we know these stories, which change each time we read them, which differ among themselves in all sorts of details, which here appear one way, there another? First from short mentions, from marginal comments, from glosses and scholia; then from later historians who attempted somehow to unify and harmonize the scattered materials, from writers comparable to our anthologists; finally, from works of art each of which takes hold of a part, a section, and actualizes this part in and of itself in a unique literary form. Nowhere, however, has the full *Sage* of this clan ever emerged as a whole. Nor do we have any epic that coherently represents the fate of the descendants of Pelops.

What does this prove? That in this case as well, *Sage* was transmitted orally; that it crept along through the Greek world – and probably earlier – from mouth to mouth; that it was known everywhere, but unlike in Iceland in the eleventh century was never realized in an integrated narrative; that – to remain with our terminology – it never made the transition from *Sage* to saga. Thus it remained polymorphous, changing its outward form from instance to instance, being narrated one way in one place or time and another way later or elsewhere, which is why it never became fixed in writing. Only in its inward structure, in its inward form, did it remain constant, only as *Sage* did it survive. Developing out of the mental disposition of family, clan, consanguinity, from a family tree it built a world that would remain constant in a hundred shimmering variations, a world of ancestral pride and paternal curses, of family property and family feud, of *raptio* and adultery, of blood vengeance and incest, of family loyalty and family hatred, of fathers and sons and brothers and sisters, a world of heritability. And a world in which good and evil, bravery and cowardice, are as little understood as individual traits as property is something thought to be subject to individual ownership – a world where everything matters solely from the perspective of family, where the fate of persons always reflects on the clan.

V. THE 'ORIGINAL FORM' IN *STOFFGESCHICHTE* – *SAGE* AND EPIC – NIBELUNGENLIED

If all this is so, then it would be very dangerous to try in the manner of *Stoffgeschichte* to push through to a so-called 'original type' [*Urtyp*] of the *Sage* of the Atreides – that is, to attempt to derive or even restore a single version from the countless 'variants' in which it is to be found, and then assert that all the other versions are 'later' modifications of this one type; or even to think that we could in this way observe the same 'story' in its various 'phases of development'.

This danger is not really present with regard to the Atreid *Sage*; but with other Greek *Sagen*, and above all with our German *Sagen*, the attempts in this direction are incessant. This is because, unlike the *Sage* of Atreus and Thyestes, these *Sagen* acquired their final, definitive character when they were realized in a unique literary form. They are no longer called *Sage*, but rather 'epic'. And in this epic, in this literary form which outlines everything, shapes everything with clarity, finalizes everything using distinctive means with distinctive laws, the *Sage* has also acquired such a definite outline that in our wonder at the new form we simply cannot imagine that the *Sage* as a simple form was once mobile, polymorphous, surging, and that in its actualizations too it was still mutable and inconstant. We do not believe that it was not formerly a coherent story representing particular events in a particular manner.

In Germany we are encouraged in our disbelief by what occurred with some of the Germanic tribes and by what happened in Iceland in the tenth and eleventh centuries. In Iceland, in oral tradition, the *Sage* developed steadily, continuously, uninterruptedly into saga: into the *Íslendinga sǫgur*. There it could easily be transcribed into written form. Thus we conclude that things will also have proceeded this way with the other Germanic tribes. And driven by this sense of wonder at the epic on the one hand, and on the other by our disbelief, we commence to botch scholarly work on the *Sage* by extrapolating from its internal character, from what is constant in it, to an actualized form that may well be gone, that may have vanished and is nowhere to be found, but which according to our convictions must once have existed and which we feel obliged to reconstruct, indeed to construct. Let me repeat: here is the great danger – it is very likely that with our jerry-built actualized forms we are violating the *Urform*, with our artificial saga the *Sage*, and that with each of these constructions we block the way to the concept. We need to know, not how a saga may have looked, but what *Sage* means – we need to know this also in order to comprehend how

Sage becomes active within the epic. The proper method is not to observe what is variable in its variability, but rather to extrapolate, from comparison of what varies with what remains constant, the meaning of what remains constant.

If we believe that the simple form *Sage* is sometimes active in works of the epic art form, then we have in the first place to ask not which actualized form, which saga is to be found in the Nibelungenlied or the Iliad, and then how this saga may have looked in its actualization before the epic took hold of it, but rather how the simple form that emerged from the mental disposition 'family, clan, blood relationship' relates to the autonomous epic art form, and how in this literary form it acquires its new, distinctive, actualized character.

With legend we saw how one of the great movements of the Western peoples comprehends itself in the mental disposition of *imitatio*, how the Crusades stand under the sign of *legend*. Here we can add that another, earlier part of that movement is connected in the same way with the concept *Sage*. Much of what we call the *migration period* [*Völkerwanderung*] occurs in terms of this mental disposition – this is not a movement oriented on *imitatio*, either in general or for each individual participant; rather, it is a matter of wandering tribes that consider themselves distinct entities, that feel themselves to be family, and within which it is again families that bind the tribe together. And thus everything that happens here becomes *Sage*: the demise of a people becomes the demise of a family, the triumph of a people is condensed in a verbal gesture to the triumph of the head of a family, of the hero of a *Sage* – and the collision of two peoples, whether migrant groups meeting each other or migrants coming upon settlers, can only be imagined in this way. It is clear how language produces, creates, interprets this experience; however, it is equally clear that although much here is actualized, in the bustle and tumult of the migrations it does not become actualized form the way it could with the leisurely Norwegian settlement of Iceland.

This fluid diversity returns in the epic – as, in epic, events of an earlier age always recur. It survives there not as saga, but as *Sage*. Nowhere are the passions and fates of a family so tangled and so expressive as in the Nibelungenlied. Here everything is family. Gibichungs, Wälsungs, Nibelungs, Burgundians are families. Yet the

Huns too are a family – they are not an enemy people, they are of the tribe of Etzel. There is in Etzel nothing of the national enemy of the Germans or of the *flagellum dei*[6] – he is a husband, he is the head of a family, he is bound through his wife to the quarrel of another family, or he lusts after the treasure in which family property is instantiated. And here, once again, there converges everything native to family: property and feud, blood vengeance, parricide, fraternal loyalty, women's quarrels, sexual intercourse – all of this escalates enormously, dissolving sometimes, when necessary, nearly into comedy.

This is how the Nibelungenlied appears to us: as an outgrowth of Germanic *Sage* far more than of any particular – let alone recoverable – Germanic saga, which allows us to distinguish it from its Romanic rival, the Song of Roland, in which all this is missing, in which it is replaced by the mental disposition of legend. The epic of the migration of the peoples next to the epic of the Crusades – coequal as a literary form, but grown from a different mental disposition.

VI. *SAGE* IN THE OLD TESTAMENT – ANTI-*SAGE* – ORIGINAL SIN – DARWINISM – GENEALOGICAL NOVEL – OBJECT AND PERSON IN THE *SAGE*

Now that we have studied the *Sage* among the Germans and the Greeks, I would like to call attention to a third point at which *Sage* has become condensed in a particular manner, and where once again an entire people is understood, and understands itself, as family. We read in a tradition that has been preserved in the canon of the Old Testament how the Israelites understand themselves as the family of Abraham, rapidly multiplied on God's orders, and of how the Twelve Tribes can be traced back to as many brothers. Here, too, all the characters are inheritors, and property is the inheritance. The most difficult trial a father can be set is the sacrifice of his son and, in him, of his family. Here the blessing of the father is so concrete, so charged with power, that it has repercussions within the lineage of someone for whom it was not intended; it can be stolen like something tangible. Here the god is a god of the fathers, a god of Abraham, Isaac and Jacob. And

---

6   'Scourge of God', i.e. Attila the Hun (c. 406–53).

here again fraternal loyalty and fraternal quarrels, family discord, jeal-ousy, and everything that goes with all this, recur as the experience of characters, of heroes in whom the *Sage* has condensed itself, and as verbal gestures.

Since I do not mean to give a history of the *Sage*, I will not pursue the Israelite *Sage* any further. I will simply point on the one hand to the events that make up the *Sage* of the Patriarchs, and on the other to what happens in the house of David and to what is told in 2 Samuel and 1 Kings. Again, for all the similarity of the material we find an utter incommensurability of mental attitudes, of mental dispositions, and we see that the form that emerges with the Patriarchs and their descendants is different from the form in which the sons of kings lived and were experienced in the era of David. In this context, family history and the question of kings were construed in relation to the state of Israel.

As with legend, however, I would like to touch on the question of how active the *Sage* may still be today.

Where we have discussed it thus far, *Sage* was linked with a move-ment of peoples. We found it with wandering Semites, and with wandering or migrating Germanic tribes. The *Sage* of the Atreides must have been formed in the time of the Doric migration – indeed, it even seems as if the Greek *Sage* includes something that was older than the migrants themselves and that the migrants assimilated in a particular way. The *Sage* was reinterpreted, debased, traced back to something evil – we have here before us *a process similar to the devel-opment of the anti-legend*. On the other hand, we have seen that what I would like very generally to call state formation or the idea of the state is a thing hostile to *Sage* – just as that which we have called very gener-ally the Reformation neutralized legend.

Let us observe this in our own sphere. Knut Liestøl has shown that in the North the saga has not ceased to develop from the mental dispo-sition 'family'.[7] But is it not still *Sage* that our own farmers experience – are property, trade, rights and events not still understood and judged by the concepts family, clan, blood relationship? Whoever is familiar with country life will recognize this *Sage*; we still encounter it today in

---

7   Knut Liestøl, *Norske aettersogor* (Kristiania: O. Norli, 1922).

stories told by farmers. Only here there is less condensation, here language could take hold less strongly; everything is faded, and the grand gesture is missing.

What about the greater picture? There is one point at which Christianity – however much it may have fought *Sage* in its very essence – nonetheless reabsorbed it: in the concept of Original Sin. In the great community constituted by Christianity, something was again heritable – something that had originated in the first parents, in the earliest ancestors; something that had instantiated itself; something that retained power from generation to generation, like the paternal curse in a clan, and which could be cancelled only in a particular sense by the deity's splitting itself into father and son, as in a *Sage*. However much a different mental disposition exerted itself to bring about the unity of this pair by binding them to a third term not belonging to family, and however much the effort was later made to eliminate the mother, the *Sage* remained effective within this relationship; and both in the inherited sin itself and in the redeeming son of God verbal gestures could be found in which the form had become condensed and in which it survived.

I believe that it is correct to bring this concept of Original Sin into relation with the concept of heritability, as a recent dissertation has done – with heritability as the nineteenth century understood it and upon which it based all manner of scientific studies: as a question of heritable qualities, of all kinds of inheritable diseases, of congenital disorders; in short, of everything we call heredity. What enormous efforts were made to observe and even to calculate this heredity in all its details! Heredity became the foundational principle of a natural system that we are accustomed to call Darwinism, after one of its most distinguished proponents. Thus did nature become *Sage* – thus was everything living brought back to family trees, to a family tree, studied with regard to its family relationships, its relationships construed in the language of family relationship. Natural science became the science of genealogy, of descent – and it was like a sacrifice that this science made to itself when, in full surrender to this foundational principle, it drew the conclusion that man's closest relative was the ape.

Once again this mental disposition has expressed itself in literary forms. It is the long prose narrative that lays hold of these concepts of heritability and filiation, that appropriates this *Sage*. I will note simply that Zola entitled his novel cycle *Les Rougon-Macquart: Natural and Social History of a Family under the Second Empire*, and that John Galsworthy, in conformity with English usage and not at all 'incorrectly', returned to the *Íslendinga sǫgur* when naming his own cycle *The Forsyte Saga*. There is no point in adding examples.

I am finished with the *Sage*. We have seen that it is a more difficult form to pinpoint because it envelops itself more tightly in its mental disposition; because – with some exceptions – its actualizations are normally less definite, less strongly marked than those of the legend; and because – to repeat – the relation of *Sage* to saga does not correspond in all respects to the relation of legend to *vita*. Its verbal gesture is also less condensed; it is not so clear and vibrant. And because the form is more modest in nature, its mode of expression is more easily disqualified, as we have seen.

Nonetheless, it stands before us as a simple form, both in its verbal form and in its characters, who here signify inheritors, and in its objects, which here signify inheritance.

Such *objects* are the family household, the family treasure, the sword of the father; such *characters* are, besides the hero of the clan and his kinsfolk, also the ghostly ancestress who represents the whole family and who appears when misfortune threatens it, or the *fylgjur* of the *sǫgur*.

A young boy is abandoned and raised in another family. Unwittingly he enters a room occupied by his own grandfather – he stumbles, and the grandfather laughs and says: I have seen what you did not see. When you came in, there was a young polar bear running before you, but when it saw me it stopped and stood still; you, however, were too quick and tripped over it. Now, I believe that you are not the son of Krumm, but belong to a more noble line.

Effectively, every figure in *Sage* carries such a fylgja with him – a young polar bear that invisibly accompanies him, but in which, when a relative approaches, the relative recognizes his membership in the clan.

CHAPTER 3

Myth

I. DEFINITIONS – JACOB GRIMM'S CONCEPTION

By the time Heyne's seminar students, who also edited the 'M' volume of Grimm's dictionary, finally reached 'My-', they must have been in a hurry to get home. They wrote:

> *Mythe*, f. – Saga, unauthenticated narrative, derived from the Greek μῦθος, with a change in grammatical gender on analogy with *Sage, Geschichte, Fabel, Erzählung*, etc.[1]

Then a meagre citation from Uhland – and that is all.

On the other hand, in the second edition of Eisler's *Philosophical Dictionary* we find the following:

> Mythos (μῦθος, speech, traditional narrative) is a fantastic, anthropomorphic conception of life and nature comprising an element of religion at a particular phase of its development, an explanation of nature founded on 'personifying apperception' and 'introjection' (q.v.). In myth, which is a product of fantasy but which also possesses its own distinctive logic, there prevails the primitive *Weltanschauung*, the 'protophilosophy', as it were; science and philosophy developed from myth, but also partly out of the conflict between myth's fantastic-anthropomorphic approach and the increasing ability of exceptional personalities to think conceptually . . .[2]

---

1 Jacob Grimm and Wilhelm Grimm, *Deutsches Wörterbuch*, vol. 6: *L, M* (Leipzig: Hirzel, 1885), 2848.

2 Rudolf Eisler, *Handwörterbuch der Philosophie*, 2nd ed., Richard Müller-Freienfels, ed. (Berlin: Mittler, 1922), p. 417.

If we compare the two definitions, we see that things are more complicated in this case than they were with the *Sage*. On the one hand, Grimm's dictionary devalues myth from the perspective of history, with the simple equation: myth = saga = unauthenticated narrative. In Eisler's dictionary, *mythos* is attacked from a different angle and once again not recognized in its autonomy. *Mythos* – so the first sentence asserts – is a conception of life and nature, an explanation of nature. Yet *mythos* comprises but one element of religion at a particular phase of its development and can only be understood as such. Then the second sentence maintains that there is present in *mythos* a primitive *Weltanschauung*, without saying whether 'primitive' here means original, simple, undeveloped, or inferior – all of these being possible meanings according to Eisler's dictionary (see under 'primitive'). In any case, the adjective 'primitive' again makes *mythos* into a precursor – this time not a precursor of history but a precursor of philosophy: into 'protophilosophy', from which science and philosophy are supposed to have 'developed'.

Thus, besides history, *Mythe* has a second enemy that denies it its singularity, that makes it a precursor, an early link in the chain of a course of development directed at higher things. We will have a chance to become acquainted with this enemy.

In the meantime, I would like to add a third citation, if only to help us recover from the dictionaries.

In 1835, Jacob Grimm dedicated his *Deutsche Mythologie* to the historian Friedrich Christoph Dahlmann, the first person in the modern era to devote extensive study to one of the sources used also by Grimm: Saxo Grammaticus. Since what this dedication, which Grimm also meant as a foreword to his book, says about our forms is more profound than what we find in the dictionaries, I shall quote it at length:

> *Sage* and history are distinct powers, whose domains may merge at the borders but each of which has its own separate, inviolate ground. The ground of all *Sage* is *mythos*, i.e. belief in gods, with all its infinite variety of nuance from people to people: a much more common, unsteady element than history, but gaining in scope what it lacks in fixity. *Sage* cannot be grasped independently of such a mythical

substratum, any more than history can be grasped independently of things that have happened. While history is being produced by the actions of men, *Sage* hovers above them like a gleam shining in between, like a scent that attaches to them. History never repeats itself; it is everywhere new and fresh, while *Sage* is ceaselessly reborn. History wanders earth's soil with a firm tread, winged *Sage* rises and falls: its lingering sojourn is a favour it does not show to all peoples. Where distant events would otherwise be lost in the darkness of time, *Sage* binds itself to them and preserves some part of them: where myth is weakened and liable to melt away, history comes to its aid. But when myth and history join together more intimately and are wed, then epic erects a loom and weaves its threads. You put it well [Grimm means Dahlmann, in his study of Saxo Grammaticus]: history unrecorded by contemporaries is liable to disappear from human memory, or – if *Sage* has seized upon it – to survive in a transmuted form, just as through culinary art, the hardest fruit can change almost randomly into the softest, the bitterest into the sweetest. I grant you the metamorphosis, the change, but not the analogy to culinary concoction. For we may not call concocted what has been transformed and altered through a quietly active, unconsciously effective power. There are very few contrived sagas – and, of these, none whose deceptiveness does not ultimately evaporate before the eye of critique, as falsified history must yield to the much greater might of true history . . .[3]

How far we find ourselves, in this paragraph, from the flattened language of the dictionaries! It is an excellent example of Jacob Grimm's language, of his style, of his way of looking at things. We see *Sage* and history before our eyes, in their disparate characters, in the specific way in which each presents itself and renders itself distinct. But is it clear now what *Sage* really is, and how exactly it relates to history? Have these lovely metaphors, which tell us that *Sage* shines like a gleam and attaches like a scent, allowed us to understand how this actually happens? Or to comprehend how *Sage* binds itself to distant events?

---

3   Jacob Grimm, *Deutsche Mythologie* (Göttingen: In der Dietrichschen Buchhandlung, 1835), iii–iv.

And, further – have we understood what 'myth' means here? Myth is supposed to be the foundation of all *Sage*, and myth itself is called 'belief in gods, with all its infinite variety of nuance from people to people'. May we conclude from this that every belief in gods is myth – or even that myth always means belief in gods? And then, in a place where we would expect the word *Sage*, suddenly we find the word *myth* instead, with the observation that myth can become a support to history. Are myth and *Sage* no longer conceptually distinguishable? Is myth the same as *Sage*? Myth and history are wed, and where they are wed, epic erects a loom and weaves. Let us stay with the metaphor – I for my part feel a pressing need to become much more closely acquainted with the bride and bridegroom before I congratulate them on their marriage; I feel a burning curiosity regarding this loom's composition: I must know the nature of this warp and woof.

There is one thing I should like to make clear: you must not believe that I lack reverence for the memory of Jacob Grimm. I have quoted this passage to show that in his work we find no smug semantic shift coming either from history or from philosophy, and that with him every concept has its own power and, as he himself says, its own 'separate, inviolate ground'. I also know the degree to which language and poetry mean, to this student of German Idealism, a great communal event occurring within the soul of a people – indeed, the greatest thing that has happened or could happen within the folk soul – and that in this foreword it was not so much a matter of explaining things in detail as of conveying a totality whose elements one could only sense. Here myth, *Sage*, history and epic were not to be sharply distinguished from one another; they were to be taken together as representatives of that 'quietly active, unconsciously effective power' that was for Jacob Grimm 'something completely different from the power of a late poet, however great'.

Yet the fact that I know all this is no reason to stop there. On the contrary – if we are truly convinced that these concepts have their own 'separate, inviolate ground', then it is our task to survey and subdivide the land, to mark out the territory. We have attempted this with legend and *Sage* – I am not unaware that with myth it will be more difficult. However, it must be possible in this case as well to push through to the form; it must be possible to define the precise nature of what Jacob Grimm suggested with images.

II. MYTHOLOGY AND *MYTHOS* – EXAMPLE FROM GENESIS – QUESTION AND
ANSWER – ORACLE – MYTH AND *MYTHOS* – ESSENTIAL NATURE: CREATION

In myth, we do not find what Catholic legend of the Western Middle Ages and the Icelandic saga of the tenth and eleventh centuries gave us. We speak of Greek and Germanic mythology, of Indian myths and the myths of primitive peoples, but in the tangle of doctrines, creation stories, heroic tales, in all the visions of metamorphosis, apocalypse and the hereafter – in short, in all that we are accustomed to call *mythology* – I know of no single point at which we might sense the presence of *myth* or *mythos* so clearly and distinctly that we would be forced, as it were, to begin our analysis there.

We therefore begin with a confused general picture, and we must attempt to put it in order. I would thus like to start off with an example, taken from Genesis:

> And God said: 'Let there be lights in the firmament of the heavens to separate the day from the night; and let them be for signs and for (the determination of) seasons and for days and years; and let them be for lights in the firmament of the heavens to give light upon the earth.' And it was so. And God made the two great lights, the greater light to rule the day, and the lesser light to rule the night; and he made the stars also. And God set them in the firmament of the heavens to give light upon the earth, to rule over the day and over the night, and to separate the light from the darkness. And God saw that it was good.[4]

What do we have here before us? Already in the translation we hear that this is not purely a statement, not a story or a simple depiction. In the sublimely affirmative – one might say: reassuring – cadences, we hear something akin to a dialogue. Something preceded this, and this something was a question, was many questions. People had beheld the heavens; they had seen how by day the sun illumined the sky and by night the moon, consistently, repeatedly. Seen, and then wondered, and then asked questions. How to name these lights of the day and the night? What is their meaning in relation to time and the phases of the year?

---

4   Genesis 1:14–8 (Revised Standard Version).

Who put them there? What was it like before the world was lit up by them, before day and night were separated, before time was subdivided? And then an answer comes to the asker. This is an answer such that no further question is possible, such that in the moment it is given, the question is extinguished. This answer is decisive, it is concise [*bündig*].

Who asks? Man. Man desires to understand the world, the world as a whole and its phenomena, like sun and moon. But this does not mean that he regards the world shyly and haltingly, that he enters it seeking and groping, that he would know it on its own terms – man stands over against the world, the world over against man, and he *asks*. Let us recall that the German verb *fragen* ('to ask'), which is derived from the Germanic root **freh*, also means 'desire', 'study', and 'demand'. Man demands of the world and its phenomena that they make themselves known to him. And he receives an answer; that is to say: he receives their response [*Widerwort*] – their word comes to meet him. The world and its phenomena make themselves known to him.

Where the world thus creates itself for man out of question and answer – this is where the form we shall call *myth* begins.

Let us imagine a king who is in doubt as to whether he should start a war. He can consider the question from all sides: Are my troops adequate? Do I have enough money? Will my allies stay loyal to me? Or: What about my enemy? Does he not have more troops, more funds? Will he not succeed in bribing my allies? The king is plagued by hopes, concerns, fears. But there is a place where the world itself – in this case, the world as event – makes itself known, declares its nature, where there is an answer to the question: What is going to happen? Not that in this place one can deploy exceptional means, unavailable to ordinary mortals, so as to learn more about something or understand it better than elsewhere, but rather such that a question resolves itself of its own accord into an answer; from question and answer, an objective reality creates itself. This place is called *oracle* – a word that instantly evokes the Greek oracle, the oracle at Delphi, and stories such as the ones told by Herodotus of the war between the Lydian king Croesus and the Persian king Cyrus, or of Themistocles. Let us regard the matter at its most general level: with the oracle at Delphi, it is not the case that future events are fixed in advance, whether by the will of the deity or in accord with some cosmic order, or that at Delphi there is a place where agents specially informed of the coming state of affairs might be prepared, under certain conditions, to dispense information concerning this state of affairs – rather, we must understand 'oracle' to mean that, in a holy place, there is a possibility of compelling the future to reveal itself by means of a question; or, better, that futurity *creates itself* in the question and answer.

Myth and oracle belong together; they belong to the same mental disposition. Both *sagen wahr* (prophesy or foretell; literally, 'say true'). For us the word *wahrsagen* ('prophesy', 'foretell') – like the word *weissagen* ('prophesy', 'divine', 'augur') – directs itself to the future, which is why we are more inclined to apply it to the story of the Lydian king than to what the first chapter of Genesis says about sun and moon. But we have to take the words *wahr* and *wahrsagen* more seriously: we must consider that *wahr* ('true') is related to *währen* ('endure') – that the world that bestows itself upon us by telling the truth of itself endures [*daß die Welt die sich uns gewährt, indem sie von sich wahr sagt: währt*], and that in this world, past and future are thus not separate. And when we have thus connected myth and oracle in the expression *wahr-sagen*, we may recall that the root we found in the word *fragen* is also present in the Anglo-Saxon nouns *friht* and *frihtrung*, which both mean 'oracle', as well as in the verb *frihtrian*, 'prophesy.'

One could use another word: revelation [*Offenbarung*]. But revelation is a dangerous word; it has been used by theology at various times in many different ways. Often what theology understands by it is an unmediated act of God – in the sense of the deity spontaneously revealing itself to man. Understood in this sense, revelation is neither myth nor oracle. The 'speaking god' who employs human speech and thought that we may know him in spirit, as 1 Corinthians 2:9–10 puts it, does not belong to this order of ideas.

Once again: the sun and the moon, as we see them in Genesis, are observed primarily as phenomena; every day, the sun appeared and lightened the day; when it went down, then the moon could appear and cast its light – in their enduring alternation, time accomplished itself as a matter of days and nights. The desire arose to understand them, and curiosity expressed itself in a question. They answered, and this answer was the 'true speaking' that permitted them to be seen; in thus speaking true, they were – in the deepest sense – perceived [*wahr-genommen*: literally, 'taken (for) true'].

Let us look at the form. Here it is not a case of the deity communicating spontaneously: 'I placed the lights in the firmament of the heaven to divide the day from the night.' What God has said, he did not say to man: the utterance refers to the sun and the moon themselves. Whereupon it was so: God put them there – now they fulfil their purpose, now they have become completely themselves. They are so much themselves that the Godhead is in a certain sense neutralized or excluded; God, too, stands face to face with them, he too sees them – sees 'that they are good'. Should we take this sentence – which recurs like a chorus throughout the prologue of the Book of Genesis – to mean that God doubted the goodness of his Creation? Obviously not. This sentence signifies that in the Creation and through the Creation, everything – light and darkness, heaven and earth, dry land and water, sun and moon – has become a concise whole and thus autonomous; it is also a final answer, a sublime truth-telling [*Wahr-sage*] of Creation itself, which declares itself 'good' before its Creator.

Myth as form is here entirely self-contained. Sun and moon are enquired after; sun and moon answer. Much more could of course be said about the deity who makes the lights appear in the firmament of the heavens; one could grasp him differently, invest him with different attributes. But that is precisely what does not happen here. The sun and the moon were put into place, and the deity is here none other than the one that put the sun and moon into place. One single phenomenon reveals itself fully in the myth and divides itself, in its autonomy, from all other phenomena.

This does not mean that other phenomena cannot reveal themselves in the same fashion in myths of the same kind. I must stress once again that I would make a distinction here – as with legend and *Sage* – between the simple form as such and its actualization. I shall do so by distinguishing myth from *mythos*: *myth* is the name of the simple form produced by our mental disposition; the actualized form, on the other hand, in which it can sporadically become present to us, is *mythos* or *a mythos*.

The longer segment, especially, that precedes the first book of the Bible – I mean Genesis 1:1 to 2:1, the introduction that exegetes call

P (or the Priestly Codex), and from which we have taken the *mythos* of sun and moon – clearly evinces a number of such distinct but similar myths. As a whole this is called 'the Creation of the world' or 'the story of the Creation', but both descriptions are misleading; for here the world is dissected into its various phenomena, and the days into which the Creation is segmented constitute more a division than a chronological sequence. Each phenomenon has its own *mythos*; coherence is however preserved by the fact that the *mythos* is effected each time by means of the very same gesture.

Meanwhile, the concept 'Creation' has taken us somewhere beyond the question of single myths. Myth is creation. I take the word once again in its deeper meaning, and recall the Germanic root *skap*, which underlies both *schöpfen* ('create') and *schaffen* ('create', 'accomplish'), and which still retains its meaning in the suffix *-schaft* ('-ship'). We have already said that in myth, the object creates itself out of a question and answer. We can also express this by saying: in myth, an object becomes creation [*Schöpfung*] by virtue of its nature [*Beschaffenheit*].

III. MYTH – KNOWLEDGE – LOGOS: PROPHECY – MENTAL
DISPOSITION, KEYWORD: KNOWLEDGE, SCIENCE

Hence we can also recognize what I called the enemy opposing myth when I cited the definition from Eisler's *Philosophical Dictionary*. Cognition and knowledge considered as process, the will to come to terms with the world actively and of one's own accord, to enter the world so as to gain insight into its nature on one's own human terms – this process in which objects do not create themselves, but are instead created, is a process that lives in perpetual feud with myth.

We could already extrapolate this conflict between myth and knowledge from a careful comparison of the Greek words μῦθος and λόγος, *muthos* and *logos*. But we must deny ourselves this as well. A few examples from Homer should make clear what μῦθος means and how it relates to the form we are calling *myth*.

In Book II of the Odyssey, Telemachos arms himself for a secret decampment. He has the housekeeper Eurycleia make ready wine and a meal from the storehouse (l. 339ff); in the evening he goes to his ship and orders his crew to fetch the supplies (l. 410ff). His mother and the other slaves know nothing: μία δ' οἴη μῦθον ἄκουσεν (*mia d' oiē muthon akousen*), 'only one woman knows what is really happening', we could translate it; or, better: 'only one woman knows the word that speaks true'.

Now Telemachos returns from his journey to Pylos and Sparta (Odyssey IV), and the suitors decide to wait in ambush for him and kill him (l. 663ff). But soon Penelope learns from the herald Medon what the suitors intend, and what she hears is again μῦθος – again, the word that embodies the truth (l. 675–6).

Finally, in Book XX of the Odyssey, Odysseus has returned home incognito, and finds the suitors feasting at his table. Ktesippos, a cocky lad from Same, is among them. He mocks the strange beggar, saying that he has had enough to eat, but that he would like to give him a gift as an expression of esteem, so that he might make a present of it to the maidservants who will wash him, or to someone else. Then he throws a cow's hoof at his head. It is only by ducking that Odysseus avoids dishonour (l. 292ff). Then the circumstances change: Odysseus has drawn his bow; with his friends he confronts the frightened suitors (Odyssey XXII). These fall one after another. Now the cowherd Philoitios kills Ktesippos, and says to him (l. 285ff) that he should no longer speak brashly and foolishly, but rather he should θεοῖσι μῦθον ἐπιτρέψαι, ἐπεὶ ἦ πολὺ φέρτεροί εἰσι (*theoisi muthon epitrepsai, epei ē polu pherteroi eisi*) – he should leave μῦθος to the gods, for they are more powerful than he. It is called cockiness, stupidity, that Ktesippos thought that the beggar appearing among the suitors was in fact a beggar, that he thought himself able to recognize him as a beggar, that based on this knowledge he treated him as a beggar. *Mythos* is that this beggar was not a beggar, but rather Odysseus. Ktesippos, starting with knowledge, missed the inner, the actual nature of the beggar: the *mythos*, which was known to the gods.

For the later Greeks, μῦθον ἐπιτρέψαι θεοῖς (*muthon epitrepsai theois*) – 'leave prophecy to the gods' – is a maxim; perhaps it was already one in the Odyssey. In any case, this turn of phrase does not at all mean that one should not ask the question that leads to *mythos*; rather, it means that knowledge is vain, that any attempt on the part of man to enter into the world and understand it on his own human terms can run aground at any moment on errors and false conclusions – and, further, that the gods know the word that speaks true, the word that prophesies [*wahr sagt*]; finally, that the *mythos* is divine, and that such divine knowledge, which derives its understanding of things from the things themselves, is *myth*.

It is not easy to find a term to describe the mental disposition from which the simple form *myth* proceeds. We could choose knowledge, science [*Wissen, Wissenschaft*], but then we must keep in mind that this does not mean all the knowledge to which cognition [*Erkenntnis*] ultimately directs itself, not even such things as are certain a priori – those strictly necessary and generally valid things on which experience and cognition are based, and which precede all cognition. Rather, we have here to do with the unconditional knowledge that arises only when an object creates itself in question and answer, announcing and proving itself by means of the word, the prophecy [*Wahrsage*].

IV. THE AETNA MYTH IN PINDAR – MYTHOLOGY

As a second example, I would like to set a Greek myth alongside the myth from Genesis. I shall choose this one once more from Pindar, from the beginning of the first Pythian epinikion; not from the part that includes the legend, but from the one that precedes it, in which the site of the celebration, of the ritual act, is established. The song begins with praise of the golden phorminx or lyre – of song. Song becalms everything, including the lightning of Zeus; it puts the eagle on the gods' sceptre to sleep, it even charms Ares, bewitches war. Only enemies of the Divine are alarmed by the singing of the Muses, like the hundred-headed Typhon, enemy of the gods. And now there follows the extensive description of the giant Typhon and of his punishment. His tremendous body lies stretched from Kyme on the Italian coast down to Sicily, where the mountain Aetna sits with its icy snow like a heavenly column upon his breast, while from the depths of the abyss he spews fire day and night, with purple flames eddying upward. A wonder to see – a wonder even to hear tell of.

We behold the mountain before us with its three zones: below, the vines; in the middle, the forests; above, the bald summit, covered for most of the year with ice and snow. But the mountain is not like other mountains; it spits fire. This is where the question arises; this is where it is resolved into an answer. In Pindar, this happens in two ways. Again, as in Genesis, we have two myths, but they are less sharply distinct. First, what is a mountain generally? The answer, gathered into a verbal gesture, is: *a heavenly column*. But then: Why does fire spray from this mountain? And the answer is: beneath it, and held down by it, lies the hundred-headed enemy of the gods, the arch-enemy. But here already we are over-interpreting something – the mountain, the heavenly pillar, *is itself*, conversely, the *giant*, the *enemy*. This phenomenon answers two times; twice, forced by a question, it declares its nature, twice it creates itself in an act of *poeisis*, of condensation into verbal gestures. The *pillar of heaven* becomes the *fire-spewing enemy of the gods*.

How little would we understand the process, the form as form, were we to say that at that time the Greeks were insufficiently informed as to the nature of mountains, the heavens, or volcanic activity, or if we were to speak of an 'interpretation of nature' based on 'personifying apperception'. It is not at all nature, in our sense, that is being explained here. In the world of our mental disposition, fire-spewing mountains are not nature – they were not then, nor are they now. And there is no direct path that could lead from the myth 'Aetna' – from the mountain's declaration – to the comprehension of geological phenomena.

There is, however, a mental reorientation – a sort of conversion in which the attempt is made to turn away from form and approach the phenomenon on one's own terms, to come by oneself to a judgment upon it, to engender the object oneself out of its determining conditions. But this conversion signifies the passage from *mythos* to *logos*.

Hieron, the victor whose praises Pindar is singing, had founded or re-founded a city, also called Aetna, on the southern slope of the mountain. He had populated it with denizens of Syracuse and Catana. It was in this city, governed by his son Deinomenes, that the celebration of victory took place – a celebration held also in honour of this son. This is where the epinikion was sung. This was the place that Pindar needed to determine, to fix. As soon as he has finished with this mountain myth, he takes up the matter of the city. Once again, myth sets in. A mountain, a column of the heavens, is now a *seat of the gods,* the place where they prevail; and thus is Aetna simultaneously a pillar of heaven, an enemy of the gods, and the place where Zeus prevails. From this myth, in the epinikion, there follows a prayer to this deity that he might protect the place founded by Hieron, grant it peace and prosperity. Then the song turns to the victors. Without explicitly saying as much, it sets Hieron's martial deeds into connection with what preceded them, and it is as if in the victories of the Sicilian tyrant over Etruria and Carthage we were hearing an echo of Zeus's victory over the fire-spewing giant. But it is precisely here that we sense the reorientation of which we have just spoken: Pindar draws on the myth, but in doing so he takes leave of the realm of pure myth. The myth is derivative in a double sense. To express explicitly what Pindar leaves implicit: what happens between Hieron and his enemies and what happened between Zeus and Typhon can be reciprocally related, can be compared. By doing so, however, Pindar no longer quite asks the sort of question that can be resolved in an answer.

Here cognition slips in. Pindar himself judges Hieron's deeds; he compares them with Typhon's defeat; he even relates them to the myth, he recognizes a relationship – but this does not amount to creating a myth of Hieron.

Seeing *mythos* and *logos* thus together, let us consider what strange compounds the Greek words μυθολογέω [*muthologéō*], μυθολόγημα [*muthologēma*] and μυθολογία [*muthologia*] are – how they 'wed contraries'. I would much prefer to strike the word 'mythology' from our set of concepts; if I must still use the word, then I would use it to indicate what Pindar does in this ode.

V. THE DERIVATIVE FORM – EXAMPLE – PLATO'S MYTHS

To make this process, too, comprehensible, we must explain a *third way* in which our forms apparently become manifest.

Up to now, we have regarded forms in two ways: as pure, simple forms, and as their actualizations. We found that alongside the legend there is the *vita*, alongside the *Sage* the saga. It is in this sense that we distinguished myth from *mythos*. But now we perceive another possibility: it is possible to take an element that does not really belong to a given mental disposition and relate it to that disposition from without, with regard to its outward shape. Jacob Grimm already speaks in this sense of an 'invented saga'. And let me recall another form, to which we shall return: we all know that there exist so-called *Kunstmärchen*, literary fairy tales. By this we generally mean a story whose outward form is deliberately based on and made to resemble the fairy tale, but whose inward nature we cannot subsume to the fairy tale genre. It is well known that there are similar things in linguistics, that certain words can adapt outwardly to others, acquiring their form. The not very useful note on *Mythe* in the Grimms' dictionary did at least show us that, when translated into German, the Greek masculine noun μῦθος acquired the gender of *Sage, Geschichte, Fabel*, etc., becoming feminine under the influence of this word series, so that in this respect it came to resemble those words. To the forms that emerge directly from a mental disposition and then actualize themselves, we may add this third variety, which we observe when something that does not belong directly to a given mental disposition nonetheless takes on the structure of the forms it produces: to the simple form and the actualized form we must add the *analogon*, the *derivative form*.

Let us look at a clear example for the case of myth. Coal, straw and bean undertake a journey together. They must cross a brook, and the straw obligingly lays itself across. The bean successfully makes it to the other side. The coal reaches the middle, where it becomes frightened of the water and stops, burning a hole in the straw and plopping with a hiss into the water, where it goes out. The bean finds this so funny that it begins to laugh – it laughs till its back bursts. Fortunately, a tailor comes along, bearing needle and thread; he sews up the bean, but alas, the thread was dark, and since then all beans have a black seam.

Here too we have question and answer. Why does the bean have a black seam? The question is well and truly resolved in the answer: it had burst; it was sewn up with black thread. And yet we sense that here things are different from how they were in the book of Genesis and in the Aetna myth. We feel there is something odd here. The question is not resolved from inside. The bean does not declare its own attribute from the inside, but instead the curious questioner himself provides the bean with an answer. To be sure, the questioner acts as if he were not the one producing the answer; while himself answering, he pretends that it is the bean that is answering. But we perceive the intention: there is no myth being made here; rather, a myth is brought to bear on the situation. The story of the burst and sewn bean does not mean that a phenomenon is declaring its nature when questioned by man; instead, it comes from a man who is anxious to imitate myth, use the form of a myth, to elucidate a phenomenon that he has observed and which has aroused his curiosity, but which his limited knowledge keeps him from being able to explain. And this is precisely what we are calling an analogy, a derivative *mythos*: a *mythos* that does not really speak true or prophesy [*wahr-sagen*], but which, because it is derivative, is no more than probable [*wahr-scheinlich*; literally, 'seemingly true'].

Everywhere a simple form arises compellingly and concisely from a mental disposition and becomes actualized, we find the derivative forms nearby. Wherever our aesthetic conscience makes distinctions, we tend – as I have suggested – to apply the prefix *Kunst-* ('art-'), to speak of *Kunstmärchen* ('literary fairy tales') or *Kunsträtseln* ('literary riddles'). Thus we express our awareness that the mental disposition as such is not present here, but that it is just being shammed, simulated. These forms are not always easy to tell apart from the true actualized forms, especially when the mental disposition from which the simple form originally arose is for some reason no longer present. We will not always have occasion to dwell on these analogies; for us, they are mostly of little value, but in the present context we must mention them, for they stand in a special relation to myth.

The small drama of the bean, coal and straw shows us where Pindar stands when he moves in his epinikion from myth to mythology; it also gives us a faint sense of the tremendous struggle that man has had to endure since the moment he first began to think.

The will to knowledge aims at the apprehension of Being and of the nature of things; knowledge is oriented to what is concrete – it seeks insight into the interconnection of things, it intends a determination of the Being and suchness of objects and of the relationships between them. Knowledge condenses itself in judgments. Every judgment is supposed to be universally valid. The true achievement of knowledge is thus that it produces its object out of the object's determining conditions.

But alongside the will to knowledge we find the mental disposition in which the world arises out of a need to be questioned and out of questions, from the seeking and proffering of answers. Alongside knowledge we have the form in which things and their interrelationships truly *create* themselves from the word that speaks true.

Alongside the judgment, which claims universal validity, there is the myth, which evokes concision [Bündigkeit].

Once again, it is not that the one precedes the other in chronological terms, that dissatisfaction with one leads gradually to the other, that a process of development succeeds in eliminating the one as inadequate so as to make room for the other – rather, always and everywhere, they stand side by side, and like the children in the folk ballad 'There once was a prince and a princess' ['Die zwei Königskinder'], they are always and everywhere divided by a body of water that is too deep, and they cannot 'come together'. But across the water, the two long for each other and bicker. We have already seen how knowledge attempts on the one hand to disparage and disavow the myth form; on the other hand, we have also seen how it reaches for analogy – especially where it becomes aware of its own limits – and attempts to complete itself in a derivative myth. For its part, where it loses its binding power myth often strives to deviate in the direction of knowledge, to support itself with the means of knowledge and thus revive itself. Knowledge wearing the mask of myth and myth disguised as knowledge are, so to speak, welcome figures in the masquerade of human thought.

If we regard literary history from the perspective of the history of philosophy, and observe the drama of attraction and repulsion that plays itself out between myth and knowledge, we begin to see clearly that this is the locus of one of the most difficult tasks of our morphology – and also how little prepared we have been for this task up to now.

Not long ago, the classical philologist Karl Reinhardt published an excellent book on the myths of Plato.[5] Not only does the book compile and compare the actualized myths to be found in Plato's works, but also, much more importantly, it allows us to see how the form 'myth' operates in Plato generally. From the moment in the *Protagoras* when

---

5   Karl Reinhardt, *Platons Mythen* (Bonn: Friedrich Cohen, 1927).

– nearly flippantly, almost in jest – the audience is left to choose between *mythos* and *logos* in order to answer the question of whether virtue is something that can be learned, to the latest, most serious dialogues, we see constantly how the mental disposition which produces the form that creates objects from question and answer is locked in a struggle against the will to enlightening knowledge. And finally, beyond these single myths and struggles, what is the figure of Socrates, as the Platonic opus, the Platonic poems construct him, but the literary form we are seeking? What is he but the Platonic myth itself – the oracle by means of which the questioned world is forced to concision in speaking truth of itself?

If we were to compare the Scholastic philosophy of the Middle Ages, that *ancilla theologiae*, we would see how here too the form 'myth' stands over against the will to knowledge – and that in this sphere as well, thoughts that have not been thought through to the end often take flight to derivative myth.

But since we have already had to dispense with a history of legend and *Sage*, we should avoid undertaking to write the still more complex history of myth.

VI. THE EVENT IN MYTHS – PECULIARITY OF THE VERBAL GESTURE

Yet we may well still ask: How does our form work? How does myth grasp the world in the mental disposition of knowing? We saw with the sun and moon, as with the mountain and the fire-spewing mountain, that the question was primarily provoked by, and aimed at, general phenomena that are at once manifold and consistent, and which thus stand out from the mobile diversity of everyday events. The world of myth is not a world in which things go one way one day and another way the next, in which something might happen but might also not happen; it is a world that seeks stability, a stable world. Thus the sun in Genesis is not a sun that shines today and is hidden by clouds tomorrow, but that light in the firmament of the heavens that always divides the day from the night and through which the consistency of time is assured. Thus too is the mountain the solid element that supports the heavens with its solidity. The volcano is likewise not a mountain that sometimes spews fire, but rather the mountain in which a destructive property, the power of spitting fire, consistently inheres. Wherever an answer annuls the question, wherever – as we have seen – this world becomes Creation, there we will always find an *event*.

The Old High German word *scëhan* and the Middle High German *scëhen* still carry the meaning 'to arrive quickly', 'hurry in', 'run'; the related Old Slavic noun *skokŭ* means 'jump'. We must keep this meaning in mind when we speak of *Geschehen*, 'event'. It is precisely the element that is universal, yet constant in its manifold nature, that myth apprehends with a swift coming-about, with an event that occurs suddenly and inevitably: it springs to light, it irrupts. 'And it was so' is how the myth in Genesis puts it, 'And God made the two great lights, the greater light to rule the day, and the lesser light to rule the night; and he made the stars also.' With this *event*, the sun, moon and stars are retrieved from multiplicity to unity. There are not *many* suns; when the great light vanishes and returns, it is not new – it is always the same sun, for in this unique event it has been confirmed, it has become the immutable Creation. There are many stars, but they are constant in their multiplicity; in their multiplicity they have been derived from the single point of their beginning. And there are many mountains, many different mountains; but where a particular mountain speaks of itself, it calls itself *pillar of the heavens* – it says it was once built to hold up the sky, or *seat of the gods*, which means that it was once placed there so that the divinity might settle upon it. Thus for the Greeks there was only one Aetna, but its continual hostile, destructive power was founded upon a unique event: the submersion of the hundred-headed monster.

Event, in this sense, defines the *verbal gesture of myth*.

When we spoke of legend, we observed how similar phenomena were condensed from the manifold of events under the sway of a particular mental disposition – how in their condensed form they were swirled together and recast into a new *Gestalt*. Things are slightly different with myth. To be sure, the mental disposition of knowing also selects, from a multiplicity, things that are similar: the form 'myth', as we know it so far, focused on those elements of the mobile manifold of visible phenomena that were at once multifarious and constant – on what consistently repeats itself, like the sun and moon, or upon what abides, like the mountain or the volcano. Yet however hazardous it might be to want to establish a hierarchical ranking of simple forms, we cannot deny that the matter with which the mind concerns itself in myth possesses a different density, a different dignity, a different degree of autonomy from what the mind addresses in legend or *Sage*, and that accordingly the verbal gesture of myth has a different solidity, a different validity, and a different integrity to its power – to use words of foreign origin: a different *dignitas* and a different *auctoritas* – from the verbal gestures of legend and *Sage*. Thus I would not want to assert that the verbal gesture of myth swirls similar phenomena together and recasts them into a new *Gestalt*. The verbal gesture of myth is different: it is like the eye of a needle. In the myth form, everything with which the mental disposition concerns itself, everything constant and multiple in the world, is pulled together, consolidated by the verbal gesture, pressed together and drawn through the unique event, receiving in this event the explanation of its constancy and multiplicity. If we wanted to put a finer point on the difference of myth from legend and *Sage*, we could say that, in the latter, mobile elements are given a *Gestalt*, while in myth *Gestalten* are rendered mobile in an event.

Let us recapitulate. What we have called question and answer can be described in greater detail. The question aims at the nature and properties of everything that we perceive in the world as constant and multiple. The answer consolidates all of this in the event, whose absolute uniqueness refers the multiplicity and the constancy back to a unity, endowing this unity with a *Gestalt* in an event that becomes a destiny.

If once again we regard the derivative form, we notice how in the story of bean, straw and coal it is precisely the *event* that the derivative myth seeks to imitate – indeed, in this case, to parody. Why do beans always have a seam? Here too the answer is cast as an event – a terrible event! But once again, we sense how this event has been brought in from outside. Only something that has been sewn has a seam; only what has burst is sewn; a person bursts with laughter. All of this is – to use a big word – a matter of cognitive judgments. But these cognitive judgments seek to shape and fix themselves in the form of an event, and this is why the tailor and his black thread are also drawn into the catastrophe.

VII. WILLIAM TELL – MYTHS OF MIGRATION – THE MYTHS OF SALVIFIC FIGURES

So far we have taken most of our examples from the realm of visible phenomena. It is self-evident that the mental disposition of knowing and the form that prophesies or speaks true in question and answer would direct itself towards those constant and multiple phenomena that seem to lead their own existence, independent of humans. Above all, it is *nature* whose properties the simple form myth and its actualizations turn into Creation. Our philosophical dictionary already spoke of the 'explanation of nature', and I need not recall that there was and still is a school of philologists, ethnologists, historians of religion, and folklorists that relates and reduces everything it understands as myth to natural phenomena – indeed, to a single natural phenomenon. The astral mythologists have gained a certain notoriety in this respect.

Yet our conception of the myth form suggests that its mental disposition does not at all limit itself to nature.

When we explored the concepts of question and answer, we hinted at the concision of myth and oracle. Now that we are better acquainted with the efficacy of form, we can separate and distinguish the two. In oracular prophecy, question and answer refer to a single case, whereas in myth, as we have shown, they are directed at recurring events. This is the reason why the prophecy involved in myth, once condensed in a verbal gesture, is confirmed in a durable actualization, while the prophecy of oracle expires with the solution of each individual case, without taking on any general form. Nonetheless, oracle proves that question and answer may be directed at something other than natural phenomena. The form that completes itself in an event can refer to events in a general sense.

Where a tyrant rules over his fellow men and oppresses them, disregarding the rights and privileges of his people, torturing individuals with senseless cruelty, where he demands the impossible, destroying public and personal security, to the point where everything in life seems to depend on his momentary caprice, man can confront the nature of this event with questions and demands; he can be met with a response, and the verbal gesture can circumscribe what is constant and multiple in this event. This is the formula: *the violent madman forces a father to shoot an apple from the head of his son.* Every single capricious act, every moment of disregard for what binds people together, is compressed into the father–son relationship (which in this case does not generate a *Sage*); the cruel demand for the impossible is called *shooting the apple.* The father stands opposite his son with the deadly weapon; the senseless target, which he has not chosen, is a small round object that can hardly be distinguished from the boy's head. But a second prophecy follows directly upon the first, a new event super-sedes everything that has yet occurred: the moment *the arrow splits the apple,* the world of injustice is shattered and freedom breaks forth. If in the first part of the myth the question was 'What does it mean when a tyrant capriciously oppresses a free people?' and the answer came: 'A father is forced to shoot an apple from the head of his son', the second part follows immediately with the question 'What happens when a people has been thus oppressed?', answering: 'Whether the shot succeeds or fails, the next arrow will split the heart of the tyrant.' But the shot cannot fail; the impossible thing demanded by despotism actually occurs, and, in occurring, it dashes the reign of violence to pieces.

One could possibly raise an objection. We might recall, first, that the myth of William Tell's arrow shot is not at all contemporaneous with the events we are supposing it is related to, that it first appears later; and, second, that similar tales may be found elsewhere – we know of a shot by the Norse hero Egil, and Saxo Grammaticus writes similar things of the Danish king Harald Bluetooth and the hero Toko and his son. It would take us too far from the point to investigate all of this in detail. Still, a few things can be said.

First: it is not absolutely necessary that an event acquire meaning through myth, actualize itself in myth, at the moment in which it occurs: the memory of things survived can use this form to create and interpret a past.

Second: when we encounter an actualization, a myth that has answered a question at another time or another place, this means that the verbal gesture has correctly seized on the constant element, upon what always repeats itself in the same way – that is, it has seized upon it in such a way that even in other times and other places one still perceives it as a definitive and valid crystallization of question and answer. Whoever speaks of a 'myth of migration' [*Wandermythos*] must give some account of the concept of migration. A migration in the sense of a wandering, an aimless erring about, a sporadic emergence first here and then there without any purpose, is inconceivable for reasons both linguistic and literary. Wherever a form or its actualizations appear, they prove themselves as carriers of meaning.

One more example. When a people and its rightful ruler, its leader, find themselves in extremis, surrounded by enemies, hemmed in on all sides, when there seems to be no possibility of escape, then a *salvific being* appears. This being is of a higher, special sort. It is not a man, nor is it a woman; instead, in this state it may be perceived in various ways: as a virgin, or a hetaera, neither of which is seen as 'woman'; it can also be a sort of androgynous deity; and, finally, it can show characteristics of all three of these things in alternation. Its attribute is a brace of horses which pull the solidly built and enduring apparatus – composed of wheels, axle and shaft – that we call a *wagon*. This being lifts the embattled leader onto the wagon, grabs the reins and leads the hero, unharmed and victorious, through the surrounding throng of enemies. Once the goal has been achieved, once the prince and the people are saved, it disappears, perishes; it can even be dragged to death by the horses.

We see this occur in the fifth book of the Iliad. The Greeks are under pressure; Diomedes, leading the fight, is wounded; the Trojans are advancing with great force. Ares and Hector drive the weakening Greeks towards the ships. Now Athena comes. She has taken off the colourful woman's dress that she made for herself. She pulls on the armour, puts on the helmet, picks up the lance – she has become a man-woman (v. 733ff). Now she speaks to the tired hero, encouraging him. She seizes the wagon-driver Sthelenos and pushes him away. She herself mounts the wagon, whose beechwood axle groans (v. 835ff). And now we move forward, straight though the enemy ranks. She herself does not fight, but she deflects the spear of Ares; Diomedes wounds the god. Ares shrieks like nine thousand men and complains to Zeus – but the Greeks are saved from their distress, and, having checked the marauder, Athena retires again to Olympus.

We find the same salvific figure in the Indian Rigveda. Its name is Ushas, and again it is neither a man nor a woman, but a divine hetaera:

'She flared up, her face painted, in the door-frame of heaven. The black dress frightened the goddess. The waking Ushas comes in a well-harnessed wagon drawn by red horses' (Rigveda 1, 92, 14). For she too has a wagon and team: 'With the finely painted, fortunate wagon on which you stand, Ushas, with that help today the glorious people, o daughter of heaven' (Rigveda 1, 49, 2). Further, we know that she is related to the twins who are themselves related to horses and are called Ashvins in India, Dioscuri in Greece: 'Come with a wagon faster than the Manas, made for you by the Ribhus, you Ashvins, with whose harnessing the daughter of heaven was born' (Rigveda 10, 39, 12). The difference between the salvific figure of the Iliad and the helpful figure of the Rigveda lies in the fact that in the Iliad the saving power is found in an event, while in the Rigveda it is derived from a natural phenomenon. We can translate *Ushas* as 'daybreak' or 'dawn', and there is no doubt that what the verbal gesture grasps in *Ushas* is the consistent and uniform recurrence of the victorious morning.

Should we consider this a case of cultural diffusion? Should we attempt somehow to translate Ushas into Athena, or Athena into Ushas? If we have correctly understood the mental disposition of knowing, if we have understood how in a simple form question and answer create their own world in a prophecy or speaking-true, then it would seem to me that in the act of demanding answers man is divining profound relationships – he is grasping how the early light triumphantly blazing a way through the surrounding inimical darkness is essentially related to the female saviour who shows a leader and a people besieged on all sides a route of escape through the enemy troops; that he is approaching both phenomena – one in nature and one in an event, and both perceived with regard to their constancy – with the same question; and that they respond to him, make themselves known to him, with the same answer.

Let us add two examples to these actualizations of Athena and Ushas.

We read in Herodotus (I. 60) that when Pisistratus allied himself with Megacles and married his daughter, the two devised a stratagem to restore the banished tyrant to power. They girded a beautifully proportioned, stately woman from the village of Paeania – she was four ells minus three fingers, let us say nearly two meters tall, and was named Phye – in full armour, mounted her in a wagon, and got her to pose in a striking attitude. Then Pisistratus drove with her to the city. They sent heralds on ahead, crying: 'Athenians, receive Pisistratus with favour, for Athena herself has shown him extraordinary honour and is restoring him to her city.' Wherever they went, the heralds proclaimed this, and the rumour quickly spread in every village that Athena herself was returning Pisistratus to his home. The residents of the city, convinced that the woman was the goddess, worshipped her and accepted Pisistratus. Herodotus finds the whole affair absurd – he laughs at the superstition. But we can recognize the myth that Pisistratus, the great admirer of Homer, is both *realizing* and *referencing* here, to his own advantage; we can also understand the people that lives this myth as experience, however derivative it may be.

Finally: in May 1429, with the English armies occupying all of France and the English king already proclaimed king of France, the French people and its uncrowned dauphin find themselves in the worst kind of distress, with no visible avenue of escape, when a salvific figure arrives from the province of Lorraine. She is neither a man or a woman, she is 'Pucelle', a virgin; an expert commission will later determine – and witnesses testify – that she makes no 'feminine' impression, that she does not awaken desire. She is a daughter of God, like Athena and Ushas; those around her call her 'fille de Dieu'. She casts off women's dress; she dons men's clothing, armour; she becomes a man–woman, and the first thing she asks for is a horse. We even know the price of this horse. Now, unseen by the enemy, she rides between two men – once again, we know the name of her Dioscuri – to the embattled king. She makes the men leave who were her charioteers, and drives it herself. She directs battles and sieges, but without herself shedding blood. She escorts the king through the enemy regiments; she liberates the people. And once she has attained her goal, she is pulled from the horse – she perishes, she disappears. This is neither a Homeric epic nor a Vedic hymn; we are standing (as it is said) on the ground of history, and still we recognize – while convincing ourselves that this is not legend, but myth – the helpful figure that we perceived in the Iliad and the Rigveda.

Here we lose all desire to think in terms of diffusion. Athena and Ushas may have belonged to spheres that we could access only with some intellectual effort, and Pisistratus may have referred to Homer, but Joan of Arc belongs to our own sphere: 'We believe in the maiden of Domremy', as one modern historian has put it. In this case – unlike with William Tell – there is no space of time between the event and the form in which it is actualized. The boundary that one could draw between a 'real' event and the 'heightened' events of myth is here fully erased. What happens in life itself is reduced – as a whole and in all its particulars – from a multiplicity to a unity: it creates form and becomes form.

In short, we could generalize: wherever living events assimilate everything into themselves and absorb themselves (so to speak) completely into themselves, or (as one thinker has put it) *wherever 'events mean necessity as freedom', there events become myth.*

VIII. APOCALYPTIC MYTHS – THE SYMBOL

I have only a little more to add.

In the first place, we could ask if the objects that, in myth, by their very nature become Creation can – by that same nature, and through the same mental disposition – cease to be Creation. Or, to put the question differently: Can the sun and the moon, can the mountain, indeed can the world – as created in myth – perish?

They can. They can do so in myth; indeed, they can do so only through myth. Just as alongside the legend we have anti-legend, so too do we find next to the myth that builds a myth that destroys. The event that reduces a multiplicity to its ultimate unity can be cancelled by an event that casts this unity back into the chaotic manifold of nothingness. Beside the creation of the world there is the end of the world. I said in discussing legend that we cannot really view the Antichrist as an un-saint; here, in myth, is the place where the arch-destroyer's actualization most properly belongs. If we consider Ragnarök, if we consider the Apocalypse, then we comprehend how the question of the last things, of the extinction of sun, moon and stars, of the world and of life, is answered in a verbal gesture. But just as the un-saint can metamorphose into the saint, so to can myth again build a new world from chaos.

Additionally, since we have seen with legend and *Sage* how the simple form can transfer its power to an object, and how this object is then charged with this power, we must establish the existence of some such object for myth. Here I would apply a word often used – and abused: we call such an object a *symbol*. With legend, we avoided construing a relic as an allegorical image, as a thing accessible to the senses that could convey a meaning; instead, we observed how the saint's body parts, clothing, torture implements, could absorb and then radiate outward everything having to do with him and his sanctity. Just as these objects become 'sacred' and vehicles of the saint's power, so also would I regard the symbol not as an allegorical image, but as an object effectively charged with myth and become an independent vehicle of myth's power. Let us recall that an oracle, too, in which futurity creates itself via question and answer, does not arise in a random place, but that it requires a sanctified locus, a site to which the force of the prophecy is effectively bound and in which it inheres.

In Genesis 28, Jacob receives a revelation regarding the future of his people. In the verbal gesture of myth, this is expressed as follows: '*a ladder is placed on the earth whose upper end reaches to the heavens, and the angels of God climb up and down upon it*'. His god speaks to him. When he awakes the next morning, he is fearful and says: 'How frightening this place is! Yes, this is the abode of God and the gate of heaven.' Then he takes the stone upon which his head had rested, sets it upright and anoints it with oil. This stone is not a memorial meant to recall past events to memory, and it is not a sensible object intended to represent God's promise; neither is it an object in which the sense of the myth is expressed. Rather, it is an object in which the myth's power is captured; it is an independent vehicle of this power, which suddenly erupts from it as a real event.

So also can a colourful cloth be a symbol as soon as – *qua* flag – it answers the questions: What is the party? What is the guild? What is the regiment? What is the fatherland?

CHAPTER 4

Riddle

I. ANTHOLOGIES AND METHODOLOGY OF RIDDLE SCHOLARSHIP

There is another form that is fulfilled in question and answer: the *riddle*.

We know what it means to ask and guess riddles. However, we know this mostly from the derivative forms in which riddling plays a part in our lives; we are familiar with it from children's school problems and the puzzle section of our newspapers. We also know to what degree the pursuit of riddles can occupy our thoughts, can possess us: allow me to recall the fervour with which both Europe and America threw themselves at crossword puzzles not too many years ago.

The scholarship – ethnography, in particular – has also examined the riddle in some detail. Richard Wossidlo's book *The Riddle* is an exemplary publication in this often slipshod field.[1] I refer you to the essay on 'Riddle' by Wolfgang Schultz in the Pauly-Wissowa *Encyclopedia of Classical Antiquity* (see also W. Schultz, *Hellenic Riddles*), which presents a remarkable collection of ancient riddles and does justice to their great variety.[2][3] I would also mention the *Comparative Riddle Studies* in which the head of the Finnish School, Antti Aarne, has compiled a massive amount of material.[4] Robert Petsch has addressed *The German Folk Riddle*.[5]

---

1 Richard Wossidlo, *Mecklenburgische Volksüberlieferungen*. vol. 1: *Rätsel* (Wismar: Hinstorff'sche Hofbuchhandlung Verlagskonto, 1897).

2 *Paulys Realenzyklopädie der classischen Altertumswissenschaft*, vol. I A, 1 (Stuttgart: Alfred Druckenmüller, 1914), 62–125.

3 Wolfgang Schultz, *Rätsel aus dem hellenischen Kulturkreis*, 5 vols (Leipzig: Hinrich, 1909–1912).

4 Antti Aarne, *Vergleichende Rätselforschungen*. 3 vols, F.F. Communications Nos. 26, 27, 28 (Helsinki: Suomalaisen Tiedeakatemian Kustantama, 1918–1920).

5 Robert Petsch, *Das deutsche Volksrätsel* (Strassburg: Trübner, 1917).

Compilations like Aarne's and Wossidlo's will serve as the basis for our approach to the riddle, as the *Acta Sanctorum* did for our study of legend. Meanwhile, here again we must draw attention to the methodological differences between ethnography and literary history. What we have in the compilations is of course actualized forms, actualizations. In such a collection as Wossidlo's, we find all the actualizations circulating at a given time and in a given place – the time and place of collection – amassed entirely without prejudice and with what could be called absolute thoroughness. What we thus have available here is a sober inventory of the riddles available in Mecklenburg at the beginning of the twentieth century.

In a collection like Aarne's, we see something different – which is already obvious from the expression 'comparative studies'. In this case, the compiler does not begin with the total stock of a particular area, but with specific riddle types. Nor does he focus on a particular place and time: instead, he surveys all the places and times where and when actualized forms that belong (or seem to belong) to a given type can be found. Based on this very large mass of material, Aarne attempts to identify, historically and geographically, the point where such a type may have originated. Since it is mostly impossible to establish this with historical precision, he proceeds 'comparatively', extrapolating, from a number of variants of common date, an original form [*Urgestalt*] that is supposed to have been the basis for all later variants of the same type. Further, he tries – again, historico-geographically – to follow the path along which these types must have travelled through epochs and peoples, and to study the transformations they underwent in their journey from culture to culture. Here the danger is great of moving in circles: one extrapolates from historico-geographical data to an original form, and then one explains the transformations of this hypothetical original form in terms of the same historico-geographical data.

But even when such circularity is avoided, the original form derived from countless actualizations still remains, in the best case, an actualized form, in the worst a derivative form or a literary form – and even if we did possess a reasonably complete collection of these so-called original forms, we would still have to find a way to move from them to the true simple form, and to make sense of the latter. However valuable such anthologies may be for the morphological method of literary history, here too our method prefers to try to define the nature of the simple form and the mental disposition that has produced it. If it succeeds in this, then it will also be able to differentiate and classify those types, those historically given actualizations, as well as to compare the new actualizations that the mental disposition continually produces with the 'historical' ones.

II. MYTH AND RIDDLE

When we compare question and answer in *riddle* with question and answer in *myth*, the first thing we notice is the superficial fact that where the form *myth* gives us the answer, the form *riddle* gives us the question. Myth is an answer in which the question is implicit; riddle is a question that demands an answer.

Just as the myth also includes the question, so too is the answer present in and through the riddle. A riddle can be asked in such a way that it is impossible for the guesser to guess the answer; indeed, the correct answer to a riddle may be lost, yet the guesser senses that there is or must have been someone who knows or once knew the answer to the question: an insoluble riddle is really no riddle at all. Further, the form of the riddle is not only such that the guesser knows that the answer is or once must have been known to someone, but also such that he is convinced that he himself can find the solution. This conviction promptly turns into another: that he *must* find it.

Here, too, we can indicate the mental disposition with the term *knowing*. But it is a different knowing and a different sort of curiosity. In myth, man inquired as to the nature of the world and its phenomena, and the world declared itself to him in its response, in a prophecy. With the riddle, there is no relationship of man to world. Here, a person who knows asks another person a question – but he asks the question in such a way that he forces the other person into knowledge. One person is in possession of knowledge – he is the one who knows, the *wise man*; opposite him stands another, whom he induces by means of the question to stake his force and his life on acquiring knowledge and presenting himself as wise. Knowledge itself is already present the moment the question is asked; unlike in myth, it does not have to be won out of question and answer.

In the myth form, we ourselves are the askers; in the riddle form, we are asked, and asked in such a way that we must answer. This is why myth is characterized by freedom, whereas riddle is characterized by constraint; this is why myth is activity, riddle passivity; this is why myth involves a sense of relief, riddle a sense of anxiety. It is no coincidence that an Old High German word for riddle, *tunkal*, means gloom, obscurity.

In both myth and riddle, the crux of the meaning is to be found where question and answer are conjoined, where the question resolves itself into an answer. But with myth this conjunction is a prophecy, whereas with the riddle it is an unriddling.

I emphasize the difference between the two forms all the more sharply because those scholars who have worked most intensively on the riddle have sensed the relationship to myth, but ignored what distinguishes the two forms. The studies by Wolfgang Schultz that I mentioned are one example of this; Ludwig Laistner's peculiar book *The Riddle of the Sphinx*, tellingly subtitled 'General Outline of a Mythic History', is another.[6]

III. EXAMINATION – COURT TRIAL – RIDDLE OF THE SPHINX – ILO RIDDLE – NECK RIDDLE

All the same, it is Laistner who first adverted to something that will permit us to see the riddle form clearly at work in our own lives: the concept of the *examination*. Indeed, the academic examination is a situation that can be compared with the riddle, however different its level and format may be. There too we have someone who knows, who asks the question, who forces the other to know, to answer the question or perish, to 'fail'. This is not a Socratic question, a question asked so that a world is created in the answer, but a question already determined by, and requiring, knowledge. If we compare a Platonic dialogue

---

6   Ludwig Laistner, *Das Rätsel der Sphinx: Grundzüge einer Mythengeschichte* (Berlin: Wilhelm Hertz, 1889).

with a catechism, we feel the difference more strongly yet. In Plato, the conversational form is what generates wisdom. A catechism is also a conversation, a dialogue, yet the answers are known in advance to the questioner; if the person asked answers correctly, then what results from these answers is not wisdom itself, but knowledge on the part of the candidate. The state of mind that prevails at exams is a good indicator that the person asking the questions, the one who has knowledge and whom we call wise, may be thought of as demonic, that this questioner is at the same time a monster who fills us with fear, aggrieves us, chokes us.

Besides the examination – Laistner missed this – there is another life situation, another event, in which we can sense the riddle as form: the court trial. In the present context, we will look at the trial not as a matter of process, as we did when discussing legend, but as a relationship between persons. In the court trial, it is the judge who *needs to know*, the defendant who *knows*. Here too it is a vital duty, a vital necessity, for the one to fathom the knowledge of the other. The defendant sets the riddle; if the judge fails to guess the answer, he ceases – at least temporarily – to be a judge.

Only a few cases are known of a riddle being expanded into a story in which – so to speak – it comments upon itself, and these examples show clearly how the riddle appears to us as a simple form, and how this situation supplies the mental disposition of the riddle.

On the one hand, there is the group we could designate as the 'riddle of the Sphinx' group. The examples are well known: they include the Sphinx story itself, then Turandot, King John and the Bishop, and Hans Christian Andersen's travelling companion, with its many variants. Here the examiner is a more or less cruel being. It can be an enchanted princess who stands in league with evil powers, or a king. The most harmless version is the king who wants to test the mental capacities of the parson whose potbelly three men together cannot encompass. But in each case the motto is: guess or die! Each is a test question in the deepest sense.

We have on the other hand a second group, often called 'the Ilo riddle', after its most common actualization. Wossidlo writes: 'This riddling fairy tale' – I would prefer just to call it a riddle – 'is widespread throughout the country. I have not found a single village in which it was not known to at least one resident; often I found it in three, four or five different variants within a single village.' In its usual version it goes like this:

> *Auf Ilo geh ich,*
> *auf Ilo steh ich,*
> *auf Ilo bin ich hübsch und fein,*
> *rat't, meine herren, was soll das sein.*

> On Ilo I walk,
> on Ilo I stand,
> on Ilo I'm pretty and sweet,
> guess, gentlemen, what can that be.

One informant's explanation is: 'A girl was accused of killing a child; in those days, when one was condemned to death, one could set the judges a riddle, and if they couldn't answer it, one would be freed. Ilo was the name of that girl's dog, and she had herself made a pair of shoes from its fur. On the day, she put on the shoes, went to the judges and asked the riddle. They couldn't guess it, and so she went free.'[7]

Besides the Ilo riddle in the strict sense, there are numerous other riddles from this group that are presented along with similar explanations: 'two legs sat upon three legs', 'unborn', and so on.

It is as if these groups had converged on each other from the two farthest edges of the mental disposition. Not to be able to answer a riddle means to die; to pose a riddle that no one can answer means to live.

Precisely because life and death here depend on the riddle's solution, these groups have been called 'neck riddles' [*Halsrätsel* or *Halslösungrätsel*]. Yet fundamentally all riddles are neck riddles, in so far as they carry within them the requirement that they be answered. It is said that long ago, on Hawai'i, those who did not solve a riddle were cast into the cooking pit and their bones preserved as trophies. For this reason there are supposed to be families who refuse to answer riddles because their ancestors perished that way – here *Sage* and

---

7   Wossidlo, *Rätsel*, p. 191.

riddle rub shoulders. And this is why some others, when riddling time comes, say: 'There is always one wager, our bones.'[8] But actually we see this everywhere we find this simple form. Be it the riddle of an exam or the riddle of a court of law – where the riddle attains its most profound meaning, it is a matter of life and death: we are playing for bones.

IV. REASONS FOR RIDDLING – INITIATION AND *'BUND'* OR ASSOCIATION

Initially, we regarded the riddle primarily from the perspective of the person obliged to answer it. This was legitimate because we always encounter the riddle in the form of a question, and because this question is always directed at us. The two groups we have called 'the riddle of the Sphinx' and 'the Ilo riddle' then suggested the importance of the person who sets the riddle, of the riddler.

We designated the activity of the guesser with the word *enträtseln* – to solve, decipher, unriddle. In order to be *enträtselt*, the thing to be unriddled must first be *verrätselt*, encrypted, wrapped up in a riddle. And with this verb we can designate the activity of the person who poses the riddle. But what is the aim, the purpose of this encryption?

We have seen that the person posing the riddle finds himself in possession of knowledge – he *knows*. On the other hand, the guesser, in guessing, shows that he also knows, that he is the riddler's equal. Thus, to set the riddle is above all to test the guesser, to investigate his equality. The question also includes a compulsion. Taken as a whole, then, from the riddler's point of view the riddle is both a test of the guesser's equality and a matter of forcing the guesser to demonstrate his equality. Here I need only recall the concept of the exam. It is obvious that this test and compulsion are not intended for random persons at random times: the tester must have a reason for testing and compelling, the person tested must have a reason for submitting to the test and to the compulsion.

---

8   Martha W. Beckwith, 'Hawaiian Riddling', *American Anthropologist* 24:3 (1922), pp. 320–1.

From this we can conclude that the sole or true point of the riddle is not the solution itself, but rather the act of *solving*. The answer was already known to the riddler, thus for him it is not a question of learning it again; what matters to him is whether the guesser is capable of giving the answer – whether he can be made to supply it to the riddler.

Let me indicate once again the fundamental difference from myth. In myth, the meaning of the answer is to be found exclusively in the answer itself. The riddle, by contrast, includes a question that is asked in order to discover whether the guesser can lay claim to a certain dignity or worth; when this question is answered, this proves that the guesser is *worthy*.

Even in the most superficial definitions of the riddle, which mostly apply to derivative forms, one can read that the riddle of today is a means of testing the perspicacity of the guesser. At a deeper level – which is where we must seek our simple forms – the objective is much less clearly defined. Here we can say that the riddler – we have called him the wise man – does not stand alone, he is not independent; rather, he represents a knowledge, a wisdom, or a group bound together by knowledge. The guesser, for his part, is not someone who answers another's question, but someone who wishes to be admitted to this wisdom, to be accepted into the group, and who proves with his answer that he is ready for this. The *solution* is thus a password, a shibboleth, that affords entry to something closed or concealed. The riddler may not confront the guesser in the terrible form of a monster who threatens to throttle him, as he does in the derivative riddling tales or in the riddle of the Sphinx – but we still sense the compulsion: the access to that concealed thing is a matter of life and death, both for the one demanding entry and for the one granting it.

The riddle is thus defined from two sides: the riddler needs to encrypt the material in such a way that the guesser can demonstrate his own worth, his equality, in the act of decrypting it.

If we ask what sort of a group this might be that is bound together through wisdom, we find that many answers are possible. We can summarize them as follows: these are groups that consist of initiates and which require an act of initiation for admittance. They thus span the range from secret societies to the kingdom of the blest, in so far as the latter is understood as a place to be reached by the path of wisdom.

Having called the riddle a password, we might add that this password leads to induction, that the entry it affords is one to a closed order.

But the purpose and task of the riddle is for the riddler to test whether the guesser is ready for admission to the order while at the same time permitting access to what has been closed off or concealed, and for the guesser to prove he is worthy of admission to the order.

V. WHAT IS MADE INTO A RIDDLE?

This brings us to our second question: What does the riddle encrypt?

To judge from the numberless riddles told daily by children and adults and printed in puzzle sections, riddle papers and riddle books, it would seem as if absolutely everything could be encrypted in a riddle. The number of objects that can thus be transformed into riddles, in all manner of ways, is endless. Yet it is clear that these are derivative forms, in which a particular method of encryption is applied to objects at random. At best, such analogies can teach us something about *how* encryption works, but they are not representative of *what*, in a deeper sense, riddles encrypt.

The difference between the riddles that we find in the puzzle section of a newspaper and the riddles that ethnographers collect and which they call 'true riddles', or folk riddles, would seem to depend on the fact that the former, once guessed or answered in the next issue of the paper, are quickly forgotten, whereas the latter 'are to be found in the mouths of the people', are 'in circulation' – that is, they are posed again and again.[9] However, this does not at all mean that the ethnographic collections do not include derivative forms, or that the riddles to be found 'in the mouths of the people' can always be understood as examples of actualized form, as forms in which the mental disposition, the simple form, is (or once was) actualized. Wossidlo's examples show that we cannot exclude the possibility of a derivative form sometimes finding its way into circulation in the vernacular, and thus expanding

9   Robert Petsch, *Studien über das Volksrätsel* (Ph. Diss, Würzburg, 1898), pp. 45ff.

the number of encryptions belonging to the common store of folk riddles. But this is just an illusion. Wossidlo's collection also demonstrates that when one surveys the entire range of encrypted objects, their number shrinks considerably – that any given mode of encryption tends to be applied repeatedly to identical or similar objects. And even in cases of apparent variety, it becomes clear that the groups are wont to converge, indicating a common point of departure. Antti Aarne has duly proved that a number of riddles from the most disparate areas with the solutions cat, dog, horse, pig, goat, sheep, camel, hare, are all to be traced back to a 'type' that encrypts cow or steer.[10]

If we proceed in the opposite direction and begin with the mental disposition, with the simple form, then we must say that the questions in which the mental disposition instantiates itself, the truly actualized riddles posed by the initiated to the initiate, can be neither unlimited nor random. Only what belongs to the initiation can be encrypted – the secret of the association or *Bund*, the things that are both native to it [*heimisch*] and its secret [*heimlich*]. Indeed, building on this root, we could even speak of the trickiness [*Heimtücke*] of the malicious riddle. The choice of what is encrypted is thus determined by the meaning of what is concealed.

We must touch once again on myth. It is possible, and it very often happens, that the meaning of the association rests on a question regarding the creation and nature of the world and its phenomena, that its secret concerns a prophecy, a revelation received in common, and that its activity consists in acts in which the meaning of this revelation is expressed and repeated ever anew. In other words, what we have here is a community whose binding element is myth and whose activity we call ritual. In this case, the riddles posed by this community will have some relation to myth – there will be a *mythos* encrypted here. I emphasize the word *mythos* because it is not the simple form that is encrypted, but its actualization. The mental dispositions of myth and riddle remain completely separate. Each time, the association's aim is to create the world in question and answer; even when what is encrypted bears some relation to this myth, it remains the

---

10   Aarne, *Vergleichende Rätselforschungen*, vol. 2, F.F. Communications no. 27 (Helsinki: Suomalaisen Tiedeakatemian Kustantama, 1919).

riddle's one goal to allow the riddler to test the guesser – the answer is never a prophecy, always an unriddling.

These two forms can reside very close to one another without ever mingling. Let us recall the oracle. There, as we have seen, future events create themselves as a simple form out of question and answer. However, this happens in the oracle itself. Is the person who 'uses' the oracle worthy of knowledge of such creation? This is not clear in advance, it has to be tested, it has to be proven. And how is it tested? The oracle itself encrypts its prophecy.

If in the story from Herodotus – mentioned above in relation to myth – Croesus *solves* the riddle, then he has thereby proved his worth, then he has accessed what was concealed, then the oracle belongs to him; if he cannot decipher it, and thus fails the test of initiation, then – here as usual, we have a neck riddle – it is all over for him. On the other hand, Themistocles proves himself as an initiate by solving the riddle of the τεῖχος ξύλινον, *teichos xulinon* ('wooden wall'), and thus grasping the sense of events to come.[11] The oracle as myth contains the sufficient, unequivocal answer, the prophecy; but this prophecy is a secret of the *Bund*. The form of the riddle necessarily inserts itself, as an ambiguity, between the oracle and its foreign questioner, the uninitiated asker.

Whether it is a question of myth or of something else, it is certain that the riddler finds himself in possession of knowledge and that he represents the group, the association. We could also express it thus: the meaning of the association – and what is encrypted for the uninitiated – is knowledge as something to be possessed.

VI. HOW ARE RIDDLES MADE? – SPECIAL LANGUAGE – VERBAL GESTURE OF THE RIDDLE

Thus we come to the third question: How does encryption occur? And this brings us to the true form of the riddle.

If what is encrypted is conditioned and defined by the meaning of

---

11   Herodotus, *The Persian Wars, Volume I: Books 1-2*, transl. by A. D. Godley. Loeb Classical Library 117 (Cambridge, MA: Harvard University Press, 1920), VII.141ff.

what is concealed, by the secret of the *Bund*, then it must be conceived in the language of the *Bund*. We could say: the test consists above all in establishing whether the outsider understands the language of the initiated.

Let us recall the idea of the catechism. Catechism – the word is derived from the Greek verb ἠχέω, *ēcheō* ('to sound or resound') – is related to the riddle, yet it differs from it in that it lacks the riddle's spontaneity. Catechism likewise enables entry into a community and the achievement of initiation, but here the questions are not solved from within: the answer is learned by the catechumen. Once again we see knowledge as something to be possessed. We saw earlier how knowledge is completed in myth, how it is produced in an act of cognition. Knowledge as a possession, however, can not only be encrypted; it can also be learned. The riddle stories express something similar. In the story of the 'grateful dead', the guesser always hears the answer from another person: he learns it.

Meanwhile, catechism shows that initiation demands that particular words be taken in a particular sense, that when we speak of baptism we not only mean water, but water subsumed within God's command and connected with God's word . . .

We find something similar in the riddle, but in a much stronger form. When we hear:

> *Ein Baum steht in der ganzen Welt,*
> *der zweiundfünfzig Nester hält,*
> *in jedem Neste sieben Jungen,*
> *doch sämtlich sind sie ohne Zungen –*

> There is a tree in the wide world,
> that counts nests five-and-twenty,
> in every nest, seven young,
> yet all of them are lacking tongues –

then we know in advance that *tree, nest, young* are not to be understood in the ordinary sense of the words, but that we must take them differently. Or if we look at the riddle of the Sphinx – Who goes on four legs in the morning, on two at midday, in the evening on three?

– then we know here as well that *morning, midday* and *evening* are not necessarily to be understood as times of day, and that the legs in question cannot simply be parts of the body.

On the other hand, we also sense that these meanings cannot be produced simply by substitution of an unusual name for some encrypted object. The words in question have a significance whose structure differs fundamentally from that of other modes of linguistic meaning: whereas linguistic meanings normally indicate just *one* state of affairs, here words like tree, nest, young, or morning, midday, evening indicate correlated states of affairs.

These examples are free-floating actualizations, riddles that have been transcribed from folk speech by collectors. The closer we come to the riddle as a simple form, the better we can understand it as a password permitting initiation into a particular community, and the better we see that the equality of which I have spoken derives from a meaning that, within this community, signifies the meaning of the world.

To grasp the riddle in a place where the simple form is still vital, it may be helpful to note that Walter Porzig, surveying synoptically the riddles of the Rigveda, found that in this material, mobile elements (sun, moon, year, foot) become *wheel* or *wagon*; coordinated elements (days, months) are *brothers*; aerial phenomena (sun, sparks, lightning) are *birds*; something from which something else issues (clouds, dawn, fire) is *cow*; what is low down is *foot*, what is high up is *head*.[12]

Thus when 'the sun shining through the clouds' is encrypted, we get: 'He who knows the answer shall tell it, the hidden trace of this dear bird. From his head the cows draw milk, and, veiling their figure, they have drunk water with their foot.'

Porzig goes on to discuss in detail the nature of such language, thus contributing to our understanding of *Sondersprachen*, or special languages. For a *special language* is what we call a language the knowledge of which affords inclusion within a closed circle, that construes the world within the secrecy of the circle:

---

12   Walter Porzig, 'Das Rätsel im Rigveda. Ein Beitrag zum Kapitel "Sondersprache"', *Germanica: Eduard Sievers zum 75. Geburtstage, 25. November 1925* (Halle an der Saale: Niemeyer, 1925), pp. 646–60.

Special languages, like common languages, constitute a world, the real world of the language community in question. But whereas the common language presents things immediately as things and is thus absolute and univocal in a strict sense, the special language conveys the sense of things, their internal imbrication and deeper meaning; this is why it is so ambiguous, as the world always is when viewed from within. The lines structuring the image of the world as conveyed by the common language are accessible only through careful study; the speakers *have* a world, but they do not *know* it. The world of the special language, on the other hand, immediately reveals the framework of its construction; this world is known well before it becomes the property of its community. These main lines of force carry so much weight that the details fade by comparison . . .[13]

Porzig then demonstrates the contrary vectors of common language and special language with an example from the domain of signification:

Our description of the character of special languages has already made clear that every given language includes special meanings within it. When we speak of the *foot of a mountain* or the *foot of a lamp*, the word 'foot' has a meaning of the same kind as in the riddles from the Rigveda in which the dawn is carried *by the foot* of the sun or the clouds drink water *with their foot*. And when we trace each phenomenon back to its 'origin', the word emphatically takes on a special meaning. These are the processes of semantic shifting that we commonly call 'metaphor' or 'figurative expression'. In reality, what we have here is a different kind of language, with a different kind of meaning. In ordinary language, *foot* means a body part with a determinate shape, understood as an existent object; in the special language, *foot* means something whose whole nature consists in supporting and carrying. To be sure, if we reflect on the *nature* of the human foot, we find that it shares this quality with everything meant in the special language by *foot*. Yet in ordinary language the object is named not according to its nature, but according to its *phenomenal*

13   Porzig, 'Das Rätsel im Rigveda', p. 655.

appearance. In modern German, both meanings coexist peacefully alongside each other, and even for the Rigveda we know that every expression in riddle language is also an expression in ordinary language, only with a changed meaning. Ordinary language and special language are thus not two linguistic fields lying alongside each other and excluding one another, but are rather strata of the same language superimposed on each other . . .[14]

For further details, I shall refer you to Porzig, whose remarks – on syntax as well – are of great significance for the concept of the riddle. Yet this quotation already shows that with this form it is possible to define more clearly what we have called its verbal gesture: without exception, the *verbal gesture of the riddle* originates in *special language*.

VII. SPECIAL LANGUAGE AND RIDDLE FORM – DOUBLE SOLUTION

When we say that as a rule the riddle contains the special language of a group, we are still far from determining its form. The verbal gesture of the riddle is special language, but special language need not take on the form of a riddle – it does not do so, for example, within the group that makes use of it. Or to take another example from real language, one at the intersection of common and special language: when I speak of the *foot of a mountain*, this is special language, but not a riddle; it would be a riddle if I were to ask: *Who has a foot, but cannot walk*?

Here we must mention a new aspect of the problem, which will allow us to judge the relationship of the riddler to the guesser. If it was the riddler's goal to establish whether or not the guesser is worthy of being accepted, the guesser's achievement, in finding the answer, was to break through to something that had been sealed off. It does not matter whether he intends to make use of this same enclosure in confrontation with others, to feel and act from now on as an initiate. The moment he speaks the answer, the secrecy of the association in fact no longer exists. The riddle stories express this by putting the riddler's life at stake. As soon as the Sphinx's riddle is solved, it dies.

---

14   Porzig, 'Das Rätsel im Rigveda', pp. 655–6.

This also determines the form of the riddle: it is not simply an encryption of the association's secret, it is also a defence, and this is where we find what I have called the trickiness [*Heimtücke*] of the riddle.

In Greek we have two words for riddle: αἶνος, *ainos* (with the related term αἴνιγμα, *ainigma*), and γρῖφος, *griphos*. If I am not mistaken, the first of these alludes more to the fact of encryption, whereas the second, which literally means 'net' – a net that catches us, in whose knots we entangle ourselves – expresses the trickiness of the encryption.

Once again, it is special language that makes the trickiness possible. If the meanings of the special language presuppose a conscious notion of the totality of the world, as well as some system of ambiguity into which everything that is effectively univocal must be integrated, then these meanings will not be readily comprehensible to the outsider. The special language of a group is incomprehensible to those who stand outside the group – as we see with such special languages as hunters' jargon or thieves' cant. This capacity of ambiguity to be incomprehensible is so to speak what the riddle form deliberately flaunts. Not only is it composed in the group's special language; it is also composed in such a way as to give the impression that this language is incomprehensible to the uninitiated. We called it special language when we spoke of the *foot of a mountain*, a riddle when we say: *Who has a foot, but cannot walk?* What does the riddle do here? It leads once again from the special language to the common language, from the foot that, ambiguously, props up and carries a whole range of things, to the unambiguous foot of man, the body part with which he advances – and in moving from ambiguity to unambiguousness, it makes the special language unintelligible from the perspective of the common language.

The riddle opens and closes at the same time; the way the riddle encrypts is such that it simultaneously contains and conceals, holds and withholds.

Question and answer are in conflict. We find this expressed in the riddling contests that still happen here and there, or which have come down – in the north, for example – in literary tradition. In these contests, forfeits are due not only from those who fail to guess the riddle, but also from those whose riddles are guessed. Here the riddle of the Sphinx coincides with the Ilo riddle. One initiation takes place alongside another, one initiate is set over against another. We know that such contests, in which the deity itself sometimes takes part, normally end with the more powerful party posing a riddle belonging to the highest level of initiation. No mortal can guess Odin's riddle, and through this secret as well the god has our lives in his hand.

But if the guesser manages, by guessing, to break through the enclosure, it is because with the riddle the riddler gave him the possibility of doing so. Every actualization contains within itself not only the possibility of a solution, but also the solution itself. Let us recall the riddle: 'What is the name of the emperor's dog?' – to which the answer is: 'What.' This form is merely a clear example of the general fact that the answer is to be found somewhere in every actualization. The riddler who encrypts also betrays himself in his own riddle. Here a new riddle inserts itself into the riddle – this is permitted by the type of special language that neutralizes the world of unambiguous factuality. The answer closes the gap, the opening that permitted the question to arise: this answer, too, is special language, it is ambiguous. The first answer retrieves and conceals a second; this answer, too, does not relinquish the deepest secret. This is what explains the oft-noted fact that 'true' riddles – unlike the derivative forms of today – have no definitive solution.

This sort of double solution becomes a game in some of our 'parlour riddles.' There are riddles that have a harmless solution in female company, a less harmless one in male company. This idea of 'male company' [*Männergesellschaft*] can be related to the type of organization that ethnographers call a 'male association' [*Männerbund*]. The female solution, too, conveys something that it simultaneously withholds. Further, we have riddles that seem to lead to a scabrous solution, but which then permit of a perfectly harmless solution – riddles whose trickiness consists in the fact that they appear to disclose something other than what they actually enclose. Wossidlo's collection demonstrates how frequent such riddles are – they remind us how ancient and widespread the special language of sexuality is.

VIII. THE MENTAL DISPOSITION OF KNOWLEDGE – EXAMPLES – THE RUNE

I have tried to show the riddle form in its many convolutions. With regard to our own era, we have seen that, on the one hand, the riddle lives on in derivative forms that have detached themselves almost entirely from the simple form as such, and on the other in folk riddles that indicate some past significance, and from which one might be able to derive a recognizable simple form, but which no longer have any relation to their original purpose. To observe the vital actualization of the simple form, we were obliged to have recourse to the riddles of the Rigveda – in our own time, both the so-called 'literary riddle' and the so-called folk riddle are merely play. Why is this? We already saw with legend and myth how, at certain times and under certain conditions, a mental disposition can be repressed and become less active, and how in such cases its actualizations, too, become thinner and harder to recognize. Something similar has happened with the riddle. In our society, the concept of the *Bund* and of its secrecy has mostly been lost, while the concept of special language, in a profound sense, is no longer active. Once again, we find evidence for this in Porzig. 'We demand even from the most "abstract" scholarly concepts', he writes, 'that they designate facts *unambiguously*. Influential scientific disciplines insist that scholarly terms cannot and should not be anything but names for matters of fact: so strong is the aversion of our age to the use of special language.'[15] Knowledge as common property, as something to be acquired by the greatest possible number of people, has displaced encrypted knowledge, knowledge as power. In the world of the nineteenth century, there was no place for the riddle. There may be other such places. Franz Boas, the greatest expert on North American ethnography, relates that northern Siberia and America both seem to lack riddles.

But wherever the *Bund* and its secretiveness are still to be found – even if only vestigially – there again we encounter the true riddle. There has recently been much talk of a society whose binding sense is supposed to be myth – of an association in which the world announces

---

15   Porzig, 'Das Rätsel im Rigveda', p. 658.

itself as a temple. This guild, too, opens and closes itself in a riddle, and the word *Freemason* is a good example of special language. In this case as well, we have observed the efforts of outsiders to demolish the insularity of this association, and we have seen how their means to this end was to reveal the answer to the riddle.

The struggle against Freemasonry shows us something else: the connection between the clandestine nature of the *Bund* and the clandestine nature of criminality. It might look as though we had lost sight of the second encryption, the one by means of which a defendant can save his own life. In fact, this situation is somewhat different – it is a reversal, but a reversal that can be explained in the same manner. The criminal, too, has closed himself up with his crime and his secret: he and his are the only initiates. Here as well, it is a matter of pushing through to him; here too the solution provides access to what had been sealed off. Whenever the outsider does not recognize the *Bund* on its own terms and in its enclosure, he performs this reversal: he accuses it of criminality, just as we see happening with Freemasonry today.

In our own era the secretiveness of the criminal, the riddle of crime, has been expanded from a short form to a longer narrative genre, the detective story. Here we have two complementary figures: the criminal, who encrypts himself and his crime but whose encryption also opens a possibility of discovery; and the detective, the discoverer who solves the riddle and penetrates the enclosure. This narrative form – which is one of the many in current literature into which the literary form of the novel is dissolving – certainly merits closer study.

To conclude: we have seen how, in the world of legend, there are objects charged with the power of the form, which in their concreteness incarnate the form as a whole; we called such an object a *relic*. In the case of *Sage*, it was the concrete object we called *inheritance* that corresponded to the relic of legend. In the case of myth, we spoke of the *symbol*. We find such objects in the world of the riddle as well, objects in which the riddle's power has installed itself, objects charged with riddles – objects containing something that they also withhold from us, which are like shelters for a solution that they also hide, which open something up while at the same time closing it off. I should like to call such objects – which murmur of secrecy – *runes*, a word related to Old Gothic *rûna* and to the Anglo-Saxon word *rún*, as well as to *Alraune*, 'mandrake'. It must remain one of our many unfinished tasks to assess how this object and its far-reaching connections – with writing especially – are related to the mental disposition of the riddle.

CHAPTER 5

Saying

To the short form of the riddle I would like to add another short form, which we normally call the *proverb* ('*Sprichwort*'). It will become clear in the course of our study to what degree this term indicates a particular actualization, and to what extent we are justified in deducing a simple form from it. The essential material for our work has already been compiled under this name. Compilations of proverbs appear quite early – much earlier than the scholarly field of ethnography – and also with thoroughly different objectives. The first scholarly collections of this sort coincide in the modern West with Humanism, and their goals are in a sense philological and pedagogical. We could mention Erasmus, Sebastian Franck, Agricola, Heinrich Bebel – and also the proverb collection that Martin Luther put together for his own use. We find details on the subject in an excellent book that I mean to use as a basis for our reflections, Friedrich Seiler's *Teaching German Proverbs*, published by Beck in their series of handbooks for German instruction in the upper grades.[1] This work, complete in every respect, will spare me from having to refer to various modern proverb collections and lexicons.

Great though the merits may be of Seiler's pioneering work, here again there are things we must formulate differently.

Seiler defines the proverb as follows: 'Self-contained sayings with a didactic tendency and elevated form, in circulation in the folk vernacular'.[2]

---

1   Friedrich Seiler, *Deutsche Sprichwörterkunde* (Munich: C. H. Beck, 1922).
2   Seiler, *Deutsche Sprichwörterkunde*, p. 2.

Shortly before this book appeared, Seiler had given a slightly different definition in a shorter work: 'Proverbs are vernacular sayings of a didactic character, presented in a form that is elevated above ordinary speech.'

If a writer changes a definition, then this means that his thinking has shifted at the place in question. Here we find that the didactic 'character' has been replaced by a didactic 'tendency', the more far-reaching word with a more careful one. Seiler seems to have felt somewhat uncertain about 'didactic' as well. The second definition also adds the word 'self-contained'. Common to both definitions is: 1) that a proverb 'circulates in the folk vernacular', 2) that it is a saying, and 3) that it displays an 'elevated' form.

Let us look more carefully at this 'circulation in the folk vernacular', or the idea of folk currency (*Volkläufigkeit*), as this characteristic is later called. Seiler himself senses that the term 'folk' is a little bit tricky. First he says: 'the thought must be comprehensible and not too high, the words commonly known and familiar to the people', and for this reason he discounts as proverbs sentences like, 'In love, all women have wit' or 'Everything earthly is transitory.' A moment later, however, he writes: 'To say that a proverb must be a true folk saying is not at all to say that every proverb must be known to the *entire* folk. Many proverbs are known only in particular locations or areas or to particular ethnic groups, in which case they often appear in dialect.'[3] And then, a bit further on, we have:

> Some proverbs, too, emerge from specific vocational spheres: soldiers', craftsmen's, peasants' and students' proverbs. Intellectual and moral education also effect certain differences in the use of proverbs. Some proverbs are more at home in the higher strata of a society, some are more at home in the lower ones. The former approach the border between the proverb and the *aphorism*.[4]

This suggests that we must imagine three social strata: low, high, and highest. The proverb is located in the first two strata, the aphorism in

---

3   Ibid., p. 2.
4   Ibid., pp. 2–3.

the third. But we do not hear how these strata are positioned in relation to the overall complex of the 'folk' or in relation to each other, and thus it is hard to imagine the relationship of the low proverb to the high or of the high proverb to the aphorism, or how these three together relate to the abovementioned proverbs from the vocational spheres. Neither is it quite correct to imagine these aphorisms as literary products, for, as Seiler adds next: 'this separation of higher from lower proverbs tends to occur when a written language detaches itself from the folk language'.[5] The higher proverb thus already coincides with the written language.

Now Seiler dissolves the difference between higher and lower proverbs – or at least, the distinction is no longer seen as decisive, for we find something else in between: 'Between the two classes there is a broad middle stratum – outnumbering both – of proverbs employed by all strata of the folk, without distinction.' Seiler even specifies when this middle stratum arose: 'These proverbs derive from a time in which the intellectual life of the folk, its ways of feeling and expression, were still homogeneous and not distinguished by differences of rank and class.'[6]

To me it seems difficult, sociologically, to imagine this epoch without distinctions of social rank, class, and so on. I would even hazard to doubt that such an idyll has ever existed in the course of cultural history. Happily, the proverbs of the middle class also derive from another era: 'they trickled down from the upper stratum into the lower'. In any case, this middle class can lay claim 'not only to the most common proverbs, but also to the majority of proverbs'.[7]

All this does not give us a very clear image of what Seiler means by 'folk', or of where in this 'folk' the proverb is supposed to arise or be preserved.

We encounter further difficulties with the concept 'folk' as soon as we reach Seiler's second chapter, which discusses the origins of the proverb and promises orientation regarding the *how* of the form. Here proverbs are sorted into two classes according to their origin: literary

---

5   Ibid., p. 3.
6   Ibid., p. 3.
7   Ibid., p. 3.

proverbs, and proverbs originating with the folk. It would thus seem that literature does not belong to the 'folk'. The literary proverbs, Seiler says, 'are much more frequent than one might think. They are at once the most widespread and the most pithy.'[8]

Since Seiler intends to discuss literary proverbs in a different book, he proposes to devote his *Teaching German Proverbs* exclusively to those arising from the folk. First, however, he means to redress a certain 'romanticizing conception': 'People have long believed that the folk proverb, like the folk song, the folktale or the folk saga, has its mysterious origin in the depths of the folk soul.'[9] This notion, which is purportedly to be found already in Aristotle and which – without reference to Aristotle – Rousseau and Herder would later make commonplace, cannot withstand the findings of modern research: even the popular proverbs did not grow in mysterious ways from the depths of the folk soul.

> 'The folk' as a whole cannot create anything at all. Every creation, invention, discovery is always the work of an individual person. Somewhere, at some point, each proverb must have been said for the first time. If it pleased the people who heard it, then they passed it on as a 'winged word'; it would then have been tweaked and remoulded until it acquired a shape acceptable to all, thus becoming a well-known proverb.[10]

This process is not entirely clear either. Every proverb is supposed to have been a 'winged word'. The folk as a whole is incapable of creating anything – but it seems perfectly able to 'trim' and 'remodel' something already available, so that it acquires a shape that can claim general validity. Yet a proverb only becomes a winged word when it has in this way acquired from the folk a shape that can claim general validity, and so on.

It is not my aim to polemicize against Seiler's book. What I would show with this argument is simply that methodologically we can no

---

8   Ibid., p. 19.
9   Ibid., p. 19.
10   Ibid., p. 19.

longer begin with the concept *folk*, and that we must admit that what we call the *proverb* appears to exist within all strata of the folk – high, low, and middle – and in all its classes and ranks: peasants, crafts-people, scholars.

II. MENTAL DISPOSITION: EXPERIENCE – THE ACTUALIZATIONS

Let us then turn to the second fundamental characteristic: *the proverb is a saying*. Generally, this means that a proverb is itself not a basic concept, but that it can be traced back to some basic concept. Within our methodological framework, this would mean that there is a simple form we call *saying*, and that this simple form is actualized in a *proverb*. We will speak later of whether, in this case, the form can be actualized in other ways.

Because there have always and everywhere been proverbs, not only in the Western world, but also in antiquity; because we need not seek them out like the true riddle or interpret them like the *Sage* or the legend, but encounter them daily, we can use this familiarity to try to determine directly the mental disposition that produces the simple form *saying* and its actualization in the proverb, without having to look to any given historical moment in which the form is especially distinct.

If we comprehend the world as a multiplicity of discrete percep-tions and discrete experiences (*Einzelerlebnisse*), we can say that these perceptions and experiences, taken in series and altogether, constitute what we call *experience* (*Erfahrung*), but also that the sum of these experiences remains a multiplicity of particulars. Each experience is understood each time on its own terms; in this respect, and in this world, a conclusion drawn from experience is binding and valuable only with regard to itself. This is a timeless world, not because in it – as in a world in which there is no more experience – the moments merge together into an eternity, but because in their scattered idiosyncrasy the moments cannot flow together as time. It is a world lacking the fourth dimension, an asymptotic world, a world of isolation – a world that knows how to add, but not how to multiply.

It is impossible to conceptualize this world, because conceptual thought is precisely the thing against which this world sets its face, and the thing that destroys this world. Here too of course there is separation and connection, comparison and correlation, classification and ordering, but separation predominates in the connections, while mere juxtaposition survives within every relation, and every grouping must still contend with the distinction of terms. In short, this world is not a *cosmos*; it is things in dispersion, it is empirical reality.

Yet we can retreat from other worlds into this world; some part of our existence takes place in this world, and whenever we find ourselves in it, then the form produced by our mental disposition and by the train of thoughts linked to it is the simple form *maxim*; or, better – even if the term somewhat limits possible usage – *saying* ('*Spruch*').

In this morphology, then, *saying* is the literary form that encloses an experience, without preventing it from continuing to be an individual detail in a world characterized by dispersion. It binds this world within itself without thereby removing it from the empirical world.

This form actualizes itself in the proverb – but unlike with the other forms, where we were less able to differentiate modes of actualization, here we can recognize other actualizations: moral maxims, aphorisms, winged words, proverbial turns of phrase, apothegms – all belong here, each in its own way.

We will however concentrate primarily on the actualization known as the *proverb*, which should sufficiently explain the nature of the form.

III. THE EMPIRICAL WORLD – THE SAGE ADDRESS (*KLUGREDE*)

Let us look once again at the saying as such. If something that could have succeeded does not succeed and we ascribe the failure to a lack of success familiar to us from experience and somehow connected with our character, then we say, gloomily: *It's all a question of luck.*

If however something unexpectedly succeeds, and we ascribe the success to a certain daring that experience shows is what it takes to reach one's goal, then again we say – but in quite a different tone – *It's all a question of luck.*

Thus does the saying appear in life and art every time an experience is understood in the manner described above. In these cases it is fully clear that we are not judging the situation critically or undertaking an explanation of the type: 'If I had acted differently, then perhaps . . .' etc. We isolate the fact or the situation, stringing it so to speak on the thread of experience, which consists only of such single pearls.

We speak of a world of experience, but it is clear that this world – precisely because it is empirical – assorts itself according to the interests, the occupations, the experiences of discrete classes and social ranks, and that these experiences are consolidated into separate worlds. This explains why we can recognize differences in the sayings that Seiler ascribes to various spheres: soldiers, craftsmen, peasants, students. Besides this we have the sayings of other strata – the humanistic, the writerly saying, and also the sayings of that great middle class in which the experiences of many individuals come together. Thus, to take one example, the experience that one should seize opportunity can be expressed as a blacksmith's experience: 'Strike while the iron is hot', or as a lover's experience: 'Fortune favours the bold'; while in the milieu that Seiler calls middle-class, both sayings can be used to isolate and categorize a given experience.

With this we have come to a word whose meaning we have seen Seiler himself restrict in his second definition, and which in my opinion we should strike completely: the word 'didactic'. The saying is not didactic; it has no didactic character, not even a didactic tendency. This is not to say that we cannot learn from experience, only that, in the world we are speaking of, experience is not understood as something to learn from. What is didactic is a beginning, something to build on; experience, in the form given by sayings, is a conclusion, an end. The tendency of the saying is retrospective, its character is one of resignation. The same is true of its actualization. The proverb, likewise, is not a beginning, but an end, a countersignature, a visible seal that is stamped onto something and with which it receives its character as an experience.

We see this most clearly where the verbal form of the proverb coincides with the mode of expression in which a *doctrine* or a *command* is normally given. The imperative in the Prussian saying 'Be always loyal and honest', or in the biblical 'Thou shalt not covet thy neighbour's wife, manservant, maidservant, cattle', and so on, is not the same as the imperative in 'Do unto others as you would have them do unto you' or 'Cobbler, stick to thy last.' The first two imperatives – one could call them categorical imperatives – envision a future; in the second two, what predominates is a past that has led to this conclusion. We also tend not to say 'Be careful whom you trust' simply out of the blue, but only when somebody has not taken care whom he trusted; we say 'Don't count your chickens before they're hatched' only when the luck of the day – the *fortuna huiusce diei*, as the Romans called it – has already begun to falter. Here as well, we employ a conclusion to associate something that has empirically already occurred with other, comparable events. We can explain the lack of moral judgment that critics have often noticed and faulted in proverbs by the fact that, in the empirical world, there is no concept of morality. Every proverb closes the stable door – but only after the horse has bolted.

'The true folk proverb', says Wilhelm Grimm, 'contains a deliberate lesson. It is not the fruit of lone contemplation, but a truth long sensed, erupting spontaneously into a higher form of expression.'[11]

Sebastian Franck also alludes to this definitive character of the proverb when he calls it *eine kurtze weise Klugred* – 'a short, wise, sage address', 'the sum of a whole transaction'.[12] *Klugrede*, 'sage address', is a nice word for the saying and its actualization, one which has alas vanished from modern German. There is in the word *Klugrede* something of what we hear in the Low German *klugschnacken* (to be a smart-alec), and this too adverts to the post hoc and grudging qualities of the proverb.

IV. THE WINGED WORD – 'FOLK' AND 'PERSONALITY' – THE
ASSERTIVE MODE – LANGUAGE OF THE PROVERB – STYLISTIC
MEANS – TONAL MOVEMENT – 'IMAGE' – ACTUALIZATION AND
MENTAL DISPOSITION – APOPHTHEGMATA – EMBLEM

With this we have come to the matter of actualizations. And here again we must ask our usual question: How does this actualization occur?

---

11 Wilhelm Grimm, 'Über Freidank', *Kleinere Schriften*, ed. Gustav Hinrichs, 4 vols (Gütersloh: Bertelsmann, 1881–1887), vol. 4, p. 22.

12 Sebastian Franck, *Sprichwörter / schöne / weise / herzliche clügreden / vvnd hoffsprüch*, etc. (Frankfurt am Main: Christian Egenolffen, 1541).

How is the actualized form produced by the mental disposition that we have suggested – indeed, more than suggested – with the words *empirical reality* or *experience*? Or, in practice: How do the proverbs 'Fortune favours the bold', 'Fortune helps those who help themselves', 'Better be lucky born than a rich man's son', 'A lucky man needs little counsel', or, conversely, 'The Devil's children have the Devil's luck' result from the life experience that we have called 'It's a question of luck'?

To take the matter of 'how' at a general level: as we have seen, Seiler imagines that the actualization occurs in passing through an individual. Like every creation, discovery or invention – so we hear – the proverb is supposed to derive from an individual personality. Seiler even describes this individual more precisely: he calls it 'a bright intellect, furnished with good mother wit, to whom the gift of the *mot juste* has also been given'.[13]

Besides the inclination – noted in my introduction – of literary scholars to consider a poet the force that gives form and structure, there is a more particular fact that has led Seiler and others to this conclusion. We do in fact possess actualized sayings known to have originated with known and named individuals: these are the so-called *winged words* that I mentioned earlier. The expression 'winged words', which originated with Homer, was revived in 1864 when Georg Büchmann first published a collection of such sayings under this title.[14] The name is perhaps not all that well chosen, but it has become established, so we shall retain it.

According to Büchmann, the requirements of a 'winged word' are as follows:

1. that its literary origin or its historical author be *demonstrable*;
2. that it is not only generally known, but has also passed into German usage and is generally *used* or *applied*;
3. that its use and application are not just temporary, but rather enduring – in which case 'enduring' need not mean 'eternal'.

---

13   Seiler, *Deutsche Sprichwörterkunde*, p. 20.
14   Georg Büchmann, *Geflügelte Worte: Der Citatenschatz des deutschen Volks* (Berlin: Haude & Spener, 1864).

Here we really have actualizations of sayings that have originated in personalities – doubtless also in individuals with mother wit, to whom was given the gift of the *mot juste*. And it is also the case with these individuals that they are *demonstrable*, but not always generally known. Who is aware, when he says of someone: 'He can be silent in seven languages', that this saying was coined by Schleiermacher, and to describe a particular person? Who knows, when he says: 'Does it have to be now?', that this phrase is based on a couplet by Nestroy? According to Seiler, this is how all proverbs came into being: they began with a single person, a poet who has remained unknown – and Seiler does not recoil from asserting that all proverbs were originally winged words.

On the other hand, we can say the following. Büchmann has nowhere established an author for the proverbs that we are calling 'generally accepted' or 'in common parlance'. I cannot estimate their number even approximately, but I will note that the first volume of Wander's *Encyclopedia of German Proverbs* includes around 45,000 German proverbs, and that the entire work encompasses five volumes.[15] Even if we factor out repetitions and various nuances of the same proverbs, we still have a few hundred thousand left over – it's a remarkable coincidence that so many individuals have gotten lost. Further, Büchmann also did not attempt to discover the authors of these 'generally accepted' proverbs. And why not? Because he knew very well that a winged word is not a proverb; because he could distinguish the two at first glance; because he understood that it was a question of another genre, and that he was interested in another kind of actualization. Once in a while the boundaries were hazy; there were turns of phrase that had been used on a special occasion or in a particular situation and which then caught on in general use, and could thus be considered winged words, but which could also be traced back to older actualizations – yet these cases were a very small minority. With the great majority, proverbs and winged words were not to be confused. One example of a turn of phrase that could thus be traced back to an older actualization is 'a storm in a teacup', supposed to have been

---

15   Karl Friedrich Wilhelm Wander, *Deutsches Sprichwörter-Lexikon: Ein Hausschatz für das deutsche Volk* (Leipzig: Brockhaus, 1867–1880), 5 vols.

coined by Montesquieu. Yet Büchmann shows that Montesquieu adapted the phrase from humanist figures of speech, which can themselves be traced back to antiquity.

I have gone into detail in order to show that, methodologically, we can do as little with Seiler's concept of the 'individual personality' as we could with his notion of the 'folk'. Since the 'folk' could not be recognized as a creative force, and since the 'folk soul' proved worthy of being consigned to the junk pile of romanticizing conceptions, it was replaced with the creative power of individuals possessing mother wit. But now these individuals had once again to be forgotten, their personal property had to become common property, and this property had further to be 'remoulded' and 'knocked into shape'. Where and when this occurred remained unknown. If one says: 'Every proverb must first have been uttered somewhere and sometime', one can of course also say: 'Every remoulded proverb must first have been uttered somewhere and sometime.' One can also say: 'Every word must first have been uttered somewhere and sometime.' And so on, ad infinitum. I will not deny that there is a circular flow between individuals and populations; I also do not doubt the significance of such circulation for literary study. I do, however, deny that it is possible to deduce the nature and meaning of a form from such circulation – also because it has just now so clearly led us astray. A proverb is not a winged word, and a winged word is not a proverb. What has been coined by an individual may lose its relation to that individual, but not its character; the name of the author may be forgotten – as so often happens with literary forms – but the distinct sense remains that an author was once there.

What the proverb and the winged word have in common is the fact that they belong to the same mental disposition. The only way to establish what they have in common and what distinguishes them from one another is to observe them in the place where the form issues from the mental disposition, where it is realized, and where we can observe its becoming actualized: in language. And here again, Seiler has done invaluable groundwork by exhaustively describing the linguistic processes of the proverb. What remains to be done is to illustrate the meaning of these processes with several examples.

Generally, the mode in which a saying indicates a state of affairs is *declarative*. This is the difference from myth and riddle, in which the form occurs in the shape of question and answer, and whose mode we therefore described as *conversational* or *dialogical*. In the saying, however, the declaration does not proceed in a connective or a deductive way from concept to concept, from judgment to judgment; rather, it refers in a unique and a categorical way to a state of affairs. For this reason we call this mode – in contrast to the *continuous* or the *discursive* – *assertive* or *apodictic*. It is obvious that this assertive mode is the only one in which what we have called experience can come to expression.

Let us now look in more detail at the language in which the saying is actualized as a proverb.

First, the words and the parts of speech. Let us take an example: *Handsome is as handsome does.* What is the word *handsome* here? A noun? Certainly not. An adjective? Not that either. A nominalized adjective? Nor is it quite that. The way it appears here does not allow us to align it with any of the usual grammatical categories. It has something of both noun and adjective, but here it has a peculiar character that distances it from the usual definitions. One could say it defends itself here against the generalizing nature of the concept – that (to exaggerate slightly) it can be used in this way only here, and in this context.

Moving on from the word and the parts of speech, we come to syntax. Here too we can cite an example: *The nearer the church, the farther from God.* We know this pattern from numerous proverbs; we also know that it is favoured as well in the South German epigrammatic genre of the *Schnadahüpfel*. One could describe this sentence form as a rigorously symmetrical parataxis – but one in which neither of the two halves of the combination has a subject, a verb or a predicate, in the usual sense. At the risk of playing on words, we could speak here of anti-phrases rather than of phrases. This entire pattern presents a syntax of multiplicity rather than one of unity, in which meaning emerges spasmodically from independent sets of contraries – which is what Wilhelm Grimm meant when he spoke of a truth long sensed, erupting spontaneously into a higher form of expression.

It is as pointless to comprehend this 'the . . . the' pattern as a combination of relative and demonstrative clauses as it is to call the equally familiar proverbial sentence pattern beginning with *Wer* . . . ('He who . . .') a conjunction of principal and relative clauses. Nor does *Wer keine Hand hat, kann keine Faust machen* ('He who has no hand cannot make a fist') exemplify hypotaxis. Rather, it is a sharp juxtaposition, with no part clearly subordinated or superordinated to the other, and in which *Wer keine Hand hat* has the same function as the word *handsome* in the proverb *Handsome is as handsome does.* The slightest change in the direction of generalization reduces the value of the actualized form. We instantly notice that the proverb loses some of its power when it is rephrased as *A person who has no hand . . .*, or, *If one has no hand, one cannot make a fist.*

We encounter the same phenomenon when we enquire as to the stylistic means of proverbial sentences. One could perhaps call *Here today, gone tomorrow* an asyndeton. But we have a sense that this sentence goes somewhat beyond what we usually understand by this term. The asyndeton, which dissolves the connection between the parts of a sentence, ceases where one cannot speak of connection in the first place. In the proverb, everything is asyndetic, and for this reason the term loses its meaning. Superficially, *Everyone's friend, nobody's friend* would appear to be an anaphora. If we look more carefully, we see that here, unlike in anaphora, the word *everyone* cannot be understood as the centre around which the parts of the sentence are grouped; the other words retain their independence, despite the repetition.

We see the same thing when we observe the melodic line of the proverb. We have already seen how a number of proverbs can share a sentence pattern in common. We can speak of a rhythmic pattern as well, and Seiler has also researched these thoroughly. When we say: *Allzu klug ist dumm* ('Too clever by half'), *Selber ist der Mann* ('Do it yourself'), *Wie mans macht, ist falsch* ('It's a no-win situation'), then we have three different proverbs constructed according to the same metrical schema (– ˘ – ˘ –). There are also more complicated patterns: *Wer den Heller nicht ehrt, ist des Talers nicht wert* ('Save a penny, save a pound') and *Wenn die Hoffnung nicht wär, ei so lebt' ich nicht mehr* ('If it weren't for hope, no one could live') (˘ ˘ – ˘ ˘ – | ˘ ˘ – ˘ ˘ –). But rhythmic patterns do not have the same function in forms of literary art and in the proverb: in the former, the patterns are there to carry the verbal images forward, whereas in the proverb they are there to close off the form. Stressed and unstressed syllables increase the isolating effect that we have noted already in the syntax; meter and rhyme are less like waves rising and falling than like the slats in a fence.

Finally, the 'image', the trope. *Lies have short legs.* We can agree what part of speech 'lies' is: it is a noun. We also have a subject, an object and a predicate. But what happens here with the noun? Something is predicated of it that is not necessarily related to it, that resides on another level. Lies are not body parts; legs are. Recall what I said about special language when discussing the riddle, where we began with the word 'foot'. Do 'legs' here have the same kind of meaning as 'foot' had in that context? Do we find comparable realities converging here in an ambiguous word? Not at all! Strictly speaking, it is not said that lies have *legs* – it is said that they have *short legs*. It is not suggested – as in the special language of riddles, where 'foot' meant something whose whole nature consists in supporting and carrying – that 'legs' here mean something whose nature consists in movement, in running away. Two unrelated things – lies and short legs – are put together *once*, suddenly, in a way that gives meaning to one of the words – *lies* – while also tearing this word from its general application, thus leaving it significance only as an experience. We make an incongruously corporeal statement about a plural noun – *lies* – that we might otherwise think an abstraction; this suppresses the possibility of abstraction and removes the word from the domain of conceptual language to that of finite objects.

It is no different when an entire proverb seems a single image; we do quite the same thing when, instead of saying 'One must seize opportunity', we say: 'One must strike while the iron is hot.' We are not comparing *opportunity* with *iron*, *seize* with *strike*; we are not replacing one concept with another. What we have here – to repeat Wilhelm Grimm's phrase – is a truth long sensed erupting into form the moment it once more becomes experience; the form removes this truth from universal validity while barring the possibility of its becoming abstract, thus returning it to the empirical realm.

We can summarize our observations on the verbal processes of the proverb as follows: the language of the proverb is such that all of its elements taken singly – in their meanings, in their syntactic and stylistic relationships, and in their melodic line – steadfastly resist all generalization and every kind of abstraction.

In its details and on the whole, the language of the proverb corresponds to the mental disposition that produces the saying. In this world, where the multiplicity of experiences and perceptions may organize itself into life experience but the sum of individual experiences still remains a multiplicity of single events, the words in their meaning and interconnection have only empirical value. Separation predominates in the connections, mere juxtaposition survives within every relation, and every grouping must still contend with the distinction of terms. Each word, each clause, each element in a syntactic sequence is, alongside others, always exclusively a *hic et nunc*. Just as in this world facts are strung like single pearls on the thread of experience, so too does the verbal gesture operate here.

We said at the beginning that we spend part of our existence in this world, that it is more familiar to our daily lives than the world of *Sage* or legend, and certainly more familiar than the world of riddles. One can also understand why we need it: we use it to ward off all those tiring consequences and conclusions that experience everywhere forces us to when it prompts us to think conceptually or in terms of knowledge: we relax in this world when we are bored with a moral world order, with the world of sobriety.

And this world is what conjures up the proverb each time. We have often already suggested in passing not only that these forms can be deduced from the mental disposition, but also that when they appear as actualized forms they naturally lead us back to the mental disposition. The form *Sage* emerges from the mental disposition of tribe and blood relationship – but as soon as we read a saga, we ourselves are no longer able to comprehend the world otherwise. In the form 'myth' there resides the highest freedom in the world, the freedom to be one's own creator – but even when we read a myth that is not our own, we find ourselves breathing more easily. With the living proverb this feeling is strong – we literally use it whenever we, so to speak, put an experience up on the shelf – but even when the proverb is spoken by someone else, we invariably feel as if we had been spared the effort to work out experiences or sensations for ourselves: *All's well that ends well!*

The fact that we are familiar with so many other types of actualization of the saying besides the proverb can be attributed to the power of this mental disposition to segregate and singularize; these all belong together in the simple form, but can be distinguished from one another in the actualization, and they even have particular names.

We will not pursue them further here; but since I mentioned 'winged words', I would like to say something more on that subject. If we sort generally through the material collected by Büchmann, we arrive at two categories: first, winged words from writers – that is to say, *quotations* that have become winged words; and second, winged words that were said by some person in a particular situation – Seiler calls these *historical* winged words, though the Greek *apophthegmata* might be a better term. Both forms belong to the mental disposition of the saying. The winged word *Ich warne Neugierige* (attributed to Berlin's chief of police in the 1910s, Traugott von Jagow, as advice to left-wing protesters: 'The streets belong to traffic: *I warn the curious*') is not meant as a prohibition, but instead a particular situation is completely isolated in the saying; the situation is singled out experientially. The same thing occurs with winged words that originate in a work of literature, that are dropped (as it were) by a work of literary art. In the literary work, too, certain situations arise that require formulation in proverbial terms. This is often the case at the ends of chapters. As products of particular situations, these experiences are also formulated empirically in sayings, and then these sayings isolate themselves further; the experience can be isolated precisely because it has become a saying. In this way the saying can leave the work, it drops out of it and stays behind, it signifies autonomously – just as in the proverb the words of the sentence relinquish syntactic connection. If we look at the process in this way, we arrive at the winged word whose author is unknown.

Emblema was the word the Ancients used for 'a small object attached to a larger one, most often made of some different material'. The scion grafted onto the wild fruit tree, the wooden peg that fastened the iron point of the Roman *pilum* or spear to the shaft, a sole inserted into a shoe, are emblemata. Every one of these small objects can indicate that the whole to which it has been joined, into which it has been 'thrown', consists of a multiplicity of disparate singularities. But emblemata are also the single set stones in mosaics; in this case, the singularities are not different, but resemble each other – and yet each stone indicates that the whole is composed of separate units. Finally, the toreutic images affixed to the bottoms of drinking bowls are emblemata, for once again these reveal a duality of artwork and use-object which can be distinguished from the unitary artwork that the bowl can become through perfection of its form.

Now, whenever an emblem not only *refers to* the composition of a whole from a multiplicity of singularities, but also itself *signifies* the multiplicity in its detached compositeness, then we have in this emblem the object that represents in the world the mental disposition with which it is charged.

Like the word symbol, the word emblem has acquired the general meaning of *Sinnbild* ('symbol'; literally, 'sense-image'). However, to our understanding it is first of all not an image, but an object. Second, it does not at all represent the meaning of the whole such that the sense of the whole as a whole is represented in it, but rather in such a way as to make clear that the sense of the whole can be understood only as a composite of disparate singularities.

CHAPTER 6

Case

Thus far, I have discussed and defined legend, *Sage*, myth, riddle and saying. We were all familiar with at least the name and existence of these forms. We had not yet connected any very distinct concepts with these names; we did not know exactly what legend or *Sage* were – but we did not doubt that these things existed. And, beginning with these names and with the conviction that these things existed, we have made an effort to comprehend in more detail what we had vaguely in mind, to distinguish what did not belong together, to define our concepts: in short, to grasp the nature and meaning of the individual forms.

Two forms remain whose names we also know, the forms 'fairy tale' and 'joke'. Before I move on to these final, familiar forms, I must pose the question: Does this list of familiar forms exhaust the entire number of forms? Or do we have other terms that we connect – however vaguely – with some concept, but which really designate forms that belong in our series?

When we speak of a *series*, it is clear that we have a *system* in mind, a finite series; it is clear that the concept of simple form – which comprehends each simple form as a possibility for the world to actualize itself in a definite way – admits only a limited number of possibilities.

Practically speaking, if these simple forms are to constitute the *basis of literary criticism*, if they are to encompass that part of literary criticism that we would locate between language as such and the constructions in which something is actualized, finally and definitively, as a literary form, then collectively they must exhaust this world

– just as, taken together, the grammatical and syntactic categories make up the world as it actualizes itself in language as such.

There are two such forms, ones that we can distinguish through careful study, that we can observe in the world, whose mental disposition we recognize, whose effects at the third level – the level of literary forms – we can assess; in short, that definitely belong to the closed system of our simple forms, but for which we lack an accepted name, so that we must (as it were) name them anew.

I mean to prove in the following chapters that these forms behave in exactly the same way as all other simple forms, that under the sway of a mental disposition they actualize themselves in life and in language, that they can be found, *mutatis mutandis*, in the same aggregate state as legend or saying, and that they must therefore be admitted into our series, if our system is to be complete.

Here, too, I would rather not proceed in a purely theoretical fashion, but would prefer to demonstrate directly how and where these simple forms – which are not always recognized as such – are operative. Hence I will begin with as obvious an example as possible.

II. AN EXAMPLE – QUALITATIVE AND QUANTITATIVE MEASUREMENT OF RIGHT AND WRONG – LEGAL PARAGRAPH AS NORM – *EXEMPLUM* AND INSTANCE – MENTAL DISPOSITION OF THE CASE – DISPERSION OF NORMS

In the third number of the *Berliner Illustrirte Zeitung* for 1928, we find a short popular essay, which the author – he calls himself Balder – has entitled 'The Grotesque and the Tragic in Penal Law'. The article narrates stories in connection with criminal law; it collects cases. Let me simply select the first of these as an example:

A pickpocket steals my wallet in a crowd; the wallet contains a hundred marks in small bills. Sharing his haul with his lover, he tells her of his success. If both should be caught, the woman will be punished as a fence.

Suppose that my wallet had contained only a hundred-mark note. The thief has the bill changed and then gives the woman fifty marks; in this case, she is exempt from punishment. For fencing, dealing in stolen goods, is possible only with the objects immediately obtained through the punishable act, not with the exchanged bills.

This case relates to two paragraphs in our penal code.

> §242: 'Whoever takes an object that does not belong to him away from another with the intention of illegally coming into possession of it, shall be punished with a jail sentence for theft.'
>
> §259: 'Whoever, for his own benefit, takes, conceals, purchases, pawns or otherwise appropriates or participates in the sale of things that he knows or must assume from the circumstances are stolen, shall be punished with a jail sentence for dealing in stolen goods.'[1]

What is happening here? Let us restrict our attention initially to the first of the two parts into which this little tale clearly divides.

We see how a rule, a legal paragraph, changes into an event, becomes an event, and acquires form by virtue of being taken up in language. Let us inspect the process more closely: it is a matter of *crime*. The concept 'crime' has already played a role in our discussion of the legend and anti-legend form; and in the current context and on this occasion I would like to show how simple forms can be superimposed on each other in a single life process, in the same sphere of life, without intermingling.

Let us recall how, in the mental disposition from which the form 'legend' emerged, the mental disposition of *imitatio*, crime could be called 'punishable wrong' in so far as evil actualized itself there, became something autonomous, a *crimen*. But at that point I already noted the fundamental provision of our penal code: *nullum crimen sine lege, nulla poena sine lege*; and I said that the law, in this sense, becomes both a norm for the behaviour to be punished and a norm of punishment.

However, we see now that the crime can mean two very different things, depending on whether we understand it as an autonomous

---

1 *Strafgesetzbuch* [StGb] *für das Deutsche Reich vom 15. Mai 1871, nach der Novelle vom 26. Februar 1876, nebst Einführungs- und Abänderungsgesetz*, ed. Karl Lueder (Erlangen: Deichert, 1876), part II, sections 19 and 21, pp. 65, 70.

object (as in the *anti-legend*) or (in the juristic sense) as a *violation of a rule*, an illegal act.

Permit me to recall the figure of Don Juan. His actions are not at all judged by the standard of whether they contravene what is to be found in Part 2, Section 13 of our penal code in the way of rules regarding crimes and misdemeanours against morality; rather, we see in his actions an active wrong, something categorically culpable that is independent of legal articles and cannot be captured by them. In the same manner, Ahasverus is not a person who has contravened the commandment: 'Love thy neighbour'; rather, in him too a wrong is objectified that does not depend on any standard: it is *absolute wrong*. Finally, as we have mentioned, Faust's pact with the Devil has been analysed with regard to its legal validity, but we instantly sense that this dissolves the form 'anti-legend', that the validity of this pact likewise cannot be judged by the rules of an agreement between two contracting parties; instead, here too concision [*Bündigkeit*] has taken a concrete form.

We saw this even more clearly with the legend itself. There was no *lex* in it, no norm or standard to which active virtue could be referred; there were only witnesses and convictions; there was only the miracle *absolutely* confirming a virtue that had become objective.

Here, however – to return to the matter at hand – we have neither legend nor anti-legend; rather, crimes or misdemeanours are referred to a rule whose validity and scope within a definite sphere cannot and may not be subject to doubt. Crimes or misdemeanours thus mean an infraction of the rule, a violation of the norm. It is not virtue and wrong that here become active and objective, but rather *law* and *norm*; actions of all kinds are referred to these, and based on them judgments are formed as to whether the actions are liable to prosecution or not.

We said that in the mental disposition of legend and anti-legend there is a qualitative difference between the saint and the good person, on the one hand, and the anti-saint and the ordinary criminal on the other. In the mental disposition we are now addressing, only quantitative differences prevail, differences determined by greater distance from, or proximity to, the norm. In the mental disposition of legend the measure is qualitative, in our current mental disposition the measure, or rather the scale, is quantitative.

Here one can indeed use the image of a scale: scale [*Wage*] is related to wagon [*Wagen*], and to the verb 'move' [*bewegen*]. On one side of the scale, there rests a law; as soon as something is laid on the other side, this side moves up or down, and in so moving, it is weighed.

Yet we saw not only that actions of all kinds, evil or good, are weighed against a law, judged in relation to a norm; we also see that this norm can emerge from its universality, make itself visible. In short: it can actualize itself in a definite manner, in a verbal gesture.

This is what happened in the first part of our story. Thieves laid hands on the property of another; accomplices appropriated this property acquired through acts that are liable to prosecution, even though they were aware of its origin; they brought it to their hall, their hideout, their hell; they hid it: they are *Hehler*, fences. What is liable to prosecution or punishable in this action is determined by a juristic norm; *the norm 'paragraph of the law'* is from now on the weight against which all acts of this type are weighed. In our case, what this norm produces is a new thief, a new fence, which exist no longer in *being*, but rather in *consciousness*: a thief and a fence in language, who represent the norm, in whom the norm is actualized.

Four points are essential here:

1. that a person takes an alien piece of personal property, with the intention of appropriating it in an illegal manner;
2. that this piece of personal property consists in this case of a sort of money that can be divided, just as it is;
3. that this person tells another person about his action and that this second person thus learns that the object in question was acquired through an illegal act;
4. that this second person takes possession of the object for his own benefit.

If we now assemble these four pieces of data in the idiom of the norm 'legal paragraph', so as to obtain the following: 'Someone takes a divisible sum of money away from another person; he communicates this fact to a third person, who, although she knows that this object was acquired through an illegal act, accepts a part of this sum for herself' – then we have a very nice instance of juristic language, but by no means a form. If however the words that betoken these actions, that illustrate them, come into play each time – that is, if the irreducible basic units of the norm become verbal gestures – then the paragraphs will actualize themselves, as in the first part of our case, in such a way that the case may appear unique; but in this uniqueness the weight of the law, the evaluative force of the norm is completely expressed and interpreted.

It is:

1. a *thief*, who
2. steals a *wallet* containing several *banknotes*,
3. then tells his *lover* about it and shares with her, and thus
4. makes her into a *fence*.

In this context, everything is evaluated according to the relevant norm; the existence, scope and validity of the rule emerge from this context.

Up to now we have limited our discussion to the first part of the case while ignoring the second part, so as to be able to observe precisely how the norm becomes visible or actualized in it. But the two parts belong together; in the sense of the form we are looking at, they constitute a whole. If we had only that first part, we would be justified in asking: Why did the author of 'The Grotesque and the Tragic in Penal Law' include this in his collection? Taken on its own, this part could be construed either as an 'instance' or as an 'example'.

What I mean by example – here I am talking of things that are *not* simple forms, so as to be able to distinguish the forms from them – is best explained with Kant's definition, also cited in Grimm's dictionary:

'Instance' [*Beispiel*], a German word, is commonly used as synonymous with 'example' [*Exempel*], but the two words really do not have the same meaning. To take something as an *example* and to bring forward an *instance* to clarify an expression are altogether different concepts. An example is a particular case of a *practical* rule, insofar as this rule represents an action as practicable or impracticable, whereas an *instance* is only a particular (*concretum*), represented in accordance with concepts as contained under a universal (*abstractum*), and is a presentation of a concept merely for theory.[2]

To repeat: viewed in their own right, the thief, the wallet with money, the lover in the first part of our case, can be understood as a particular instance of the practical rule that we saw laid down in the legal paragraph on theft and the fencing of stolen property; and they can also count as a theoretical representation of the concepts of theft and fencing. However, if we bring the first part together with the corresponding second part, we understand both as – intentionally – constitutive of a whole, and we see that it ceases to be possible to speak either of 'instance' or of 'example'.

Very little has changed in the second part. What has remained constant is *thief, theft, wallet, communication, lover*. Only the alien piece of personal property illegally appropriated by the thief has been transformed: it is no longer divisible as such; it is no longer a question of *banknotes* – it is *a banknote*. But this immediately makes the lover no longer a fence: she is no longer liable to prosecution. Her action and her conduct remain the same. But thanks to the way in which this paragraph was written, her action can no longer be evaluated as it was in the first part.

According to the legal code, the thing she appropriated is no longer the thing that the thief stole, even though she knew that the latter had been acquired through an illegal act.

What is revealed in this second part, in contrast to the first, is not the positive but the negative side of §259; what was presented in the first part is dissolved in the second part. Taken together, both parts point not to a law, but rather to a hole in the law. What becomes manifest in this totality is the fact that here a weight fails to weigh properly, a standard fails to measure correctly. At the same time, something else occurs. As the inadequacy of §259 becomes manifest, a higher norm also becomes manifest, and in the following way: the lover can no longer be *prosecuted* according to §259, but she is *guilty*. She is guilty when weighed against the higher

2   Kant, *Metaphysics of Morals*, AA VI, pp. 479ff, note, transl. Mary Gregor (Cambridge: Cambridge University Press, 1996), p. 223.

norm from which the inadequate norm must have issued; at this point we would also like to see her culpability measured against her guilt. In this totality the lover is thus no longer measured against a norm, but rather this norm is measured against another norm. Practically speaking, the correlation of the first and the second halves, the whole thing together, is meant to show that §259, measured by the norm of our moral and legal consciousness, has been weighed and found wanting, that the standard of the law is here an inadequate measure of value – and from this intention arises the form.

For this form I would like to select a name that it already carries in its actualizations, when it appears in jurisprudence, ethics and elsewhere: *Kasus*, or 'case'. What we observe in this whole composed of contradictory parts reveals to us the true meaning of the case: in the mental disposition that imagines the world as one that can be judged and evaluated according to norms, not only are actions measured against norms, but norms are also measured against norms, in an ascending series. Where a simple form is generated by this mental disposition, there becomes manifest a measuring of standards against standards. Staying with the image of the scale, we can say that in the end a weight remains on each side of the scale, and these weights are weighed against each other.

We have thus also sharply distinguished the case from the instance and from the example. If we had dealt only with the first part of our case, it would simply have illustrated the special case of a practical rule or the theoretical representation of a concept. Illustration, however, does not lead to form – form is realization. This is why, in the first part, all the details were already oriented such that something could become realized through its connection with the second part, in relation to the totality. We can define the result as a divergence – or, better, a dispersion – from the norm.

Before I adduce other cases to clarify what a case means, I will return once more to the case that we have been discussing, so as to take this occasion to show how simple form, actualized simple form, and literary form relate to each other, for the case and for simple forms generally.

III. INTERCHANGEABLE PARTS – TRANSITION TO
THE LITERARY FORM – NOVELLA

Not only did the essay 'The Grotesque and the Tragic in Penal Law' supply us with this first case, it also includes a number of details beyond the four pieces of data that have allowed us to visualize the norm. We heard that the action took place 'in the crush of the metropolis'; it was not a wallet, but 'my' wallet. For generating the form, these additions are beside the point; they are not essential to the matter at hand. But they do have a recognizable aim: the weight of the law must be interpreted with regard to a singularity; these additions, insignificant in themselves, amplify the feeling of singularity, increase the poignancy of the case.

We can say something more of these *additions*: they are interchangeable. Instead of 'in the crush of the metropolis, a pickpocket steals my wallet', we can say, for instance, 'a pickpocket steals the wallet of a sleeping man with whom he is sharing a railway compartment . . .' – without changing the case. What we have called its intensity is simply increased in a different manner.

How, from a literary point of view, do these additions differ from the intrinsic components of the case?

A component like *thief* must be produced by the form itself – it is only through this word, this verbal gesture, that the thing comprehended in the norm, the 'he who takes an alien piece of personal property with the intention of appropriating it in an illegal manner', is made manifest. By contrast, a component like 'in the crush of the metropolis' is not necessarily produced by the form; it remains free to a certain extent; or, better: it is left – in some measure – to personal choice.

There are no interchangeable parts in the proverb. We cannot add anything to 'Try before you trust!'; we cannot change anything without the phrase ceasing to be itself, ceasing to be a proverb, ceasing to correspond to the mental disposition that produced it. As Seiler put it, the proverb is 'self-contained'; it 'erupts spontaneously' – thus Wilhelm Grimm – 'into a higher form of expression'. This self-containment typical of the proverb is not to be found with the case; it can accept help from outside when expressing itself.

Here we find ourselves at one boundary of the world of simple forms. For what happens, or can happen, here means that although the case is itself a simple form, it also indicates the path leading beyond an actualized simple form to a literary form; indeed, to a degree the literary form is sketched out in advance. For things that are interchangeable, things that can be left up to personal choice, can lead to the forms we call art forms. By *art forms* [*Kunstformen*] we understand such literary forms as are determined precisely by personal choices, personal intervention – forms that assume a final, definitive verbal shape in which it is no longer something in language that is composing and compressing, but where maximal concision is attained in an unrepeatable artistic act.

Practically speaking, the case we have been discussing can already be set at the boundary of this art form thanks to the additions amplifying its poignancy; the art form, on the other hand, represents a poignant event in its singularity, which – because it is an art form, a literary form that we call the *novella* – it no longer means as a case does, but for its own sake. The thief and the fence, his lover and the theft, which were produced by the norm as a simple form, which actualized the norm, have been endowed with a personal aspect thanks to these minor additions, so that what we see happening here almost ceases to represent either the norm or the legal paragraphs. It would take only a few further additions connecting the first and the second parts of our case to rob it entirely of the character of a simple form.

If we turn from interchangeable additions inessential to the matter at hand to the components whose necessity is certain because, taken together, as a simple form they correspond to the four given facts of the legal paragraph, we find that, despite their necessity, these, too, cannot be called absolutely stable. The thief as such needs to remain a thief, but the fence need not be a 'lover' – it could also be a male fence, a brother, a friend of the thief; it does not have to be a question of 'a hundred' – it could also be fifty marks, the wallet could be a purse with silver coins in it, and so on. These components are not interchangeable in the same sense as what I have called the 'additions' – the essence of the matter is still expressed in them. One notices that *wallet, hundred-mark note, lover* tend to characterize this essence as sharply as possible, but still the verbal gesture is not so stringent; it does not take hold of things with the unconditional assurance we observed with the other simple forms. The verbal gestures in our case seem pale when compared with those of legend, in which events were irresistibly whirled up together: *the wheel with sharp blades*, *gods that explode*; or with those of myth: the mountain as *fire-spewing giant*. We shall have to see if we cannot find *cases* in which the verbal gesture is more tightly constructed.

IV. FURTHER EXAMPLES – SPIRIT AND LETTER OF THE LAW

Let us return to the mental disposition of the case. I shall present two additional cases from the essay 'The Grotesque and the Tragic in Penal Law', so that we may better observe the various ways in which the standards can be arranged.

> The attempt on an inadequate object with inadequate means is still punishable today: if a woman who is not at all pregnant, but imagines herself to be pregnant, takes a fully harmless herbal tea in order to get rid of the foetus which exists only in her imagination, then she may be found guilty of attempted abortion.

Here we are first of all concerned with a crime or a misdemeanour against a life, namely against 'budding life', thus with §216 of the penal code:

> A pregnant woman who deliberately aborts or kills her fetus in the womb shall be punished with up to five years in jail.
>
> If there are mitigating circumstances, then a jail sentence of not less than six months shall come into effect . . .[3]

There is no crime or misdemeanour here, only the attempt at a crime or misdemeanour,

> §43: Whoever has put into effect the decision to commit a crime or a misdemeanour through actions that include the beginning of the execution of this crime or misdemeanour, is, if the intended crime or

---

3   StGb, part II, section 16, p. 59.

misdemeanour has not progressed to completion, to be punished for
the attempt . . .[4]

As the essay's author notes, what is at stake is the question, often
debated in juridical circles, of whether it is possible to make a criminal
attempt 'on an inadequate object with inadequate means'. Of course,
for practical legislation, especially, this is an extremely tricky question.
Here one encounters such hard-to-define concepts as 'absolute inadequacy' (a murder attempt on a corpse, an attempt at poisoning with
too low a dose). One could place the accent on 'dangerousness' – that
is, on the possibility that the action could end in success; however, in a
plenary session (24 May 1880), the Supreme Court of the Reich laid
emphasis on the criminal intention and proclaimed the 'attempt on an
inadequate object with inadequate means' legally culpable. Now a new
case arose from this way of looking at things: it generated a *woman
who imagined that she was pregnant*, just as §242 generated a
pickpocket.

One cannot speak here of a legal loophole. On the contrary! With
the lover who really received the money and was actually aware of the
crime, the rule was written in such a way that, although the awareness
of her guilt was everywhere present, she still could not be adjudged a
fence according to the legal paragraph, and thus could not be punished.
With the judgment of the Supreme Court the matter stands thus:
although the action of the woman who imagined herself to be pregnant not only had no consequences, but was also not a true act in the
proper sense, still the act had to be judged against a higher norm – that
is, according to the intention – and had therefore to be punished. But
here again we have one norm being measured against another.

In both instances, the act of weighing is realized in the case. In the
second part of the first instance, the case showed that the scope and
validity of the existing regulation – measured against the norm 'guilt'
– were inadequate; in this last instance, what is shown is that the
Supreme Court's evaluation of the concept 'attempt' according to the
concept 'intention' acquires validity and scope even where things seem
not to have happened in fact.

---

4 StGb, part I, section 2, p. 13.

I shall relate a third case from this essay:

> With a charming smile, an actress visits her colleague, who is rushing to study a role for that evening. She contrives to make use of a moment in which she is alone in the room to tuck the manuscript of the play behind the wardrobe. The colleague cannot study her role, for despite all her efforts she cannot find the manuscript; her performance is a total flop, and she loses the role. The malicious rival has not committed any offence against the legal code.

The writer introduces this case with the following sentence, which so to say supplies us with commentary, explaining the case: 'Under certain circumstances, cases of exceeding meanness and perfidy shall remain unpunished, for they do not break any laws.'

This case goes considerably beyond the ones already mentioned. In the first part of the first case the norm itself became manifest; in the second part of the first case and in the second case what became manifest was the conflict between two norms in the law, between what we call the spirit and the letter of the law. With the fence, the spirit was lamed by the letter; with the woman who imagined herself pregnant, the letter achieved an unanticipated effect through the spirit. Here, finally, it becomes clear how the scope and the validity of the law are fully inadequate: an action by which someone has been most seriously aggrieved, with deliberate intent, cannot be grasped as such according to the norms contained in the legal code. There is a general awareness that guilt is present – even in the legal sense – but yet the action is still not punishable.

V. THE INDIAN CASE

Now that we have derived the simple form 'case' and the mental disposition from which it emerges from examples of our own era, let us cast about more widely to see if and where we may find it elsewhere, in some concentration.

I shall begin with an example from Indian literature. In the second half of the eleventh century an Indian, Somadeva, collated a great number of stories then in currency in Kashmir and elsewhere, and called the new collection he had edited *Kathāsaritsāgara* – the ocean of the stream of stories. This collation can be compared with collections we know from other eras and other areas: with the *Gesta Romanorum*, the *Thousand and One Nights*, the *Decameron*. Within this 'ocean' we find stories that belong together and collectively constitute what we call a frame narrative – a concept that one can apply, at a pinch, to the entire 'ocean'.

One of these interpolated frame narratives is entitled 'Vetālapañcaviṁśatika', the five hundred stories of Vetāla.[5]

A beggar came every day to the famous king Trivikramasena, each time giving him a piece of fruit in homage. After ten years, the king discovered, when a monkey took one of these pieces of fruit to play with, that they concealed invaluable jewels that had accumulated in a great pile in the treasury, through whose window the treasurer always threw them. When the king asked the beggar why he was paying him homage in such a spendthrift way, the beggar answered that he needed the help of a hero – the king, in the Indian sense, *is* a hero – in order to work a magic spell. The king finds himself obliged by the gifts and the pleas of the beggar – the king in the Indian sense *must* help when asked, when homage is paid to him – and the beggar asks him to come to the cemetery one evening at the time of the waning moon. The king arrives at the appointed place in the graveyard, which is full of blazing pyres and horrid ghosts, and is sent by the beggar to a faraway fig tree on which hangs the corpse of a man: he is to bring the beggar this corpse. The king goes and cuts down the corpse, which, when it falls to the ground, begins to scream piteously. At first, Trivikramasena believes that he has before him a living person, and he begins to rub him; but then the corpse shrieks with laughter and the king realizes that it is possessed by a Vetāla, a fiend. But when he boldly addresses it, it is again suddenly hanging upright in the tree. The king thus understands that he has to keep quiet; he climbs up in the tree again, cuts the corpse down again, slings it over his shoulder, and leaves the place in

---

5 The tales that follow can be found in Somadeva, *Tales from the Kathāsaritsāgara*, trans and with an introduction by Arshia Sattar and with a foreword by Wendy Doniger (New Delhi: Penguin, 1994), pp. 190ff.

silence. Then the Vetāla suddenly says to the king that he wants to tell him a story, so as to shorten the way. He tells the story, and it becomes apparent that this story includes a question – it is a case: a matter of establishing who was guilty of the deaths of two men. At the end of the story the Vetāla challenges the king to give his opinion by threatening him with a curse: may his head explode if he should arrive at a judgment, but withhold it. This curse is the confirmation of a duty, the doubling of a compulsion the king stands under in his capacity as king: the king in the Indian sense is a wise man; he *must* pass judgment in cases of conflict, he must decide the Vetāla's question. This is the king's duty. But in so doing, he violates his vow of silence – and finds the Vetāla hanging once more from the fig tree.

Thus it goes, twenty-three times, until in the twenty-fourth story the spirit puts a case before the king that he cannot decide; but because he cannot decide it, the silence he keeps does not violate his duty. The Vetāla is now so convinced by the courage and wisdom of the king that he advises him to kill the beggar who wanted to sacrifice him to gain mastery over the spirits, and thus himself to gain mastery over the spirits of heaven. So it happens; and the frame narrative closes with the king wishing that the stories of the Vetāla might everywhere become renowned, and with the Vetāla promising that evil spirits will have no entry anywhere these stories are read or heard.

The king's wish was partly fulfilled: a number of these stories have become known throughout the whole world. I will give an instance that will show us the case – the second story.

A Brahmin has a beautiful daughter. She is barely grown when three suitors appear, all of them equally high-born and admirable. Each one of them would rather die than see her married to one of the other two. For his part, the father fears offending the others if he gives her to one of them, so the daughter remains unmarried for a time. Suddenly she becomes ill and dies. She is cremated, and the first lover builds himself a cottage over her ashes, in which he lives ever after. The second gathers her bones and carries them to the holy river, the Ganges. The third wanders through the world as a pilgrim. One evening this third lover comes upon a Brahmin's family; a child is behaving badly at table and screaming. The mother becomes angry and flings the child into the fire, where it burns up. The pilgrim is horrified! But the father reassures him; he fetches a book of magic, pronounces the formula, and the child is suddenly sitting there once again, just as before. During the night the third lover steals the book. He comes home and brings the virgin back to life. Because she has gone through the fire, she is much more beautiful than before. Now the three suitors commence to bicker once again, but between the first conflict and this one there is something new, an action: each of the three has acted according to a definite norm, doing what he believed was the right thing to do as a lover and Brahmin. Now it should be possible to determine who is to have her. 'And now, king' – the Vetāla says – 'you must decide their dispute.'

What should the king do? He weighs the actions against each other, he interprets them. The man who brought her to life is her father; the one who carried her bones to the Ganges did what children should do for their parents according to Indian custom, thus he is her son; finally, the man who stayed with her, slept with her, loyally abided with her, that man is her husband. The king has spoken – the corpse again hangs in the fig tree – it all can begin again – a new case.

I have already mentioned that Somadeva adapted older stories in his collection. And thus there are numerous earlier and later versions of this case in India. There are some in Europe, too. We see them as soon as the Italian novella begins to stir. The transformations of this case have been collected in an essay by W. H. Farnham, 'The Contending Lovers'.[6] Uhland's poem 'Three fellows once crossed over the Rhine' is a pale, weakened version of the same story.

For us the point is not to follow this story through its metamorphoses in literary history, but to understand it as a case.

First, this case shows us something that was also to be found in our collection of legal cases, but which we could not observe there quite as clearly: in the case, too, there is a relationship to the *question*. In myth, the world declares itself as question and answer in its phenomena, becomes Creation by virtue of its nature. The riddle used question and answer to test and announce inclusion in an order. With the case, the form arises from the use of a standard for judging actions, but what the

---

6   W. H. Farnham, 'The Contending Lovers', *Publications of the Modern Language Association of America*, 35:3 (1920), pp. 247–323.

actualization does is inquire into the value of the norm. The force, scope and validity of various norms are weighed, but this act of weighing includes the question: Where is the weight? By what norm should we judge?

This is precisely the question set with the case of the 'contending lovers'. In this story the duty of judgment is imposed on the wise man, the king; but in the case as such this duty lies at a deeper and more general level. In our first legal case, too, we sense this duty to render judgment; the story of the lover who was not a fence but who also *was* a fence also implicitly led us to reflect on the question of whether or not she should be punished, whether or not our law code should remain as it is or be changed. What should count – the letter of the law or its spirit?

The special character of the case lies in the fact that it asks the question, but cannot give the answer; that it imposes the duty of judgment upon us, but does not itself contain the judgment – what becomes manifest in it is the act of weighing, but not the result of the weighing. The weighing device with two bowls is called in Latin *bilanx*, which in the Romance languages produced the terms *balance, bilancia*. In German we have from the same source the verb *balancieren*, which also carries the meaning of trying to find the equilibrium. The case presents us with the charms and difficulties of balancing – we could say that the swaying and swinging of the mental disposition of weighing and judging is what becomes manifest in this form.

And thus it is the special character of the case that it ceases to be completely itself whenever the duty to decide is relieved by a definite decision. This is the second thing we can observe in the Vetāla stories, and it is what is expressed by the stories in their entirety.

In connection with the first case, that of the thief and the fence, we established that the case has a tendency to expand into an art form – we added: to become a novella. That is what happened with the Vetāla stories. But in this way the literary form, in its autonomy, destroyed the simple form from which it developed. The decision was made; with that, the case ceased to be a case. Now, however, the frame narrative continues, and – as tends to happen in the world of norms – one case is hardly decided when another appears. Indeed, the disappearance of the one is what makes the other appear – which the story conveys as:

the corpse hangs again in the fig tree; the king must begin again. This captures the world of the case with great subtlety, for the king's actions within the frame are also determined by this form: whether he answers or does not answer the Vetāla, we here have the form 'case', for to answer is to fulfil the duty of a king, while not answering is to comply with the command to keep silent – and ultimately he cuts the corpse down each time because he has assumed an obligation to the beggar. The story can only end with the case remaining a case and undecided, but thus also never really becoming a novella – and this is what happens in the twenty-fourth story, when the king cannot arrive at a decision. There we read: 'The king weighed the Vetāla's question again and again; he found no answer. So he continued on in deep silence.' Here everything is in balance – we know few examples in literary history of a form thus instantiating itself in all its particulars.

The Vetāla stories tell us yet another thing: where to look for the case when we find ourselves in the world of the scale.

More than other peoples, the Indian has a need to live according to norms. Nowhere is the concept of the 'manual', in the sense of a collection of rules, so vital as in India. Not only are there textbooks on how to attain and combine the three great goals of life, there are also textbooks for all sorts of other things, and in all of these Sūtras and Śāstras, conduct is measured against norms. In a well-known Indian drama – *Mrcchakatika* – we witness on stage how a burglar executes a burglary. In our own context, we might establish the legal paragraphs according to which the burglar has made himself liable to prosecution; here, things go considerably further. The burglar breaks and enters by the rules of a 'manual for thieves' – while working (for burglary is his work), he cites single paragraphs from this 'law book', he follows the rules, he works by the book. We no longer possess this illicit handbook; we may doubt that it ever really existed. But a world like this, in which life's fulfilment is gauged and judged against norms, must everywhere produce cases. Indeed, a great number of the cases in circulation, and partly recognizable as such despite their closure, are of Indian origin.

VI. CASES OF FEELING AND TASTE – LOGIC – *MINNE* – THEOLOGY
– REWARD AS OBJECT – CASUISTICS – PSYCHOLOGY

In the West, our lives unfold rather differently – but here too we find the form 'case' every time things are weighed in this manner.

It would be a good exercise to tell the story of the case and of the migrations and transformations of single cases, but I will not do this here. There are some cases in very widespread dissemination. We might recall the Princess and the Pea, or the story of the gourmands who would test the quality of a very old barrel of wine; one of them detects a slight taste of iron, the other an equally faint taste of leather: and indeed, when the barrel runs empty, they find a tiny key attached to a small leather loop, which must have fallen into the barrel at pressing time. These two cases, with their countless variants, reveal a sphere in which it is difficult to pass judgment, but where norms are still called for: the sphere of sensory perception, of feeling and taste.

The norms of logic, too, can yield a case, as we see already in antiquity. Thus the tragic fallacy known as the *Crocodilina* manifests itself as a case. A crocodile has stolen a child and has promised the mother to give it back to her if she will tell him the truth about it. The mother says: You will not give my child back. The crocodile answers: Now there is no way you will get the child back, whether on account of what you just said if you spoke the truth, or based on our contract if you told a lie. The woman says: I must get my child back in any event – based on our contract if I told the truth, or, if what I said is not true, according to what I asserted. Here the variants ensue of their own accord.

We see in other spheres how the case proliferates at certain moments in Western culture, how cases spring from the ground like mushrooms.

I am thinking of the age of the great *Minnekultur*, the culture of courtly love – a time when a particular kind of love shaped life, an age in which nearly every activity was brought into relation with this love and received its significance, its power, from love. Where courtly love, *Minne*, provides the standards, there ensue the norms, the rules, the legal codex of *Minne* with its paragraphs; there we find the *Minnehöfe*, or courts of love, in which infractions of *Minne* are judged, where the problems of *Minne* are weighed and, if possible, adjudicated. The tension of *Minne* can be heard in the *Minnelied* or courtly love song. The way of *Minne* is illustrated in instances or examples, while the values of *Minne*, its weighing and judging, express themselves in the case.

The cases of *Minne* have thus come down to us through a number of different channels. We have them in their first beginnings as theoretical questions, such as: Should a man love a woman who stands above him in social status and wealth, or a woman who stands below him in this respect? Or: Which is a greater pleasure for the courtly lover, to think of the beloved, or to gaze upon her? We then see how the question gradually becomes form: A girl is beloved of two young men; she takes the garland of the one and sets it upon her own head, while upon the other she bestows her own garland. To whom has she shown the greater proof of her favour? Gradually the form becomes more distinct, the case is rounded out: A young man loves a girl. Thanks to the help of an ugly old pander they manage a rendezvous, but they are surprised by the girl's brothers. The brothers grant the lover his life on the condition that he must live a year with the girl, but also a year with the ugly old woman. One expects the question: Will he accept life? In the source I am citing, however, the question is: 'With whom should he spend the first year?' Or: A girl is beloved of two young men; by an unlucky turn of events she is condemned to be burned at the stake and can only be saved if a knight proves her innocence with the sword. The first youth is prepared to fight for her; but the second, who has been late in hearing of the duel, accepts the part of opponent and allows himself to be beaten. Who has shown the greater proof of his love?

Some of these *Minne* cases are so intricate and contrived that we might think we are seeing derivative forms – but indeed it is difficult to think through a life-form like *Minne* in all its norms and consequences. In any event, we can see from the cases just cited how here too, as with our first legal cases, the case tends toward the novella; but also how, here too, the novella dissolves the case by requiring a decision. In fact, the art form we know specifically as the Tuscan novella emerged to a great extent from the *Minnehof* and the *Minne* case. But that is beside the point here.

We have spoken of *Minnehof*, of 'infractions of the law', of 'judgment'. These are all expressions that bear on evaluative love, but which also designate concepts belonging to evaluative justice. We see then how the same mode of expression can unify domains in which the mental disposition of evaluation, of weighing and judging, of norms and standards, is established. These in turn are not transferred meanings or figurative expressions; rather, we have in them the *special language of the evaluative world*. It is not quite the same as with the riddle, but we can still recognize the same ambiguity. Reviewing further expressions of *Minne* language, we can see that their meanings can encompass another sphere beyond that of love and justice: the sphere of religion, or rather of theology. Words like *mercy*, *service* or *reward*, which we encounter at every turn, occur also in theological language – where they likewise have an evaluative meaning. Just as on the one hand the legal court and the court of love can be classed together, just as both accord the duty of judgment to a king or a queen as their highest authority, so can one also set *Minnedienst* and *Gottesdienst* – service to the beloved and service to God – alongside one another. Allow me to summarize: it is a peculiar quality of the special language of casuistry that it combines within itself the spheres in which evaluation occurs according to norms. And also: it is the charm of the *Minne* language that we can hear resounding within it the language of justice and the language of theology.

To put it in musical terms: the common language supplies notes, the special language, chords – we have this kind of concord in *Minnesang*.

There is one expression or verbal gesture attached to the case that we must especially emphasize: *reward*. Reward can be an object, and as an object it can be charged with the force of the case, with everything that the case signifies. Reward, in this sense, can represent the swinging and swaying that we find in the case, or it can represent the case's decision. As objects, love's reward and God's reward are to the case as the relic is to the legend, or the symbol to the myth.

With this we have reached a sphere in which the case has played a very significant role in the life and literature of the West – the sphere of theology, and in particular of moral theology, the doctrine of duties.

In this sphere we find very extensive collections of cases. The books that contain them make up a whole library. Indeed, in its general usage the word *casuistics* usually means the practice of moral theology as it has evolved in the Catholic Church, principally since the end of the sixteenth century. Such casuistry has often had a very bad reputation, and since Pascal those who have had to deal with it, within and outside the Church, have most often used it as a weapon. Casuistics are seen as a standard of measure for Catholic morality generally; when we say casuistry, we mean *reservatio mentalis*, mental reservation, or Jesuitism, in a bad sense.

Of course, this is not the place to go into this sort of casuistics as such. I would just like to show very quickly how the form of the case becomes manifest here, just as it did with the *Minne*. Unlike with the kind of morality given in the Commandments as absolute norms, and the morality that advocates the free ethical force of belief, we have here a morality that weighs various norms against each other, a morality with mobile judgments of value, a morality – I use the word in all seriousness – that *balances*. The contrast of this morality with a Scholasticism that sought to define virtues and vices as objectively as possible seems obvious to me; it is equally obvious that such valuation was meant in a thoroughly humane sense, that it not only shielded the penitent from the opinions and whims of individual confessors, but also protected him from despair before the Absolute, and smoothed the way to Heaven.

To be sure, the nature of casuistics was such that it led perforce to numerous controversies. A very precise survey of these controversies may be found in Ignaz von Döllinger's *History of Moral Controversies in the Roman Catholic Church since the 16th Century*. From the many concepts that Dollinger works with, I shall select for our purposes just one – the most important: that of *probabilism*.

'In many cases', he writes,

> there is no way to be fully certain regarding whether a given action is a duty, whether it is allowed or disallowed; in which event we have two opinions standing over against one another, each of which is supported with reasons; neither is *certa*, each is only *probabilis*. If this is the case, either each position can have an equal number of reasons in its favour, both thus being *aeque probabilis*, or one can have more reasons in its favour than the other, which makes the one *probabilior*,

the other *minus probabilis*; if the weight of the reasons for one is substantially greater than for the other, then one is *probabilissima*, the other *tenuiter probabilis*. The probability can be based either on internal reasons, *probabilitas intrinseca*, or on external ones, i.e. on the authority of people who are considered experts, *probabilitas extrinseca*.[7]

And so forth – once again, we will avoid following up on the practical consequences of this way of looking at things; the quotation suffices to show us yet again, in its entirety and with complete clarity, the mental disposition with which we began. There is little we still need to add. Out of this mental disposition, life and literature must produce the case; only in this form can the moral world we see here become manifest.

The cases engendered by these moral controversies remained within a small circle, at least when they were not used or exploited by one or the other antagonist. And yet it seems to me that their influence on literature has generally been of importance. Or perhaps we should say that what occurred in the Catholic Church within the limited sphere of moral theology also had an effect on literature as a whole. What we tend to call the *psychology* of eighteenth- and nineteenth-century literature – the weighing and measuring of motivations of actions according to inward and outward norms, this mobile criterion of the judgment of characters in literary works and of the literary work of art as such – to me seems very similar to what we perceive in Catholic casuistics. But neither does this belong to a morphology of the simple forms.

---

7 Ignaz von Döllinger and Franz Heinrich Reusch, *Geschichte der Moralstreitigkeiten in der römisch-katholischen Kirche seit dem sechzehnten Jahrhundert*, 2 vols (Nördlingen: Beck, 1889), vol. 1, p. 3.

CHAPTER 7

Memorabile

I believe that we need to admit another form into our series of simple forms. I would like to derive this one, too, directly from things that we see on a daily basis.

On my desk I have an old newspaper that was used to pack up a book for shipping. I straighten it out and I read:

> **The Suicide of Councillor of Commerce S.**
> The motive for the suicide of Heinrich S., Councillor of Commerce, who shot himself last night in his home at Kaiserallee 203, is to be sought in financial difficulties. S., who was born in Turkestan, used to own a vodka factory, which however he sold long ago. The 62-year-old had already expressed the intention to kill himself some time before, and he used his wife's attendance at a concert yesterday evening to execute this intention. The pistol shot was heard by *Asta Nielsen*, who occupies the adjoining apartment. Ms Nielsen was then the first to notify a doctor and the police.

The purpose of this notice is apparently: 1) to give a short summary of the life of the deceased Councillor of Commerce Heinrich S.; 2) to explain why an elderly, respected man voluntarily chose death; 3) to provide information about the way he committed suicide.

To achieve the first aim, the article relates where Heinrich S. was born; at what age he killed himself; how he had earned his fortune; where he lived. The second is served with the mention of 'financial difficulties' and of 'expressions of suicidal intention'. To the third belong the information that he shot himself; that he chose the evening his wife was absent to do so; that a neighbor, her attention drawn by the crack of the pistol, notified the police.

Written as a report, the notice could read as follows:

> The 62-year-old Councillor of Commerce Heinrich S. shot himself last night in his apartment at Kaiserallee 203. He was born in Turkestan, used to own a vodka factory, and had sold the factory a long time ago. He was in financial difficulties and had often expressed the intention to kill himself. He chose an evening when his wife was absent to execute his plan. A neighbour, her attention drawn by the crack of the pistol, notified the police and a doctor.

Our original notice, however, looks different – it contains more information, it includes other details. And these details are not at all literary – they have not been chosen freely by the writer of the notice in the way we saw happening with the case, in the first court case that we cited. Also, these details are non-conceptual; they are drawn from the concrete course of events; they are historical.

Let us regard these details with greater care. Mrs S. was not only absent, she was *at a concert*. This fact has no direct connection with what the notice intends to relate. For understandable reasons of feeling and taste, S. wanted to choose a moment for his suicide when his wife would be absent. But Mrs S. could equally well have been paying a visit to relatives in mourning or spending time with friends. And yet the historical fact of the *concert* is here brought up explicitly. Why? Because in this concert there is an element of entertainment, pleasure, enjoyment of art; because this pleasure contrasts with the lonely man at home facing the difficult decision to kill himself, and because together the wife in the concert hall and the husband alone at home put special emphasis on the matter at hand: *suicide*.

These two historical facts – the wife at the concert, the man at home – are neither linked causally, nor do they explain each other; rather, they are coordinated so as to give an autonomous value to the governing fact of suicide among the events narrated.

Let us look further. If the neighbour had been some random bachelor or Mrs X, Y or Z, she would doubtless have notified the police and the doctor as well. Yet again it is mentioned explicitly that this neighbour was Asta Nielsen.[1] How often has our sublime film diva witnessed or even enacted a suicide on screen? How often has she held her hands to her ears at the crack of a pistol shot, opened her eyes wide, torn out her hair, revealed herself in close-ups? But now: wall-to-wall reality! It is clear that we do not ask how pleasant it may have been for Ms Nielsen to read her name in the papers on this occasion. We ask: What is happening in our newspaper notice? And there again we see how two facts – the revolver shot and the movie actress, which are linked neither causally nor as explanation with regard to this event – are nonetheless coordinated so that their polarity gives value to the governing fact of suicide, thus shaping the fact in such a way that it sticks in our minds as an autonomous entity.

In the *report* that we composed from the facts to be communicated, an event was presented as such: the report contained nothing that was not directly connected with the Councillor of Commerce S. and with his suicide. The historical facts were ordered in a way that showed their relationship to each other, but which did not show the meaning governing the facts taken as a whole.

In the *newspaper clipping*, however, facts were adduced that had nothing directly to do with Heinrich S. and his suicide, despite being quite as historical as the facts given in the report – yet these facts were coordinated with one another and with the whole in such a way that the governing event gained autonomous value and the sense of the whole was apparent.

It is, we are told, a matter of suicide. The meaning of suicide does not emerge from the fact that someone was born in Turkestan or owned a vodka factory – nor from the fact that he lived at Kaiserallee 203 – but from such circumstances as the fact that he is alone and his wife is at a concert, or that an artiste lives next door who has played all this often enough, but who is now drawn into real events by the crack of the pistol. Ultimately, the form attempts to endow the event with additional meaning: *suicide of a councillor of commerce*, of a man who used to be rich and who now can no longer rescue himself from

---

1   Asta Nielsen (1881–1972), Danish silent film actress, active in Germany 1911–37.

financial difficulties. Such are the times we live in! This singular event, standing out from the rest, is a sign of the times.

To recapitulate: the clipping is bent on extracting something unique from the general flow of events that will convey the total meaning of this event; within this totality, the details are ordered in such a way that – taken individually, in their relationships and as a whole – they emphasize this meaning through explanation, comparison and contrast.

II. A CLIPPING FROM HISTORY

I would now like to set an extract from history alongside our newspaper clipping. I will select an incident from Dutch history, namely the murder of the Prince of Orange, William I, the Silent.

I need only sketch the course of events. William of Orange was born in 1533 at Dillenberg Castle, and was raised in the circle of Charles V. He was a favorite of the emperor, who recommended him to his son Philip II upon his own abdication. He was appointed governor of Holland, Zeeland and Utrecht, and a member of the State Council in Brussels. Gradually, conflicts arose – the secession of the Netherlands was gathering steam in the 1560s; it was already considered a revolt in 1558. The prominent role William played in it as a politician and general is well known. Towards the end of the 1570s, when the focus of the revolt had shifted ever more strongly to the north, and the actions of Alexander Farnese in the south had given new strength to the Spanish hegemony, the northern provinces entered into a union at Utrecht on William's instigation, thus laying the ground for a united Dutch Republic. William was officially ostracized by Philip II in 1580; he lost all legal rights; his murderer was promised a pardon for the crime, ennoblement (assuming he wasn't a noble already), and 25,000 gold crowns. The first murder attempt quickly followed, in 1582 – without success. The prince was injured fairly badly on the cheek, but he recovered. An attempt of 1584 was successful. The murderer, a certain Gérard, had planned the attack for several years; he was encouraged from several quarters. In May 1584 he managed to gain access to the prince's Calvinist court chaplain, Villiers, by passing himself off as a victim of Catholic persecution; he was sent to the ambassador of the

Estates General in France with a small mission, and then he returned to the Netherlands with a message for the prince himself. The first time he was admitted into the prince's presence, he was unarmed.

I will quote the further course of events from P. J. Blok's *History of the Netherlands*:

> On 8 July, [Gérard] appeared at the prince's court in Delft, in order to note the exits and work out opportunities of flight. When he was discovered, he explained his presence there by his reluctance to show himself in the church across from William's house dressed in the shabby clothes he was wearing. The prince, hearing of this, sent him a sum of money to better outfit himself. With the money he bought a pistol and shot from a soldier in the bodyguard and on Tuesday afternoon, 10 July, he proceeded to the court, where he asked the prince, who was just entering the dining room with his family, for a pass. The princess was much alarmed at his sinister appearance, but the prince paid this little notice and ordered that he be supplied with what he desired. At two o'clock, after the meal – at which he conversed with his guest, mayor Ulenburgh of Leeuwarden, on the state of affairs in Friesland – the prince, wearing his stately robes, slowly and thoughtfully left the dining room with his family, passing through a small vestibule in the direction of a stairway leading to the floor above. Suddenly the murderer jumped out from a small dark archway leading to a narrow corridor and fired his pistol; two bullets struck the prince in the region of the lungs and the stomach. The wound was fatal. The prince cried out: 'My God, have pity on my soul. My God, have pity on this poor people', answered with a weak 'Yes' when asked if he commended his soul to Christ's hands, and in a few moments gave up the ghost . . .[2]

What we have here are exclusively historical facts; the information came from eyewitnesses, from the murderer himself, from trial records. But once more we see that this is not a simple report, not a protocol.

Although he had prepared his enterprise over a long period of time, Gérard still could not act according to a thoroughly thought-out

---

2   P. J. Blok, *Geschichte der Niederlande*, transl. O. G. Houtrow, 6 vols (Gotha: F. A. Perthes, 1902–18), vol. III, p. 356.

plan – he was dependent on circumstances. When he was discovered spying out the exits on 8 July, it was probably fear that prompted the lie he used to cover himself. Had he not obtained money in this way, he would have acquired weapons some other way, for as he himself said on cross-examination, he was firmly resolved to murder the prince, 'be it while he was on his way to the sermon, or when he came down to eat, or when he was returning from his meal'. Nonetheless, this lie needs to be mentioned here, as it is in fact through the lie that the murder weapon was acquired. The lie and the murder attempt here stand in a causal relationship – but beyond this, mentioning the lie also sets the fact of the murder into another sort of relief. The benevolence of the prince is thus contrasted with the dastardliness of the murderer, who does not shrink from accepting money from his victim, indeed from using it to buy the weapon.

In addition, however, we find details that are completely unrelated to the murder itself. The princess was alarmed at the man's sinister appearance; the prince had seen Gérard many times before, as had many people belonging to the prince's circle, foremost among them his good friend, the court chaplain Villiers. Were these people less sensitive to knavish faces, or did they think that one should not judge a man by his outward appearance? We do not know. It is certain however that this – attested – historical fact is mentioned here because it places a special kind of emphasis upon the main event, the murder. It represents what in a literary form we would call a retarding element: we hesitate a moment – could this judgment or prejudice of the princess possibly have prevented the danger that threatened . . .?

Finally: the prince, wearing his stately robes, slowly and thoughtfully left the dining room, where he had been conversing with his guest, mayor Ulenburgh of Leeuwarden, on the state of affairs in Friesland. All of this, too, was attested to by eyewitnesses, by the people themselves, but here we have completely departed from any causal or explanatory connection. Might Gérard have abandoned his plan if the prince had been differently dressed, or had he left the dining room differently or spoken with the mayor about something else? Yet still these facts are adduced; in this context they still fulfil their purpose – for again they explain and gloss the event, they stress its governing meaning by means of comparison and contrast. We see the prince in this moment; we interrelate the solemn attire, the pensive stride, the discussion of state affairs; we connect them with the sudden death of the great, indispensable man, with what is happening here.

In themselves, these historical details are unimportant. We can go further yet – we can say they are so irrelevant that they could be entirely different; indeed, they could be changed into their opposites. Imagine: the prince, dressed in a short, colorful doublet, leaves the dining room with a quick step, where he has been joking with his young wife Louise de Coligny – and then he is shot in a dastardly fashion. The picture is different, but we imagine it in the same way. Again we see the prince – but now we feel the difference between vibrant life and a sudden death, between merriment and assassination. Certainly, what we have presented here fits the character of William the Silent rather less well – also, it is not a matter of historical fact, but a derivative form that we have fabricated ad hoc. But even in the derivative form we can see how the classed and coordinated details interfuse with each other in quite the same manner as before, so as to bring out the governing meaning.

III. ACCUMULATION AND CONGELATION – MEMORABILE AND HISTORY

Let us survey the process once more. We have a set of events that we can summarize quickly as follows: from a complex of territories that had been held together by the Habsburgs since the end of the fifteenth century, and which reached its greatest importance and extension under Charles V, a portion secedes at the end of the sixteenth century because it no longer feels itself to belong in respect of religion or government, a national consciousness awakens within it, and so on. A single personality, William of Orange, participates in this event to such a degree that we bring this entire independence movement into relation with him, we attribute it to him, we judge it with regard to his actions: we recognize him in the event, and the event in him. This personality dies: he is murdered at the behest of his enemies. Obviously, both the event and history go on, and – equally obviously! – it remains our historical task also to study what happens afterwards: the disengagement of the Netherlands from the Spanish–Habsburgian complex. However, in the moment in which this person retires from history, in which history must continue on without him, something rises up out of the chain of events, becomes autonomous, achieves a governing meaning. The connection with history is not interrupted, but the event is grasped differently in this moment.

The event accumulates, it labours on from stage to stage. From the event 'The Dutch Revolt' there arises the person to whom we attribute the event; he governs the event – we see the revolt in him. At the decisive moment when this person leaves the story, however, something else comes to govern *him*: the *murder*, the *political assassination*; we see a murderer spurred by fanaticism and greed for money who murders a man unknown to him, a man who has done something good for him at a moment when this man, surrounded by family, is occupied with his duties in life.

The meaning of the event shifts from level to level. We want to learn something about the Dutch Revolt – and William of Orange becomes a vehicle of meaning; we follow the story of William of Orange – and the moment he leaves the story, it is *murder* that represents the sense of the whole.

What we are doing here is neither historical scholarship nor philosophy of history; we are observing a linguistic–literary process; we can see how the event, developing steadily, unstoppably, condenses at certain places, solidifies, how the flow of events congeals at such places, and how in the places where it has solidified, congealed, language takes hold of it, and it acquires literary form.

What is more, we see once again – not in the sense of literary history, but in a linguistic–literary sense – how this form is produced by a kind of *accumulation*. All the details of the event, details which belong to it and which must in fact run and flow with it, turn suddenly here in a different direction, direct themselves towards something that governs them, towards something that *stands*: in their arrangement and taken together, each and all of them emphasize this governing meaning. By informing the governing meaning and being informed by it in turn, the coordinate details make of the whole a *static* form that conveys the sense of the event in process.

In the case of the suicide of Councillor of Commerce Heinrich S., we spoke of a 'newspaper clipping' [*Zeitungsausschnitt*]. With this term we do not actually mean something that we have cut from a newspaper with scissors, but something that cuts itself out of current events, detaches itself and becomes autonomous within the paper, something that takes on form. In the same manner, we called the murder of the prince of Orange an extract from history. Here too it seemed as if we were cutting something out from a more complete overview – in reality, though, we took hold of something that had cut itself out from history, something that had become solidified, congealed, within the historical event, in which it had taken on *form*.

I have named this form *memorabile* – the Latin translation of a somewhat awkward Greek word: ἀπομνημόνευμα, *apomnemoneuma*. What the Greeks understood by *apomnemoneuma* seems to me to have come fairly close to the form I mean here. When after the death of Socrates the conflict broke out between Plato and Antisthenes on the subject of Socrates' personality, Xenophon – then living in Corinth – wrote his *Apomnemoneumata*; he may have been the first to use this word as a book title. His goal in this case was not to represent Socrates' personality according to his own personal opinion of him, as the two opponents in the debate were doing, but rather to allow a sense of it to emerge from events as they had impressed themselves on his memory. The Christian apologists of the second century do much the same thing when they distinguish the records of the Evangelists, as *apomnemoneumata*, from the lying tales of the pagans. Here too it seems that the way to present a personality is to show it solidifying out of real events in progress, rising up from them, coming to govern them.

Of course, for Xenophon what was at stake was the personality of Socrates, while for the Evangelists – according to the apologists – it was a matter of the person of Jesus. For our part, we must proceed in reverse – from the form; we must attempt to explain how, in this form, something that was fluid congeals.

IV. THE MENTAL DISPOSITION OF FACTUALITY – CONCRETENESS – THE DOCUMENT AS OBJECT

The mental disposition that produces the memorabile is defined fairly well by what we have said so far. If we require a word to suggest this mental disposition, that word could be *factuality*. Both the memorabile of the suicide of Councillor of Commerce S. and that of the murder of the prince of Orange absorbed nothing that was not, in fact, a part of the event, but from the series of correlated facts there simultaneously emerged a governing factuality to which all the details were now uniquely and ingeniously referred – a bound factuality materialized from free facts.

When many things that are severally engaged in a process of growth grow together in a specific place, and we observe these several things in the locus where they are conjoined, we describe the process with a word derived from the Latin verb *concresco*, 'coalesce'. In this sense we can say that the memorabile is the form in which *the concrete* is produced. And what becomes concrete in this form is not only the governing factuality to which the several details ingeniously refer, but also each and every detail, in and through its relationship with this factuality.

Let us recall – to stick with our last memorabile – the *solemn robe*, the *measured step* of the prince. The purpose of these details was to assert the fact of *murder*; through them the murderous deed was singled out, made available to isolated inspection – in a word, it was made concrete. But here, suffused as they are with the governing event, these factual details – unimportant in their own right, as we have seen – come into their own. The prince always wore clothing, he always moved in a particular way: in the ordinary flow of events, these facts could not become noticeable, we did not perceive them. Not until the event congeals into this form, in which every single detail suffuses the governing factuality and is suffused by it, do we cease to see the prince as a representative of the event – the Dutch Revolt – and begin to see him as a man: we see how he is dressed and the clothing itself, we see how he walks and stands, we see him as a fully fleshed-out personality; we see him *concretely*.

There is one more thing I should mention regarding the prince's robe: the robe itself, along with the entire suit of clothes that the prince was wearing the day he was murdered, are in a museum in The Hague, while in the 'Prinsenhof' in Delft one can still see the spot where the bullet that pierced him was stopped by the wall.

Once again we have before us an object and something objective that are charged with the power of the form. If the prince of Orange were an *imitabile* and his story a legend, then these objects would be relics. As seen here, this clothing, the hole in the wall, become means for us to visualize both person and event in the strongest concreteness

– they are *documents* of the event, located where it has coalesced into the most intense concretion. The entire activity of this form, too, can likewise be lodged in an object.

V. EXAMPLES – CREDIBILITY – THE WORLD OF HISTORY

Thus far we have discussed single memorabilia; at this point, I would like to present an example that shows how, in a verbal phrase, the form 'memorabile' emerges spontaneously from an event. This example will lead us in the direction where we must look for the memorabile.

We have already established that some of the stories that the brothers Grimm collected in their *German Sagas* did not correspond to our simple form *Sage*. Among the stories at the beginning of the second part of this collection, published in 1818, we can recognize quite a number of memorabilia. I will select one of these stories – the death of Athaulf:

> The death of King Athaulf, who had conquered Spain with his Visigoths, is told in *Sage* in a number of different ways. By some accounts, he was stabbed with a sword by Wernulf, whose ridiculous figure the king had poked fun at. According to others, he was standing in a stall inspecting his horses when he was murdered by Dobbius, one of his attendants. The latter had earlier been in the service of another Gothic king whom Athaulf had eliminated, and had afterwards joined Athaulf's household staff.[3]

Dobbius had thus avenged his first master upon his second.

This story includes two versions of the tradition – two memorabilia that refer to the same event. We will not discuss the second memorabile; I will quote the first from the Grimms' source, the *Getica* of Jordanes:

> Once a kingdom was established by the Goths in Gaul, [Athaulf, king of the Visigoths] began to lament the misfortune of the Spaniards. Planning to save them from raids by the Vandals, he left behind his

---

3   Jacob Grimm and Wilhelm Grimm, eds, *Deutsche Sagen*, 2 vols (Berlin: Nicolaische Buchhandlung, 1816–1818), vol. 2, p. 11.

property and the unwarlike population with certain trusted men in Barcelona, and then entered into the inner parts of Spain. There he struggled frequently against the Vandals. In the third year, after he had brought Gaul and Spain under his sway, he died, pierced through the groin by the sword of Euervulf, whose height he had been accustomed to mock.[4]

In the original text the entire story is related in a single sentence. In the first part of the sentence, the event is in a state of flux, and the personality in whom we perceive the event, the Goth Athaulf, is himself perceptible only in the event. He has entrenched himself in Gaul with his Visigoths, and is now encroaching on Spain; using Barcelona as a military outpost, in continuous battle with the Vandals, he is pushing ever more deeply into the country. But now he is assassinated, and suddenly single details appear in the sentence that have nothing directly to do with the event – the campaigns of the Visigoths – but from which the person and the murder of the king emerge and converge.

We see how Athaulf *mocked a man on account of his small size*; and this person, too – who does not himself make the choice to intervene directly in the event but whose act does affect its progress – appears in person. It is Euervulf; Athaulf falls by the sword of this Euervulf. Now the manner of death becomes concrete in its details: Euervulf is small, he has been ridiculed for his squatness, but this shortness of stature defines the manner of his revenge. He does not split Athaulf's skull in battle; instead, he unexpectedly stabs him *in the abdomen* with his sword. This is murder; this is how a small man kills a great man – but at the same time it is how history accumulates and congeals, how the historical event seizes upon a form in which all the factual details, even if they do not stand in a direct relation to the event, are nonetheless referred both to a governing meaning and to each other: a form that bears the meaning of the event and in whose fusedness both the details and the whole achieve concretion.

We said earlier that a very considerable part of the world of the Middle Ages would be revealed to us if we were to demonstrate in

---

4 Iordanis, *Romana et Getica*, ed. Theodor Mommsen (Berlin: Weidmann, 1882), *Monumenta Germaniae Historica*, vol. 31, p. 163.

detail all the points where the mental disposition of *imitatio* is operative in the life of medieval man. Similarly, we could assert here that a considerable part of the modern world might be revealed to us if we could demonstrate all the points where the mental disposition of *factuality* is operative in the life of modern man. In any event, no form is as familiar in modern life as the memorabile: wherever people have understood the world as an accumulation or system of effective realities, the memorabile has been the means of fractionating and differentiating this undifferentated world, of making it concrete.

Yet, precisely because this form was so current and familiar in its time, this time was perhaps less inclined than others to recognize it as a form. When a form takes the lead before other forms, becoming the form par excellence, form as such, people stop comparing it with other forms or including it among other forms. Thus for a while it seemed (and still seems) impossible to comprehend events in any way other than as a memorabile. A philosophy of history is prepared to say: 'History does not occur until by being set in a temporal series arranged from an evaluative perspective an occurrence acquires the character of an event.'[5] This is a direct conversion of the concept of history into the simple form memorabile. On the other hand, a philosophy that would understand general concepts as handy heuristics, instruments, mental devices, convenient fictions, has itself crossed the line to the memorabile.

In any case, the proliferation of this form explains the quality that people tend to associate with the memorabile in the world of fact: when factuality becomes concrete, it becomes *credible*.

Here we arrive at the *process of meaning transfer* that I mentioned in my introduction to the *Sage*. At that point I used the word 'history' [*Historie*] and spoke of *the world of history*, while putting off specifying the nature of this world. In the simple form memorabile, we now see this world before us. The mental disposition in which factuality becomes concrete is concerned with credibility – but it finds credibility only in its own form; it only considers 'attested' what takes on the form of the memorabile. We called that the tyranny of *Historie* – at this

---

5 Theodor Lessing, *Geschichte als Sinngebung des Sinnlosen* (Munich: Beck, 1918), p. 10, quoted in 'Geschichte', in *Eislers Handwörterbuch der Philosophie*, 2nd edn, Richard Müller-Freienfels, ed. (Berlin: Mittler, 1922), p. 243.

point we can apologize to history and its muse, and express ourselves more precisely. Wherever the mental disposition we are discussing becomes dominant, domineering, something occurs in the relationship to other forms that can be compared with what occurs in the memorabile itself – a sort of accumulation happens, and in this accumulation *Sage*, legend or myth appear only in relation to what this mental disposition tends to call history, to what its form has rendered concrete, to what it itself is prepared to recognize as credible and attested. Thus, in the mental disposition concerned with factuality and in the verbal gesture of the form memorabile, the form *Sage* becomes a 'precursor'; the word *Sage* loses its significance and comes to mean that which is unattested or incredible.

Although it does lead away from the sphere of simple forms, we should perhaps also point to the fact that literary forms, to the extent that they strive – for whatever reason – to represent a fictional element as something factual and thus as concrete and credible, often employ the resources of the memorabile. We saw with the clothes of the prince of Orange how an ensemble of factual details could be meaningfully interrelated, as well as related to a governing meaning. We have seen – and we will see every time events assume memorabile form – how gaiety before a mishap produces the contrast happiness–unhappiness, while seriousness before a mishap produces a presentiment of calamity; how a mishap on a beautiful summer's day once more produces the contrast, while one that follows a stormy winter's night yields the relationship of congruity – and how (to repeat the point) the mishap is made concrete by the confluence of all this, how we believe in it and how it impresses itself on our memory. Yet where things that happen do not coalesce in the memorabile, where it is not a question of a factual mishap that is to be made concrete but of an imaginary mishap, we see that in order to be credible, this mishap must be represented in the same way as in a true memorabile; it is surrounded with similar specifications of detail, all of them oriented towards it and towards each other in a meaningful way. And this can go so far that – as is often the case with modern literature – we can hardly feel the difference between the derivative form of the memorabile and the literary art form 'novella'.

CHAPTER 8

Fairy Tale

I. NAME – TYPES – GRIMM GENRE – LANGUAGE AND POETRY

The use of the word *Märchen* to designate a literary form is remarkably limited. The words *Sage*, *Rätsel* ('riddle') and *Sprichwort* ('proverb') can be found in several Germanic languages; the word *Märchen*, used in this sense, exists only in High German. Even Dutch, which otherwise tends to parallel High German in its terms for these forms, here has another name: *sprookje*. French employs a variant of the word *conte*, story: *conte des fées*; English has the word *fairy tale*.

In fact, *Märchen* first acquired its meaning as a name for a particular literary form when the brothers Grimm used the word in the title of their collection *Kinder- und Hausmärchen* ('Children's and Household Tales'). To be sure, this was a word that had already long been in use – also to describe such stories as the ones they collected. In the eighteenth century there is already mention of *Feenmärchen* ('fairy tales'), *of Märchen und Erzählungen für Kinder und Nichtkinder* ('Fairy tales and Stories for Children and Non-Children'), of *Sagen*, *Märchen* and *Anekdoten*. Musäus published his *Volksmärchen der Deutschen* ('German Fairy Tales'); Wieland, Goethe, Tieck and Novalis each used the term with a slightly different nuance but in a basically consonant sense – and yet it was the brothers Grimm who collected all this earlier material under the one umbrella concept, while their anthology would become the model for all later nineteenth-century collections. It is also the case that, for all its disciplinary variety, fairy tale research has proceeded since then in the manner pioneered by the brothers Grimm.

At the risk of giving a circular definition, one could almost say: a *Märchen* is a story or a history of the kind collected by the brothers Grimm in their *Kinder- und Hausmärchen*. When they appeared, the tales of the brothers Grimm became a benchmark for judging similar phenomena, not only in Germany but everywhere. Generally speaking, one tends to recognize a literary object as a *Märchen* when it corresponds more or less to the stories we find in the Grimms' *Kinder- und Hausmärchen*. And so, until we have defined the concept 'Märchen' in our own terms, we will speak likewise of the 'Grimm genre'.

Our understanding of the word *Märchen* cannot be derived from the basic sense of the Old High German word *mâri* and the Gothic word *mêrs* ('known, renowned'), nor from the fact that the noun *Märchen* is a deprecatory diminutive form of *Märe* ('story, report, tradition'), meaning a little story, or a vague circulating rumour whose accuracy it is hard to assess. What we have here is a form with very different names in different languages, but whose essential nature is universally thought to have been expressed in the Grimms' collection.

The *Kinder- und Hausmärchen* first appeared in 1812. The collection stands in a very close relationship with another, published several years previously, without being its sequel: Achim von Arnim and Clemens Brentano's *Des Knaben Wunderhorn* ('The Youth's Magic Horn'), which in its turn followed certain currents of the century before, those vital currents of romanticism which testified to a 'hunger and thirst for the living force and the inward beauty of native folk life' reaching far beyond Germany's borders, but which Herder represented – indeed, embodied – for Germany. Just as Arnim and Brentano collected the poetry and the music that survived in native folk life, so too did Jacob and Wilhelm Grimm undertake to copy down folk narratives, in all their manifold forms.

And yet there was an enormous difference between Achim von Arnim and Jacob Grimm; this Castor and Pollux conceived of the artefacts they were recording, and indeed of poetry generally, in contrary ways. The contrast between them is so important to our study of this form and to the principles of its definition that we must take the time to explore it. Beginning with this conflict, which was essential for romanticism, we can define the relationship of language and poetry, this definition being where every conflict of the sort that we see between Arnim and Grimm must lead. The *Märchen* or fairy tale form, especially, demands a preliminary investigation – one that will lead us to a fundamental consideration of *language* and *poetry*, and constitute both the conclusion and the introduction to all of the simple forms.

II. GRIMM-ARNIM – NATURE POETRY AND ART POETRY
– SIMPLE FORMS AND LITERARY FORMS

In the correspondence between Arnim and Jacob Grimm,[1] we can witness the back-and-forth of a conflict of opinions, circa 1811, that we must quickly sketch – a conflict centring on the catchwords *Naturpoesie* ('natural poetry') and *Kunstpoesie* ('art poetry'). For Arnim, there is no opposition between these two concepts; for him, Jacob Grimm's 'favourite distinction' does not exist. 'I am convinced', writes Arnim, 'that you will understand why I definitely and generally reject all *oppositions* of the sort that philosophy loves to create these days, whether in poetry, in history or in life; thus I also see no opposition between folk poetry and meistersinging . . .'.[2] To which Jacob Grimm responds:

> Poetry is what passes directly from the soul into words; it arises continually from a natural urge and an innate ability to express it. Folk poetry emerges from the soul of the collective; what I am calling art poetry emerges from the soul of the individual. This is why modern poetry calls its poets by name, while ancient poetry does not know any names – it is not at all something made by one or two or three people, but rather it is the sum of a whole; as I said earlier, it remains inexplicable how all this came together as a made object, but this is no more mysterious than the process by which the waters coalesce into a river and flow on together. I cannot conceive of the existence of a Homer or of the author of the Nibelungen.[3]

I will mention in passing that Jacob Grimm also includes in natural or folk poetry some forms that we call literary forms. For us this is not the

---

1   Reinhold Steig and Herman Grimm, eds, *Achim von Arnim und die ihm nahe standen,* vol. 3: *Achim von Arnim und Jacob und Wilhelm Grimm*, ed. Reinhold Steig (Stuttgart: Cotta, 1904).

2   Ibid., p. 110.

3   Ibid., p. 146.

point of the exchange; what is important for us is the attitude of both men, as it emerges from this opposition.

A number of conceptual antitheses develop out of this difference in attitude over the course of their epistolary debate.

For Jacob Grimm, art poetry is a 'concoction' [*eine Zubereitung*], natural poetry 'a spontaneous creation' [*ein Sichvonselbstmachen*],[4] and 'modern poetry' is something 'fundamentally different from ancient poetry'; this is why nothing at all, not the slightest tittle or jot, may be changed in ancient poetry as we find it; this is why every rearrangement, to whatever purpose, is evil; this is why translations or even paraphrases in modern language are completely worthless! What we see here is not an anxious philologist sticking fearfully to his text and its letter, but a thinker with convictions who refuses to blend disparate elements.

Arnim, on the other hand, feels personally somewhat stung, for he knows that in *Des Knaben Wunderhorn* many a tittle was changed and quite a lot added that could hardly be counted as 'ancient poetry'. Yet he too is sure of himself. There is no such thing as folk poetry in the Grimms' sense – there are only *poets*: 'the more a folk has experienced, the more uniform it is in its facial features and in its ideas; every poet who is recognized as such is a folk poet . . .'[5] Authors' names are forgotten – they get lost. Naturally, it is the mission of the poet to make poetry out of the people's concerns or bring his poetry to the people:

> I would consider it a blessing of the Lord to be given the honour of using my head to endow the world with a song that was adopted by a folk, but such things are up to the folk; I will be satisfied with what I have done in my life if even only a few find something in my work that they, too, have sensed, sought, without being able to express it . . .'[6]

Grimm disagrees with this, and answers at length:

---

4 Ibid., p. 118.
5 Ibid., p. 134.
6 Ibid., p. 135.

If you believe as I do that religion originated in a divine revelation and that language has an equally marvellous origin and was not brought about by human invention, then you must perforce also feel and believe that ancient poetry and its forms, the wellspring of rhyme and alliteration, likewise arose as a totality, and that neither work-shops nor the reflections of individual poets can account for this.[7]

I will remind you that Seiler speaks of a 'romanticizing conception' in his *Teaching German Proverbs*, according to which the folk song, the fairy tale, and so on, have their 'mysterious origin in the depths of the folk soul.'[8] This exchange of letters shows how the alternative notion, too – the idea of the poet as a creative force – could equally have been labelled 'romanticizing', at least on the grounds that its representative is the indubitable romantic Achim von Arnim. 'Art poetry' and 'natural poetry' – and all that these concepts entail – are romantically conceived notions of the opposition we are facing here, which in fact has a deeper meaning.

The polemic rested a while. Arnim visited the brothers Grimm in Kassel in 1811, accompanied by his wife Bettina. There he looked into the new anthology – and was enthusiastic. He reported on it to Brentano, and pressed for publication as quickly as possible; later on, in Berlin, he took over negotiations with the publisher. When, after Arnim's death, Wilhelm Grimm dedicated the *Kinder- und Hausmärchen* to Bettina, he wrote: 'He was the one who pushed us to publish . . . Of all our collections, he liked these tales best . . .'[9]

However, their differences were not reconciled. In 1812, on the tales' publication, the debate about ancient and modern poetry recommenced. Jacob Grimm was pleased that Arnim had enjoyed the *Kinder- und Hausmärchen* more than Brentano's adaptations of fairy tales: 'I am very pleased that Clemens's reworkings don't sit well with you, and I only regret the time and the thought that he's put into them; he can

7 Ibid., p. 139.
8 Friedrich Seiler, *Deutsche Sprichwörterkunde* (Munich: C. H. Beck, 1922), p. 19.
9 Wilhelm Grimm, 'An die Frau Elisabeth von Arnim', *Kinder- und Hausmärchen gesammelt durch die Brüder Grimm*, 3rd edn, 2 vols (Göttingen: Dieterich, 1837), vol. 1, p. iii.

arrange and embellish them all he likes, but in the end our simple, faithfully collected stories will certainly put his to shame every time.'[10] Now, however, he let himself slide into an attack:

> My respect for epic material, which I consider incapable of invention, grows daily, and I could possibly become one-sided, and not care for anything else; this is the kind of pure and good innocence that *is simply there of its own accord*; with all your efforts, you modern poets cannot produce any new colours, but only remix them; indeed, you cannot even apply them without mixing them . . .'[11]

Arnim does not take this lying down; in his answer, he accuses Jacob Grimm of not *knowing* the modern poets. Not in the sense of not having read them, but in the sense of not having understood them. Then he defends Clemens Brentano, even though he is fully aware of his weaknesses. Brentano's fairy tales are not 'something lived among children that can be transferred directly to children without being further digested, but rather a book that inspires the art of invention in adults, that shows every mother who finds herself in a pinch – the truly educated ones perhaps excepted – how to transform a situation whose charms they perceive into a longer tale for lasting entertainment'.[12] For Arnim, the significance of the *Märchen* lies in this inspiration to *invention*. If it does not inspire us, if it does not show us how to tell stories, the ancient tale loses its value and its charm. The point is sharply emphasized: 'Fixed *Märchen* will be the death of the whole world of *Märchen*.'[13] The value of old things is in their capacity to inspire new things and take them further – 'poetry is neither young nor old and has no history at all; we can only indicate certain series of relationships based on external characteristics'.[14] Thus the modern poet timelessly continues work on what the ancient poet composed. It is here that Arnim's position comes fully into view; it is also the position from which he compiled *Des Knaben Wunderhorn*. New things

---

10   Steig, *Achim von Arnim und Jacob und Wilhelm Grimm*, p. 219.
11   Ibid., pp. 219–20.
12   Ibid., p. 223.
13   Ibid., p. 223.
14   Ibid., p. 225.

exist: they are the essential thing, they must be encouraged and further perfected by every available means – also by means of tradition, through what is ancient or of folk origin. Old things are not collected for their own sake, but precisely to serve this end.

It is easily understandable that Grimm should have felt wounded by this in turn. He summarizes Arnim's opinion in his own words:

> Thus there is no history of poetry, it's a joke to distinguish between natural poetry and art poetry . . . by saying this, you attack what is most dear to me . . . all of my work, I feel it, depends upon learning and showing how a great, epic poetry has lived and prevailed all over the earth and how people have forgotten and squandered this poetry bit by bit, or perhaps not entirely – how they still live from it, even now.[15]

Now Grimm's poetic profession of faith follows in six paragraphs, beginning with the words 'I believe', uttered in deepest earnest. The first sentence runs: 'Just as Paradise was lost, so too was the garden of ancient poetry locked, although everyone still bears a small Paradise in his own heart . . .'[16]

I repeat: this debate is identical with our own conceptual distinction. The question that preoccupied the two romantics Arnim and Jacob Grimm more than a century ago is also of greatest importance to our own era: it is the question of *poetry* and *language*. My aim with these definitions of form is to try to find a new version of both of these oppositions, to use a morphology to define the concepts that were then called *natural poetry* and *art poetry* and which appear to us now in the guise of *simple forms* and *literary forms*, and thus bring the problem closer to its solution.

In the correspondence we next encounter a curious assertion that returns us to the fairy tale. Arnim responds – here sticking with his poet; indeed, in a sense, turning the tables – that what the brothers Grimm have done with their *Märchen* collection is poetic work:

---

15 Ibid., p. 234.
16 Ibid., p. 235.

The most recent object that the scholar can access historically will only just satisfy him: the true audience of the poet, the non-academic contemporary, understands only this realization of a more general phenomenon. I do not mean to surprise or wound you with the assertion, but I cannot avoid it: I will never believe the two of you when you say such things, even if you believe that you transcribed the fairy tales for children precisely as you received them; the structuring, creative drive in man overcomes all intentions and is absolutely ineradicable. God creates, and man, his likeness, labours at carrying on His works. The thread is never broken, but a different sort of flax must always appear . . .[17]

And with that Arnim hit home, for Jacob Grimm was much too serious a philologist and too honest a man not to see that there was something true in all this, even if ultimately it did not shake his basic intentions or his deepest convictions. He answered – and this is the last quotation we shall draw from the letters:

In this case it is a matter of fidelity. A mathematical fidelity is completely impossible, nor is it to be found in even the most truthful and stringent history; but this does not matter, for we feel that *fidelity* is something real, not a sham, and this is why we can truly contrast it with *infidelity*. You cannot tell a story in an entirely adequate way, just as you cannot crack an egg without leaving some egg white sticking to the shell; this is how human life is, and also a matter of how the story is told, which is always changing. To continue with this metaphor: for me, true fidelity means not breaking the yolk. Even if you doubt the fidelity of our *Märchen* book, this last you cannot doubt, for it is there. As for this matter of impossibility: someone else, or we ourselves, could have retold the tales in different words and still not with lesser fidelity; nothing at all has been added to or changed in the thing itself.[18]

Let us stress and retain the fact that Jacob Grimm recognized in the fairy tale a 'thing itself' that can remain completely itself, even if it

---

17   Ibid., p. 248.
18   Ibid., p. 255.

is narrated by other people with other words. Before we proceed in our own way to understand this 'thing itself' as a simple form and define the mental disposition from which it derives, we will want first to look elsewhere in the Western world for further examples of the 'Grimm genre'.

III. THE TUSCAN NOVELLA – HISTORY OF THE FAIRY TALE

In another place I undertook to outline the history of the fairy tale in Western literature;[19] here, where it is a question of form, we can make do with an extract. Whereas with other simple forms we cannot really speak yet of a history, we do have enough data to be able to study at least part of the history of the *Märchen*. The deeper ground of this history lies in the confluence between the simple form and the literary form of the fairy tale. This will lead us again, from another direction, to our opposition language/poetry, simple form/literary form.

In fourteenth-century Europe, we see the beginnings of a short narrative form that we are accustomed to call the art form *novella*. Tuscany seems to be this form's point of origin; in any case, the way in which it first appears in Boccaccio's *Decameron* is normative for the history of the novella. For this reason we have called it the *Tuscan novella*. It is always written in the local vernacular – for the few extant Latin examples, we can say that Latin was the vernacular of the Humanists.

Shortly thereafter, two variant types of novella emerge: novella collections and single novellas. The novella collections most often take on the form of their great precursor, the *Decameron*; the individual stories are held together by a frame narrative that expresses – among many other things – where, on what occasion, and by whom the novellas were narrated. I need not mention that this form of frame narrative is older than the Tuscan novella.

Moving outward from Tuscany, both the frame narrative and the individual story form spread through all the lands of the literary West;

---

19   André Jolles, 'Het sprookje,' *De Gids* 78: 1 (1923), pp. 72–102, 380–411; 78:2 (1923), pp. 212–40; 'Het sprookje in de wetenschap,' *De Gids* 92: 10 (1928), pp. 235–50.

they undergo certain modifications, they flow here and there into different literary forms, but they are always recognizable as such. Without going into all the details, I would note in general that the Tuscan novella strives to narrate an incident or event of urgent importance in such a way as to give us the impression of an actual event, and such that the event appears more significant than the persons experiencing it.

In the sixteenth century we already find something else within the tradition of the Tuscan novella. We must emphasize that in its general form this other thing is tightly linked to the initial example of the Tuscan novella, as found in Boccacio's *Decameron*. In 1550, Giovanni Francesco Straparola published a frame narrative – *Piacevoli notti*, 'Facetious Nights' – that sticks closely to the model as far as the frame narrative is concerned. Here, too, we find ladies and gentlemen who have been brought together by exceptional circumstances, and who literally pass the time by telling stories. The difference from the Tuscan frame narrative consists in the fact that a number of the stories are not novellas in the sense we have just defined, but stories such as the ones we know from the Grimms' anthology – stories that do not at all give the impression of actually having happened. Here we even find certain material that we encounter again in the *Kinder- und Hausmärchen* or in later collections, such as 'Puss-in-Boots', 'The Thankful Animals', 'The Master Thief', and so on.

This phenomenon remains isolated – the novella continues on its course. But the same thing happens at the beginning of the seventeenth century. In 1634–36 there appears a posthumous frame narrative in Neapolitan dialect by Giambattista Basile – *Cunto de li Cunti* ('Tale of Tales'), later known as the *Pentameron*. Once again, the author closely follows the model of the *Decameron*. But there is a difference, in that the frame story does not give the impression of really having happened, but rather belongs to the Grimm genre, while the individual stories must equally be included in this genre. It looks as though the author, who parodies Boccaccio in his frame but is also bent on recording as many expressions from the folk vernacular and describing as many folk customs as possible, is intentionally opposing this manner of storytelling to that of the outmoded Tuscan novella – and accordingly one can read in the works of the fairy tale scholars of the nineteenth century that Basile was the first collector of fairy tales. We can add that his book includes such stories as 'Cinderella', 'The Seven Ravens', and 'Sleeping Beauty', all of which we know from the *Kinder- und Hausmärchen*.

For the brothers Grimm, the 'true fairy tale collections' begin – as they note in the third volume of the *Kinder- und Hausmärchen* – in France at the end of the seventeenth century, with Charles Perrault. Thus we skip over La Fontaine, who in his *Loves of Cupid and Psyche* had presented something from antiquity in a new form that is comparable to the stories of the *Kinder- und Hausmärchen*, and we come to Perrault's *Contes de ma mère l'Oie* ('Mother Goose Tales'). Prior to the publication of these prose narratives, Perrault had written three stories in verse between 1691 and 1694: 'Griselidis', 'Donkey Skin', and 'The Ridiculous Wishes'. In their outward form, these verse narratives imitated the notorious *Contes* of La Fontaine. However, whereas La Fontaine's *Contes* were for the most part reworkings of novellas from the Tuscan school, in 'Donkey Skin' we again find an instance of the Grimm genre. After this, in 1697, the *Mother Goose Tales* appear under the title *Histoires ou Contes du temps passé avec des Moralités* ('Stories or Tales of Times Past, with Morals'). In fact, the book is no longer a frame narrative, yet something of the old frame still shimmers through: Perrault pretends that the stories had been told by an old nanny to her son, and that he himself had heard them from this son. In any event, the *Contes du temps passé* are among the tales in the *Kinder- und Hausmärchen*, and here too we find such stories as 'Little Red Riding Hood', 'Sleeping Beauty', and 'Mother Holle'.

Very soon after the publication of the *Contes* of Perrault, a storm of similar stories broke out all over France and Europe. One can say with confidence that at the beginning of the eighteenth century this genre dominated literature: on the one hand, it replaces the narrative long form of the seventeenth century – the novel; on the other, it supersedes everything that still remained of the Tuscan novella. It is hardly possible to estimate the number of these stories. Next, between 1704 and 1708, the first translation of the *Thousand and One Nights*, by Galland, added the oriental narrative to the mix, and afterwards the literature of the eighteenth century was suffused with stories of this kind. One need only look for this in Wieland's works to get a sense of how significant and multifarious the genre's influence was.

It is precisely Wieland who gives us a clear image of how the eighteenth century understood this genre, in the many remarks we have from him on the subject. The *Märchen* – he uses this word as well – is a literary form, and indeed an art form that unites and satisfies two contrasting propensities of human nature: the predilection for the marvellous and the inclination towards the true and the natural. Since the predilection for the marvellous and the love of truth are both innate to humanity from the beginning, there are fairy tales everywhere, and there are very old fairy tales. But with this form of literary art, everything depends on bringing these two inclinations into proper interrelationship; if this does not happen, then the fairy tale loses its charm and its value – and it is a matter of taste and the artist's business to produce this relationship. Wieland expresses himself sharply: 'Products of this sort must be works of taste, or they are nothing. Old wives' tales, told in the manner of old wives, may propagate themselves by oral tradition, but they need not be printed.'[20]

We can now speak of romanticism. I need not mention that, for Novalis, this genre has a different and higher meaning than for Wieland; but however different their opinions may be, and however much poets and poetry may acquire a deeper meaning for Novalis, for him as well the fairy tale is an art form, and 'the true fairy tale poet is a visionary into the future'.

IV. FAIRY TALE AS SIMPLE FORM – FORMATIVE LAWS IN NOVELLA AND FAIRY TALE

This short survey will have sharpened our eyes for the question: Is the fairy tale a simple form?

We have on the one hand a form of which we have said that it strives to narrate an incident or an event of urgent importance in such a way as to give us the impression of an actual event, and such that the event appears more significant than the persons experiencing it.

---

20 Christoph Martin Wieland, *Dschinnistan, oder auserlesene Feen- und Geistermärchen, teils neu erfunden, teils übersetzt und umgearbeitet*, 3 vols (Winterthur: Steiner, 1786–1789), vol. 1, p. xv.

We see how, in the course of literary history, this form is confronted by another form, timidly at first, but then ever more assertively. Although this second form initially mimics the first in its outward characteristics, it has a different tendency from the start. To put the point negatively: first, it no longer strives to convey an event of urgent importance – instead, jumping from one event to another, it conveys an entire chain of events, a chain definitely completed only at its end; and second, it no longer strives to represent this chain of events so as to give us the impression of an actual occurrence – instead, it continually works with the marvellous.

We will call the first form *novella* and count it among the art forms; we will call the second *Märchen* or fairy tale, and assert that it is a simple form. Or, to use Jacob Grimm's terminology once more: we will say of the first form that it is art poetry and 'a concoction', and of the second that it is natural poetry and 'a spontaneous creation'.

It is clear that this distinction cannot be derived from the way in which the two forms present themselves in the literary–historical situation of the West from the sixteenth century on. Both the novella and the fairy tale are connected with the names of authors: the novella with names like Boccaccio, Sacchetti, Bandello, the fairy tale with names like Straparola, Basile, Perrault, Madame d'Aulnoy, Wieland.

Nor can we say that the difference depends on the fact that the tales can be shown to have been in circulation among the folk, and that they then passed into literature from the vernacular, while the novella was freely invented by its authors. We know that – to stay with Boccaccio – at least ninety of his hundred novellas had already appeared, in written form, in other works of literature; we also know that, for the most part, he did not draw these from the apposite Indian, Arabic and Latin sources, but that they were told to him orally, that he knew them from 'hearsay'.

If we would rather not assume, as Wieland did, that both are forms of literary art, and that in the novella only *one* human tendency comes to expression, the penchant for what is natural and true, whereas the fairy tale mixes *two* human tendencies, the penchant for what is natural and true and the predilection for the marvellous; if we would prefer instead to stick with our assertion that what we have here is a basic formal difference, then we must derive this difference from the form itself, without recourse to the literary–historical situation.

Surveying the world of the novella, we perceive an infinite variety of incidents of the most diverse kinds; what gives them coherence is the way they are portrayed. Further, we see how other incidents – provided they suit the requirements and have a certain intensity – can always be portrayed in this manner, and thus become a novella. Boccaccio took incidents and events of this sort from a literary tradition – we know, however, that it is equally possible to make choices freely: one can apply the form 'novella' to any part of the world, and each time we do so this part of the world will appear as a novella. What is more, we know that our freedom of choice is so great that with our imagination we can produce a literary construction that will autonomously embody this part of the world in this form.

If we survey the world of the fairy tale, here too we recognize a wealth of incidents of all kinds, which equally seem to owe their coherence to a specific mode of representation. Yet if we attempt to apply this form to the world in a similar way, we instantly sense that this is impossible – not because the incidents in a fairy tale need necessarily to be marvellous, whereas in the world they are not marvellous, but because incidents such as the ones that we find in fairy tales are conceivable only in fairy tales. In short: we can bring the world to the fairy tale, but we cannot bring the fairy tale to the world.

If we regard the activity of the novella, we can observe how it intervenes in the world in a structuring manner, how it defines some part of this world, binding it in such a way that this part is now simply and definitively incarnated by this form.

If we speak of the activity of the fairy tale, we see that what it constructs is above all itself, and that, in so doing, it prepares itself to admit the world into itself in the shape of this construction.

We can summarize all this as follows: Both the novella and the fairy tale are forms, but the laws informing the novella are such that we can use this form to construct every incident in a definite manner – be it traditional, factual or invented – as long as it has the common characteristic of intensity; the laws informing the fairy tale, on the other hand, are such that wherever we insert this form into the world, the world transforms itself *according to a principle reigning only within this form and defining only this form.*

V. SOLID, PARTICULAR, SINGULAR – MOBILE, GENERAL, PLURAL – THE VERBAL GESTURE

What we are saying here about fairy tales and novellas can however be generalized: it is the difference between simple forms and literary forms. This is also the difference that Jacob Grimm was talking about. Where we approach the world with a form, reach constructively into it, render concise a part of it that seems coherent thanks to some common attribute, Grimm speaks of *concoction*; conversely, where we allow the world to enter into a form that has evolved according to a principle prevailing solely within and determining only this form, and where the world now transforms itself in accord with this form, there he calls it a *spontaneous self-generation*. We recognize with him the basic difference of structuring laws – but we do not agree that the one form belongs to a past time, the other to the present. If this were the case, one could observe the one, but only collect the other. Grimm drew this conclusion as well. Our opinion is that both are always and everywhere active, and that observing them in their disparity and in their relationships is one of the basic tasks of literary criticism.

If we pursue for a moment the trajectories of the novella and the fairy tale, we can say this: what is crucial for the novella, which brings some part of the world to completion, is that everything it includes in this concise completion must have a *solid*, *particular* and *singular* shape; in the fairy tale, on the other hand – which holds itself open to the world and takes the world up into itself – the world retains its *mobility*, its *generality* and what I will call its *pluricity*.

Then again, we can say that this holds not only for the novella and the fairy tale, but for literary forms and simple forms generally; and in so doing we can recall what we said about the relationship of the *case* to the literary form.

If we now look at *language*, we can say that, in the literary form, language strives so much to be solid, particular and singular that ultimately we can only imagine it as the language of an individual person, of an individual who, thanks to an eminent gift, is in a position to achieve, in a final completion, the highest degree of concision [*Bündigkeit*] – but only *here*, only *now* – and who can give this work the solid, particular and singular imprint of his own personality. We express this by saying that the literary form can ultimately be realized only by an artist, a *poet*; here we naturally understand the poet not as a creative force, but as an executive one.

On the other hand, in the simple form, too, language stays mobile, general and plural. We tend to say that one can retell a fairy tale, a *Sage*, a legend 'in one's own words'. With the saying and the proverb, and also with the riddle, we saw that these 'own words' can sometimes be very limited in their range. With legend, *Sage* and fairy tale as well, the form lost its validity whenever we omitted or changed what we called the *verbal gesture*. And yet there is some truth in the notion of 'telling the story in one's own words', for it is not in the words of an individual that the simple form is realized. The individual is not understood as the final executive force that brings the form to unique realization while also giving it his personal imprint; this final executive force is language itself, in which the form can be plurally realized. With both the literary form and the simple form we can speak of 'own words'; with the literary form, however, we mean *the writer's own words*, in which the form is finally achieved, whereas with the simple form we mean *the form's own words*, in which the form can be realized each time anew in this same way.

We can extend what we have shown here regarding language to everything that we find in both forms – to personalities, to places and to events. We shall not go into this in detail; suffice it to say that, in the simple form, these things preserve the character of mobility, generality and pluricity – if one sets a fairy tale princess next to a princess from a novella, one senses the difference.

We have often used the word *actualization*; this term, too, can be applied to both forms. For it is entirely conceivable that another poet could bring the same part of the world to completion in a literary form. But then we see once again that this completed work strives equally to be solid, particular and singular, while the actualization of a simple form always points back to the mobility, generality and pluricity of the form itself.

With this last point we have returned to the literary situation that arose with the appearance of the fairy tale in Western literature, and which we can sketch as follows: a guild of poets and writers that has concerned itself for centuries with literary forms believes itself obliged and able to actualize a simple form in the same way it actualizes its literary forms; a series of novellas undertakes to treat the fairy tale like a novella, to bring it to closure in the same way, to give it solid, particular and singular shape, to impress it with personal character. It would be of great scholarly importance to study what can happen generally, and what does happen each time, when a specific simple form converges, in literature, with a literary form – in short, to determine what such crossings yield – but this we cannot do here. At this juncture, we can only say that, in the present case, the simple form baulks at the convergence: it resists being remodelled in this way; it remains itself. It resists this to such an extent, it remains so much itself, that, despite countless transmutations and displacements, perceptive and linguistically and formally sensitive men such as Herder or Grimm detect the hybridity, the disparity in the mixture; they perceive the simple form as such, and thus arrive at distinctions such as we find in Herder's *Voices of the Peoples in Song* or in Grimm's reflections on 'natural poetry' and 'art poetry'.[21]

Thus we have come to the last part of Jacob Grimm's and Arnim's debate. Each time a simple form is actualized, it takes a step in a direction that can lead to a definitive form such as we finally have in the literary form; it sets a foot on the path to solidity, particularity and singularity, and thus forfeits something of its mobility, generality and pluricity. We have already seen this in our discussion of the relationship of legend to *vita*, *Sage* to saga, myth to *mythos*. This is where the rebuke directed by Arnim at Jacob Grimm applies, when Arnim says: 'I will never believe you when you say . . . that you transcribed the fairy tales for children precisely as you received them.' In our terms that would mean: every actualization distracts from what the simple form intends to convey. Grimm responds: 'For us, it's a matter of fidelity', and he employs the image of the cracked egg. Translated into our parlance, this would mean: we cannot avoid the actualization, but this actualization must be such that it refers back to the simple form as such in as direct a manner as possible, while tending as little as possible towards the solidity, particularity and singularity of the literary form.

This is why Jacob Grimm ceased to occupy himself with fairy tales

---

21 Johann Gottfried Herder, *Stimmen der Völker in Liedern* (Tübingen: Cotta, 1807), a revised third edition of his *Alte Volkslieder* (see p. 7, note 6, *supra*).

derived from literary sources – he went to the folk. It would require a special study to establish to what degree the *Kinder- und Hausmärchen* are 'faithful' in this sense, and to what extent they are in fact still influenced by eighteenth-century literary processes. No matter how the *Kinder- und Hausmärchen* turned out, it is certain that *Jacob Grimm understood the fairy tale itself as a simple form.*

VI. MENTAL DISPOSITION: NAIVE MORALITY – THE TRAGIC WORLD – VERBAL GESTURES OF THE TRAGIC FAIRY TALE – THE SELF-EVIDENCE OF THE MIRACULOUS – VERBAL GESTURES OF THE FAIRY TALE – THE OBJECT OF THE FAIRY TALE

We have said that in the fairy tale the world is transformed according to a principle obtaining only in this form, and defining this form alone. With all the simple forms, we called this principle the 'mental disposition.' We will do this with the present form as well, and attempt to define the mental disposition of the fairy tale.

It is curious that in the period that we have sketched, whenever novella and fairy tale are opposed to or compared with each other a certain fond emphasis is placed on the notion that the fairy tale is a moral story. We need not pursue this here in detail; it will suffice to recall that Perrault called his stories *Histoires ou Contes du temps passé avec des Moralités*, that he did in fact close each fairy tale with a rhymed *moralité*, and that in his introduction he says:

> Virtue is always rewarded in them and vice is always punished. They all try to show the advantages of being honest, patient, prudent, diligent and obedient, and the evil which overtakes those who are not . . . However frivolous and odd the events in all these tales may be, they definitely instill in children the wish to be like the people they see becoming happy, and, at the same time, fear of the misfortunes into which malicious people have fallen through their malice . . . These are seeds being sown; at first they produce only spurts of joy or sadness, but they seldom fail to result in a propensity for good.[22]

---

22 Charles Perrault, *The Complete Fairy Tales in Verse and Prose / L'intégrale*

At first glance, this might seem contradictory: If the stories are frivolous, *frivole*, how are they then to sow the good seed in the hearts of youth? If they are quirky, *bizarre*, how are they to serve as proof of fixed life-rules? If we look more closely, we notice that certain persons do become happy here, but the degree to which it is virtue that is rewarded and vice that is punished is more than questionable. Take 'Puss-in-Boots', for example. How do we know that the miller's boy is modest, patient, prudent or industrious? He is obedient, to be sure, for he does everything the cat orders him to. And this cat himself: he lies and deceives from beginning to end; he compels others to lie by persuasion and threats; last but not least, he devours a magician who has done him little or no harm. Is Snow White so very virtuous, or the Prince who goes about kissing sleeping girls at the drop of a hat? Nor do Tom Thumb and Little Red Riding Hood exactly seem heroes of virtue to me. On the other hand, we cannot say either that the devious Puss or the frivolous Prince impress us as immoral.

Now, if the characters and events of the fairy tale fail thus to impress us as truly moral, still we cannot deny that they do give us some satisfaction – and this satisfaction has less to do with the stories' satisfying our 'predilection for the marvellous' together with our 'penchant for what is natural and true' than with the fact that in these stories things happen as we feel they *should* happen in the world.

In 'Puss-in-Boots', we see a poor miller's son. He has two brothers, who have both inherited something valuable – the mill and the donkey; he himself has received something worthless – the cat. In itself, this fact or situation is not immoral, but it does give us a sense of injustice and a feeling that this injustice must be corrected. In the course of the narrative this desire is satisfied – and in such a way that precisely this worthless thing, the cat, becomes the means of correction, and that the happiness of the disadvantaged son exceeds his brothers' in the same measure as his happiness had at first fallen short of theirs. This is certainly not an ethics in the philosophical sense of the term; nowhere are we told who is virtuous or who is not, what is virtuous or what is not. The miller who

des Contes en vers et en prose, ed. and transl. Stanley Appelbaum (Mineola, NY: Dover, 2002), p. 7.

treats his older sons better than the youngest is not called evil; nor, in this tale, are the two older brothers worse than the youngest. This all means nothing other than that our sense of justice has been troubled by a state of affairs or by given incidents, and that a series of incidents, an event complex of a special kind, has satisfied it and restored it to equilibrium. The situation is realized somewhat more sharply in Cinderella, where a poor girl is set over against an evil stepmother and two evil stepsisters; but here too the emphasis is less on the intrinsic evil of the relatives than on the evil of the injustice; and the satisfaction we feel at the end arises not so much from the fact that an industrious, obedient, patient girl is rewarded as from the fact that everything that happens corresponds to what we expect and demand of a just universe.

This expectation of how things should really happen in the world seems to be normative for the form 'fairy tale': it is the mental disposition of the fairy tale. Perrault and others correctly saw that it is 'moral', but not moral in the sense of a philosophical ethics. If we say with Kant that ethics responds to the question, 'What should I do?' and that accordingly our ethical judgment includes a valuation of human behaviour, then the fairy tale does not belong to the sphere of ethics. But if we say that there is an ethics beyond this that responds to the question, 'How should things happen in the world?' and an ethical judgment concerned not with *actions* but with *events*, then we see that this judgment is captured in language by the form 'fairy tale.'

In contrast to philosophical ethics, the ethics of actions, I call this ethics the *ethics of events* or *naive morality*, here using the word *naive* in the same sense as Schiller when he speaks of naive poetry. Our naive-ethical judgment is a judgment of feeling. It is not aesthetic, for it speaks to us apodictically and categorically; it is neither utilitarian nor hedonistic – the standard here is neither utility nor pleasure. It stands outside of the sphere of religion, since it is undogmatic and independent of divine guidance – it is a purely ethical, and hence an absolute, judgment. If we use this to define our form, we can say that in the fairy tale we have a form in which events, the way of the world, are ordered so that they correspond fully to the demands of naive morality – that is, so that they are 'good' and 'just' by the measure of our absolute judgment of feeling.

As such, the fairy tale stands in the sharpest contrast to what we normally observe to actually happen in the world. The way of the world corresponds only rarely to the demands of naive morality; it is mostly not 'just' – the fairy tale thus contraposes itself to a world of 'reality'. But this world of reality is not the world in which general validity is ascribed to the way things are, but a world in which events contradict the demands of naive morality, a world we naively feel is immoral. One can say that here the mental disposition is active in two directions: on the one hand, it apprehends the world negatively as a reality that does not correspond to the ethics of events; on the other hand, it affirmatively grasps another world, in which all the demands of naive morality are fulfilled.

We call this world of naive immorality, the 'real' world negated here, 'tragic', and once again we do not mean this as an aesthetic judgment, but as a judgment that speaks to us categorically and apodictically: a judgment of feeling. It is tragic – so it has been said, succinctly but accurately – when something must be that cannot be, or when something cannot be that must be. By this logic, what is tragic is the resistance of a world naively felt to be immoral to the demands our naive ethics makes of events.

We might expect that this doubly directed activity of the mental disposition would also produce two forms, that besides the form in which the way of the world is ordered so that it answers completely to the demands of naive morality we would find a form in which the naively immoral world, the tragic world, is condensed: in short, that there must be an anti-*Märchen*, an anti-fairy tale. This is in fact the case. If we take the story of the two royal children who could not come together because the water was too deep, and which ends in death, or the story of Pyramus and Thisbe and the lion, we find ourselves faced with an obvious actualization of this simple form. These stories correspond to the world of tragedy; the tragic way of the world is condensed here into a verbal gesture called *much-too-deep water, lion*, which carries within it separation and death. It would not be difficult to locate a number of these anti-*Märchen*, or – to use a *contradictio in adjecto* – of these tragic fairy tales; they seem to have been especially prevalent in antiquity, and we find them in Celtic tradition as well. The form as such is unrecognized and thus lacks a name, first because – as we saw in our examples – in more recent times it is conjoined with literary forms and is familiar to us only in such actualized form; and second because the second form, the one produced by the mental disposition of naive morality and in which its doubly directed activity is also entirely actualized, has suppressed the unilaterally active form. When we come to the literary forms, we will see the necessity of distinguishing the tragic fairy tale as a simple form.

The *Märchen* form is thus the form in which the mental disposition appears in its double effect – the form in which the tragic is both established and dissolved. We already see this in the way it combines dates and incidents. There is a preference for situations and events that clash with our feeling for justice: a boy inherits less than his brothers, he is smaller or dumber than those around him; children are abandoned by poor parents or abused by step-parents; the groom is separated from the true bride; people come under the power of evil fiends, they are required to execute inhumanly difficult tasks, they must flee, they are persecuted – but invariably this all is overcome in the course of events; it finds an end that corresponds to our sense of justice. Abuse, misjudgment, sin, guilt, despotism – they appear in the fairy tale only in order to be gradually and definitively abolished and dissolved by naive morality. In the end all poor girls find their prince, all stupid and poor boys their princess – indeed, in the fairy tale even death, which is in a sense an acme of naive immorality, is overcome: '. . . and they lived happily ever after'.

The moral satisfaction that we have discussed arises from this internal structure of the fairy tale: as soon as we enter the world of the fairy tale, we destroy the world of reality that we experience as immoral.

This destruction is carried out in every detail. This is what explains the quality of the marvelous that the poets who dealt with the fairy tale found characteristic of it. Where a mental disposition equates reality with the naive–immoral, the incidents cannot be realistic. This is the origin of the apparent paradox that forms the true ground of the fairy tale: *in this form, the marvellous is not marvellous, but rather self-evident.* We can compare the fairy tale to the legend in this respect. With legend, the *miracle* was the only possible confirmation of a virtue that had become active and had thus actualized itself; here, the *marvellous* is the only possible guarantee that the immorality of reality has come to an end. Just as the miracle permits us to understand the legend as such, just as with legend the miracle is necessary and self-evident, so does the fairy tale become comprehensible only in the marvellous. It is not marvellous that the poorly dressed Cinderella gets the best clothes, or that the seven young kids re-emerge from the belly of the wolf – it is what we expect, what we demand from the form. It would be miraculous – that is, senseless within the bounds of the form – if this did *not* happen, and if the *Märchen* and its world were thus to be lost.

A second feature seen in the fairy tale can be explained in the same way. The setting is 'a land far, far away', the time is 'long, long ago'; or the place is nowhere and everywhere, the time never and always. As soon as the fairy tale acquires historical traits – which sometimes happens when it overlaps with the novella – it loses some of its force. Historical settings, historical time, approach the sphere of immoral reality and break the power of the self-evidently and necessarily marvellous.

This holds as well for the characters in the fairy tale: they too must have that indefinite certainty against which an immoral reality is smashed to bits. If the prince in a fairy tale were to bear the name of a historical prince, we would be transferred immediately from the ethics of events to the ethics of action. We would no longer ask: So what happened with the prince? Instead, we would ask: What did the prince do? And this would raise doubts about the inevitability of what was happening. Thus it is, too, with those beings that play such an important role in the fairy tale that in France and England the genre is named for them – with the fairies and their attendant fiends and ogres. These, too, are clearly constructs of the mental disposition, which they represent in both of the cited directions. The fiend, the monster, the cannibal, the witch, represent the tragic direction; helpful fairies and everything connected with them and with their magical powers are, on the other hand, the best means of escape from reality. Both are marvellous; neither acts truly as a person but only as the executor of the ethical event, which can be inhibited by one sort of character, or guided by the other in a direction consonant with our judgment of feeling. Puss-in-Boots is not set over against a being that has done him little or no wrong and which he deviously kills; rather, what happens here is that the means by which a just settlement must occur, the worthless cat through which the poor miller's boy receives more than his fate has withheld from him, triumphs over a being that, by its nature, stands in the way of the just event, in the path of happiness; the evil magician's treasures do not belong to him – they belong to the one who received too little at the beginning.

We finally arrive at the verbal gesture of the fairy tale. This comes so strongly to the fore, and events are organized in such a definite way within it, that it has been considered the true 'content' of the fairy tale. Fairy tale scholarship has shown an exceptional fondness for the word 'motif', which we have avoided for reasons suggested earlier; these are the 'fairy tale motifs' that are frequently used to classify the fairy tales. It has even been argued that the fairy tale is nothing more than a fairly random collection of such motifs, that one could, so to speak, decompose it into its motifs and rebuild it from others: that fairy tales are made from motifs as mosaics are made from stones. We need not waste many words on this argument. Fairy tale is event, in the sense of naive morality; if we banish the event, with its tragic beginning, its progress towards justice, its tragic obstructions, its ethical conclusion, what remains is a meaningless skeleton that can afford us no moral satisfaction, and which can at best serve as the mnemotechnical scaffolding for a reconstruction of the form. We *can* say, however, that this event – which, as a whole, is what constitutes the form produced by the mental disposition – can be divided into units that are themselves indivisible, and that these units, charged and impregnated with meaning by the whole, can be grasped as verbal constructs. Just as in legend the verbal constructs are charged with virtue and miracles, and in *Sage* with kinship and everything that can result from kinship, so are they charged in fairy tale with tragedy and justice, in the sense of naive morality. In this sense, injustice is called *being stupid, being clothed in rags*; tragedy: *in one night, sorting out a pile of various grains*; *undertaking an endless journey*; *fighting a monster*; justice: *receiving a treasure*; *marrying a prince*. But this verbal gesture is always charged with the thing that destroys the immoral reality; like time, place and characters, one way or another the gesture always signifies the marvellous.

Is there an object or something objective in the fairy tale that we find charged with the power of the form? Precisely because the fairy tale stands opposed to what we are used to regarding in the world as real events, because the world of the fairy tale is more radically distinct from a world of reality than any other form, we find it more difficult to find such objects in a world understood as reality and therefore negated – objects charged with the power of fairy tale that could represent the fairy tale, just as the relic represents the form 'legend' or a rune the form 'riddle'. Still, it seems to me that we have something similar in objects that the fairy tale extracts from reality in order to transform them according to the laws of a world of marvels. When in Perrault's 'Cinderella' the biggest pumpkin from the garden is not a pumpkin but a coach, when the mice from the mousetrap are not mice but horses, or when in other fairy tales a nut contains not a kernel but a dress or a golden hen with chicks, then I would count this not entirely as a matter of verbal gesture, but would say instead that the pumpkin, the mice and the nut remain real objects, objects so charged with the marvellous, according to the demands of naive morality, that reality itself no longer recognizes them as its property.

Yet I must confess that I have discovered no name for objects of this kind.

CHAPTER 9

Joke

With the last form that we shall discuss, we need not ask whether or
how it survives to the present day – there is no era and probably also
no region in the world where jokes cannot be found, in being and
consciousness, in life and in literature.

This is not to say that jokes have always and everywhere been
valued in the same way. There have been times when the joke reaches
into the highest genres and forms of literature, and there have been
times when it has had to make do with being popular, in the broadest
sense of the word. Yet wherever the joke has been popular thus, it
always characterizes the folk, the group, the era from which it issued:
we can distinguish the American joke from the English, the English
joke from the Irish; in Germany, we have jokes typical of Berlin, of
Hamburg, of Munich – as well as Jewish jokes. Likewise, jokes from
antiquity, the Middle Ages and the Renaissance cannot be confused
with each other, and the hunter's joke is different from that of the criminal. This is probably also why the names for this form are so various,
and why we find so many subcategories within the purview of the
general term. *Witz*, joke – which can also mean 'wit' or 'reason' – is the
usual name for this form in High German; Dutch and Low German
have *grap*, with uncertain etymology; English has *joke*; French has *bon
mot*; Italian *scherzo* – and so on. Besides this, we have words in New
High German that designate variants of the form, like *Kalauer*, which
comes from the French word *calembour*, and *Zote*, probably from the
French *sotie*; then we have the English *pun*, the Irish *bulls*, and so on.
The joke thus affords us the best possibility of understanding how,

given the same mental disposition, a form may be differently actual-ized depending on the people, the era, or the style of the times.

For us it is not a question of differences, but of the mental disposi-tion as a whole. We can begin by saying that in the joke form, wherever we find it, something is released or *undone* – that the joke *unbinds* something bound [*irgendein Gebundenes entbindet*].

We will illustrate this with several examples. If we begin with language, we find an extremely widespread manner of joking that we call 'wordplay'.

In so far as language is a way of communicating with other people or of making oneself understood to others, it is clear from the start that every part of language must possess the quality of intelligibility. As long as language aims at intelligibility, each verbal form can thus be used only in its intelligible sense. If, however – given this same activity – I use a word in another sense, or if I really mean one thing with it while appearing to mean something else, or if I replace a comprehen-sible word with another that sounds the same but has a different mean-ing, what arises is not what we called 'special language' in our treat-ment of the riddle – *ambiguity* – but rather a *double sense*: that is, the communicative intention of language is abrogated, the intelligibility of language is undone, the bond of relationship between speaker and listener is momentarily unbound. Yet this undoing is precisely the purpose of playing with words, of wordplay.

A Frenchman is asked for a play on words, *a jeu de mots*, about a raging epidemic, and he answers: 'Je ne fais pas un jeu de maux' ('I don't play games with sickness'). By replacing the word *mots* with a word that sounds the same but has a different meaning, he has abro-gated the necessary condition that, in a conversation, question and answer must refer to the same state of affairs – thus producing a double meaning. But he has also done something more: in pointing out to his interlocutor that one should not make a game of serious matters, he has undone the entire concept *jeu de mots*.

A north German walks into a Saxon department store on a cold winter's day and asks the manager for *Ohrwärmer*. After thinking for a moment, the manager (who has understood not *earwarmers*, but *Ohrwürmer*, earworms) answers: 'Bird food department.' Double mean-ing once more, arising from the fact that the north German and the

Saxon do not 'understand' each other. But once again, something else, something more has been undone: first, the fact that, thanks to dialect differences, two people who speak the same language may nonetheless mean different things with words that sound the same; and second, the manager's conviction that he must have every article in stock.

As we see, even a simple joke is already a complicated structure. Yet all the parts of this structure aim at the same thing: every time, they undo something, unbind something bound.

The means that a given language has at its disposal to effect such undoing are almost as numerous as the means it has at its disposal to bind things. Every mode that language has of expressing a state of affairs, and every verbal form that arises in consequence, has its comic antipode in the joke. We need only view an abstraction concretely, or take a metaphor literally, and the witty undoing is there.

What is possible for language per se can be applied also to logic. Any thought process, all conditions, principles, laws and norms of proper thought, can be spontaneously undone. One need only interrupt the sequence, replace one link in the chain with another, jump from one logic to another; each time, the absurd, contradictory, unthinkable result takes the the form of a joke.

A Greek dreams that he has been with a famous hetaera, and he goes and tells of it in the Agora. The hetaera hears of this and demands payment. The case comes before a judge. The judge orders the man to lay the money on the table; he has a mirror brought, and permits the hetaera to take the mirror image of the money as payment for the dreamed pleasure. We find a parallel to this logic in the story of the traveller who brings a stuffed ichneumon from Egypt to kill off the snakes that his brother in Berlin, who suffers from delirium tremens, thinks he is seeing – and who answers the objection 'But that isn't a real ichneumon' with the response 'Correct! but the snakes aren't real either.'

It is much the same with ethics. Let us take the well-known moralistic narrative of the man sitting under a tree pondering why the oak bears such tiny, unattractive fruit, while the big, beautiful pumpkins in his garden grow on paltry creepers. Nature and the Creation seem to him not entirely purposeful. But while he sits and thinks and doubts, an acorn falls on his head and he sees the light, and is happy at least that pumpkins do not grow on oak trees. The story seems certainly to betray a serious tendency; equally certainly, it reveals certain gaps – it shows that *something here is not quite right*. Now it is a pleasure to watch how the joke exploits these gaps in order to take control of the story, and how it uses what isn't quite right to destroy and undo the ethical aspect of the story or the moral satisfaction that it could afford. The story can also be told as a joke: A vicar is walking bareheaded one summer evening while indulging in pious thoughts on the wonders of Creation. A sparrow flying overhead does its business upon his bald spot. The clergyman clasps his hands together and speaks: 'Lord, I thank You for not having given cows wings.' Here, everything is undone. The doubt in the layman's mind is replaced with the certainty in the vicar's soul. Instead of two comparable fruits, acorn and pumpkin, we have two incomparable animals, sparrow and cow. Finally, indecency is called upon. For just as in jokes absurdity is what undoes philosophical logic, indecency undoes what practical morality, decency and good manners prescribe to us.

Proceeding further, we notice that it is not only language, logic, ethics and suchlike that can be undone in this way, but also that everything we have called simple form up to now is undone in the joke. If we ask such a riddle as: 'Under a plum tree there lies something blue with a pit inside. Guess what it is?', and we answer the person who guesses 'a plum' that it is 'a blue Hussar who has swallowed a plum pit', but to someone who knows the Hussar solution we say that this time it is 'a plum', then with this we undo the form 'riddle', which depends on the possibility of its being guessed – which here it cannot be. If we rearrange the saying 'Learn to suffer without complaint' into 'Learn to complain without suffering', then we undo the experience that was condensed in the saying. With the story of the bean, the straw and the coal, we saw that, where one approached the world and its phenomena with a pseudo-question, the myth form slackened and dissolved and could turn into a joke. We could go through the entire series of simple forms in this way, and we would find that they can all be dissolved into jokes.

We find the joke everywhere, with its exaggerations upwards and downwards, with its transpositions, with its capacity for turning things on their head. The means that it uses are endless, because – once again

– its means are as many as the means used by language, logic, ethics, and the simple forms to achieve their goals of fixation [*Bindung*]. Under certain conditions, every attempt at fixation can be undone at a given point, and acquire the form 'joke.'

II. COMEDY – INADEQUACY – MOCKERY

We are wont to call the mental disposition that yields the joke by a Greek name: 'the comic,' or comedy. I would like to do the same here, but with a restriction. Just as with the concept of the tragic, a philosophical aesthetics, proceeding primarily from the art forms, has addressed the concept of the comic, arriving at certain results, at certain definitions; it has even declared comedy an extra-aesthetic value. In contrast, our task is and remains morphological: we have everywhere kept a distance from aesthetics, and we will do the same here as well; the relationship of comedy to tragedy, to the Sublime, to the Characteristic or the Beautiful, in the aesthetic sense or in works of art, will not concern us here. We will understand comedy the same way we did tragedy in our discussion of fairy tales: as a mental disposition that produces a simple form.

Yet if we replace what we have discussed thus far with comedy, this initially seems to be something negative. We have spoken everywhere of *undoing*, and everywhere we found that there was something that was being undone – language, logic, ethics, simple forms. It was not as in the fairy tale, where a world felt to be immoral was transformed and then destroyed in its tragedy; there had to be something else there, something had to exist to be seized upon and undone by the joke.

This raises the question of whether and to what extent this undoing agent is itself in a position to create a new form, or of whether and to what extent the object undone remains itself despite the undoing. The question can also be put in this way: Does comedy construct its own self-enclosed world like the other simple forms, or does it only achieve the undoing inversion of another world?

Recalling what we said in our introduction about producing and creating, we can use several examples to examine the morphological significance of this question.

It is obvious that a vessel without a bottom – thus a vessel that neither corresponds to the concept 'vessel' nor meets the requirements that we make of a vessel – has nonetheless not ceased to be a vessel. We could call it a vessel with the valence reversed. Even if it were to turn out to be the case that one could put this bottomless vessel to use – say, to bash in the skull of an enemy – and even if one had modified this vessel in this particular way, like a Bavarian beer stein, to make it more useful for this particular purpose, one would nonetheless have to say that, although in this case the vessel had served as a weapon, still it remained a vessel. On the other hand, we can say of a piece of gut that we take from a sheep or a cat, that we prepare and then stretch on a bow so as to shoot arrows with it, or which we stretch on a sounding board so as to coax sounds from it, that this gut in its altered state can no longer be linked with either the concept or the object 'gut', but that it has now become a *string*, and that this 'string' cannot possibly be understood as 'gut' with the valence reversed.

We can now tentatively pose our question regarding comedy as follows: Is the thing that the 'undoing' turns into a joke a bottomless vessel, or is it a string? Or again: Is what has become comical this same thing with the valence reversed, or has comedy made something different come into existence?

To be able to decide this, we must speak for a moment about the *intention* of comedy and of the joke.

Since the joke is a means of undoing something, it is obvious that we will want to deploy it wherever we meet with something that we regret, deplore, detest, or – to use a more general word – that we *condemn*. Not everything that is reprehensible can be recast or undone through comedy. We already saw with the moralistic narrative of the dissatisfied man sitting under the tree and with the French *jeu de maux* that there had to be something in what is to be undone that was not quite right, something that bore the beginning or the nucleus of dissolution within itself – indeed, something that was already part way to undoing itself – and for this we can use the word *inadequacy*. The necessary precondition for being able to undo something reprehensible, or indeed any structure at all, and to give it the form of a joke, is that this structure is inadequate. We must add that the concepts 'reprehensible' and 'inadequate' need not necessarily coincide, but that in some circumstances they can coincide very well, so that ultimately inadequacy will suffice to produce a comic solution.

What is produced in a joke – in so far as its intention is to undo something reprehensible beginning with an inadequacy, or something inadequate beginning with itself – is the thing we call *mockery*.

III. SATIRE – IRONY – IN LITERARY FORMS – STRICTNESS – JEST

At this point we can distinguish two forms, depending on the greater or lesser distance between the reprehensible object undone by mockery and the mocker who undoes it: *satire* and *irony*.

Satire is mockery of that which we condemn or abhor, and which stands at a distance from us. We want to have nothing in common with what we condemn, we sharply confront it, and thus we undo it without sympathy, without pity.

By contrast, *irony* mocks what we condemn, but it does not confront it from a distance – it feels sympathy with it, it is concerned. Irony is thus characterized by a sense of *solidarity*. The mocker shares with the object of his mockery a feeling for what is being mocked; he knows it from his own experience, but he has recognized it in its inadequacy, and he is revealing this inadequacy to someone who seems not to have noticed it. This is why solidarity here acquires a deeper meaning. We sense in irony something of the intimacy and familiarity between a superior and an inferior. And the great pedagogical value of irony lies precisely in this solidarity.

Satire destroys – irony educates.

But the awareness that one is familiar with the thing one is mocking, that it is a part of us, can lead to a combination, in irony, of comedy with the entire range of nuance from melancholy to pain. Bitter satire is embittered with its object; bitter irony is bitter because it is embittered at finding within ourselves what we mock in others.

Meanwhile, the relationship between the mocker and what he mocks can lead to their increasing coalescence with each other. The fact that irony targets and undoes itself can also become the reason why it falls in love with or becomes fixated on itself.

The spirals and byways of irony thus belong to the highest achievements of which comic form is capable. The first part of the *Praise of Folly*, by Erasmus, can serve as an example of such appealing and difficult paths; the second part of the book, which is far less profound, gives us a good example of satire.

The expressions satire and irony are often confused in colloquial speech. No wonder – there are great works of literature that began as satire and ended as irony, works in which the poet believed at first that he needed to stand off at a distance from his object to mock it and hoped to be able to undo it without pity, but where he gradually came to see how closely related he was to what he was mocking, how deeply affected he himself was by his mockery. We need only recall Cervantes and his *Don Quixote*. There are other works of literature in which we find both forms running continually alongside each other, in which satire and irony seem always to be nipping at each other's heels, and here we might think of Ariosto, of Rabelais, or of many a German romantic.

With these authors, however, we have already left the domain of simple literary forms for that of literary art forms, which was not our intention.

Yet at the same time we did see that irony, whose mockery arises from what we have in common with things we consider inadequate, took us in a new direction. Here we perceive how the intention of comedy or of jokes can be more profound than the undoing of what we condemn or abhor, and that the form need not signify vain derision.

Our life and our thinking take place in a constant state of tension. Tension within us and tension outside of us. Each time this tension verges on overload, we try to reduce it, to ease it. One means of getting from tension to relaxation – sometimes the only one, often the best one – is the joke. In so far as comedy has the intention of easing tension, it contrasts not with the *reprehensible* and the *inadequate*, but with what is *strict*. Here we must understand strict, *streng*, in its deeper meaning. The German adjective *streng* is related to the noun *Strang*, cord; the verb *(sich) anstrengen* ('to strain oneself, make an effort') also applies here. We find ourselves within an etymological group to which many other words belong, including the Latin *stringo* and the Greek στραγγάλη, *strangalē*. The meaning of this group can be derived from a cord that acquires resilience by being spun, but is thus also ever more tightly tensed. In itself, strictness is nothing reprehensible, and not in the least inadequate; on the contrary, it is – as we have already noted – a necessary condition for living and thinking. And yet, in order to enforce strictness as strictly as possible, we need to be able at times to revoke it or free ourselves from it. The writers of the Renaissance who addressed themselves to the concept of comedy, to the *facetie* (witticism) and the joke, speak in this context of a *relaxatio animi*, a relaxation of the spirit. Indeed, in the joke our spirit does have a temporary means of freeing itself from itself, when need be.

In so far as comedy and the joke have the goal of undoing tension in life and in thought, and of freeing the spirit, we can call the form that it takes not *mockery*, but *jest*.

In contrast to mockery, jest can be understood as what happens when comedy addresses not a single case, but a general state of affairs. Jest goes beyond mockery, for in jest the negativity that at first seemed inherent in comedy ceases. For the liberation of the spirit that is effected by the release from, or dissolution of, a tension, is not at all the negation of a state of being bound or tense, but means instead a positive freedom. We feel how much liberation means freedom whenever comedy liberates us from the strictest or most stringent tensions of exhaustion or dilemma.

Having distinguished the two aims of comedy as mockery and jest, we must quickly add that the literary form 'joke' means a dual unity in which mockery and jest are simultaneously distinct and conjoined. Without exception, every joke both undoes an inadequate structure and dissolves a tension. Even when it is the aim of the joke to undo something reprehensible in a particular case, still its effect is to release us from a general tension. Even the most biting satire and the most bitter irony fulfil this double task: however much we may insult and wound our enemy with the first and ourselves with the second, still both liberate the mind from an inward tension. And contrariwise: even when the main intention of our comedy is to dissolve a tension, still our most innocent joke begins with an object, a particular case, whose inadequacy is undone.

Naturally, we can say that in any given joke the centre of gravity lies more on the one side or on the other. But the joke that lacks one of the two intentions of comedy necessarily loses its form: it misses its point, or it becomes an insult.

Keeping this in mind, let us come back to our question: Does comedy have its own world? What does the joke do with what it undoes? What is the relationship of the old form to the new?

IV. DOUBLE FUNCTION – AUTONOMOUS FIGURES
– THE WORLD OF COMEDY – CARICATURE AS AN OBJECT

If we begin with the concept of mockery, it might seem as if the joke simply repeated the thing it condemned with the valence reversed. There are forms of mockery – parody, for example – that bear a certain resemblance to an imitation. They repeat what they mock, but using comedy to emphasize the nucleus of the solution already present within it, thus repeating what is mocked in such a way as to undo it in its entirety. We found repetitions in the joke of the Frenchman, with the Greek judge, with the pious vicar – and were we to search further, we would often find similar things. In so far as the joke, proceeding from an inadequacy, undoes an individual case in language, logic, ethics or elsewhere – that is, in so far as it remains *mockery* – we can understand it as a repetition with the valence reversed.

Yet we also saw that the joke has another effect – that its intention is not only particular but also general, in that it liberates the mind by dissolving a tension. Just as the freedom of the mind is not the negation of a restriction, but something positive in itself, so is the joke not just a form that repeats another form with the valence reversed, but thanks to its double function it is always also a form that autonomously creates.

We can observe this process especially clearly with jokes that, building on the defects and weaknesses of certain circles or human types, spontaneously produce sharp sketches of autonomous figures and characters – by which I mean jokes on the hunter, the dandy, the cook, the lieutenant, the hoodlum, the princeling, the nouveau riche, the miser, the drunk, the schoolmaster, the teenager, and similar figures, which are as popular in modern newspapers as in the farces of days gone by. Comedy here apparently begins as mockery. Proceeding from inadequacies, it attempts to dissolve or undo the more or less reprehensible qualities that inhere in each of these characters. But at the same time such comedy is jest, whereby it succeeds in transforming – indeed, binding! – the same characters into very positively individualized elementary forms. What is mocked in the hunter becomes 'Münchhausen' in the joke;[1] relaxation of the mind turns the inadequacies of the princeling into a sharply sketched figure like Serenissimus;[2] finally, a figure like Frau Raffke[3] consoles us for what annoys us about the new rich.

The force of these newly minted, fully autonomous humorous personalities is so great that they are able to draw to themselves all the mockery of the past, every older joke with the same intention or tendency, and to relate all this to themselves in a new way. They become magnetic poles until another era dissolves and replaces them.

Yet every joke does the same thing in microcosm: beginning by undoing what is reprehensible – thus with the negative – it becomes binding in its own right through the freedom it affords our mind by dissolving a tension, and thus creating its own positive world. This world of the joke can be wholly understood only in the dual unity of mockery and jest. In other words: *the world of comedy is a world in which things become binding in being dissolved or in being undone.*

The comparison with the bottomless vessel did not work. Was our comparison of the gut with the string any better? Perhaps we can add a third possibility. Just as, thanks to their composition, certain materials can undergo chemical metamorphosis and take on form through a complex process of fermentation through which their effect is completely altered – in short, just as grape juice and milk, honey or rice or potatoes, can be fermented to produce something that excites and intoxicates us, so also does it seem as if mental substances can be

---

1 Hieronymus Carl Friedrich von Münchhausen (1720–97), a German aristocrat whose life became the basis of numerous tall tales, most famously in Rudolf Erich Raspe's comic novel of 1785, *Baron Munchausen's Narrative of his Marvellous Travels and Campaigns in Russia.*

2 See *supra*, 'Introduction', note 8.

3 A Weimar-era comic type of the well-dressed wife of the *nouveau riche*, with chauffeur and mink stole. See for example Kurt Tucholsky, 'Unsere Zeitgenossen, die Raffkes' ('Our Contemporaries, the Raffkes'), *Berliner Illustrirte Zeitung*, no. 31, 25 June 1922, p. 26.

brought through comic fermentation to yield something new, to produce a form with its own character and a new function.

Objects exist that accomplish a dissolution in the sense of this mental disposition, that thus once again represent our form as objects charged with our mental disposition. When Wilhelm Hauff introduces a monkey dressed in human clothes into human society, he is using literary means in a particular way to undo 'society' in its 'humanity'. But does not a real monkey, marvelled and gawked at by a crowd as it drinks from a glass or eats from a plate or rides a bicycle or smokes at its trainer's command while dressed in a tail-coat – in short, a monkey that acts like a human – do exactly the same? And cannot a knightly ancestral portrait on the walls of the room of a parvenu, amid a hodge-poge of eras and styles, represent the entire attitude of the new rich in such a way as to undo it?

I would like to call this sort of object, in which an undoing occurs in one particular place and there alone, *caricature*. Normally, caricature means an overloaded (*caricato*) portrait that undertakes an attack (*carica*) on a character, that attempts to dissolve a bodily and mental complexion by emphasizing and exaggerating certain of its traits. Here, however, we see an object attacking a character, a complexion, a situation in the same way; charged with our mental disposition, it caricatures them, undoes them.

CHAPTER 10

Perspectives

So now we have them before us, those forms of which we said initially
that they exist in a different 'aggregate state' from literature proper, and
that they have not been properly understood by the disciplines that
describe how works are constructed from verbal units and articulations to yield definitive artistic compositions; those forms that – we
feel this is worth insisting upon – are so deeply anchored in language
that they even appear to resist that eternal conscience of language,
writing.

We have seen how all these forms are completed, in life and in
language, how they are perceived on the level of being as well as on
that of consciousness;

how every one of them can be derived from a particular mental
disposition;

how we can recognize them as a *pure simple form* and as an *actualized simple form*, and how ultimately this can yield a *derivative form*;

how, finally, the simple form can always transfer its power to an
object, charging the object with the power of the form.

We might perhaps have expressed all this in a more systematic
fashion from the beginning, stressing more sharply and more schematically what the simple forms have in common, their inner coherence. But we preferred to allow each form to develop so to speak out of
itself, to allow each to remain in its world so that they might indicate
their common traits only when these emerged naturally from the separate study of each form. The great danger, in a work of analysis, is that
it can lead us to evaluate falsely the relationship of the parts to the

whole; it is the fate of all analytical studies that, on their completion, we are faced with the debris of our 'beautiful image of the world.'[4] If we chose this approach nonetheless, it was because we felt obliged to combat the sort of casual use of language that we saw in the dictionaries, which proved no longer able to make rigorous distinctions between words with various meanings, as well as to fight a way of thinking in which concepts had begun to fade and to blur. To separate and delimit appeared our first order of business; building a deliberate system seemed a matter for later concern.

The next step would thus have to be a comparison among the simple forms themselves.

This would require a great deal of effort. I have often indicated in the course of this essay where certain points might be expanded or pursued further. I could – and probably should – have done this more often. With a study like this, one feels what is missing at every turn; gaps appear everywhere, and when one surveys one part or another of the whole, one cannot help sighing and saying: we are just at the beginning; the place we are stopping at is where the work really ought to commence.

In defining the simple forms, we remained within a fairly small ambit. We spoke of antiquity, the Migration Period, the Middle Ages and modernity. Our goal was to demonstrate how phenomena that appeared – perhaps in their clearest form – in one part of this span of time, retained their validity throughout the entire timespan, if sometimes with less definition: how the mental disposition from which a form emerged was present continuously and ubiquitously over this timespan, if not always in the same measure. On the other hand, we spoke of the peoples of classical antiquity, of the *Germanii* and the Romans, of Semites and Indians, and also, less frequently, of indigenous peoples. We tried in this way to show as well that the same mental dispositions prevail everywhere, that everywhere they have produced the same form, and that it was only their actualization whose character changed from moment to moment. Yet the timespan of world history is greater, the global spread of peoples more extended, than what we have been able to draw into our field of study. Before we can properly speak of incessancy and ubiquity, before we can understand a mental

---

4 Cf. Goethe, *Faust*, lines 1608–11.

disposition in its generality and thus also the meaning and nature of a form – however different the actualizations may be from which we proceed – we will need to extend considerably our ambit of observation, both historically and geographically.

We are well aware of the difficulties posed by such a project. They reside in the just-mentioned differences of character between the various actualizations.

The path we followed to recognize the single forms led through the actualized forms. The actualization was where the form was initially available to us; starting with this, we were able to penetrate to the simple form as such; in the simple form, we could discern the mental disposition. Jacob Grimm had proved that this path was possible; in an era that could no longer recognize the simple form *fairy tale* in actualizations that had become distanced from the basic form and combined with literary forms, he picked out the idiosyncrasy of that simple form, its 'spontaneous self-generation'. We have tried to follow his example – but we must not forget that the 'discovery of the fairy tale' also began within the very small circle of the scholar's intimate friends and family.

Were we to collect and study actualizations of all kinds from times long past or from more distant peoples – let us say from the Egyptians, the Chinese, the North American Indians – with the aim of determining if what we found there confirms what we have seen in our own closer context, would we always be able to recognize the simple forms in these actualizations, which differ so much in character from our own?

Let us recall, for example, that we discovered the mental disposition that yields the simple form *legend* in a saint's life in the Middle Ages, in part of the epinikea in antiquity, and in a sports report in the modern age. If a Chinese or a North American actualization of the simple form *legend* were to diverge as much in character from all of our actualizations as a sports report does from a saint's life, then it will certainly not be easy to ascertain whether they are the same.

We have only one means if we would arrive at valid conclusions rather than settle for superficialities.

Let us repeat: under the sway of a particular mental disposition, similar phenomena are condensed from the manifold of being and of events; they are swirled together by language, condensed and recast into a new shape; they are present to us in language as indivisible units impregnated and charged by the mental disposition, units we called *individual verbal gestures*, or *verbal gestures* for short.

It is a common characteristic of all the simple forms that they are realized in language through these individual gestures; on the other hand, these individual gestures are what permit us to distinguish the simple forms from each other as linguistic units charged with the power of a mental disposition, and thus to perceive them morphologically.

We are thus faced with another challenge besides comparing all the simple forms as such: to study the task, function and structure of the verbal gestures of each simple form, and then to compare the verbal gestures of the various simple forms among themselves. Once we have determined the verbal gestures of our own cultural sphere and become acquainted with the inward and outward structure of other spheres, we must observe whether and to what extent the verbal gesture is confirmed wherever we think we have recognized the mental disposition in these other languages, albeit with certain changes and displacements.

In these chapters I have been able only occasionally to point out such paths of possible inquiry. A rigorous study of verbal gestures, however, would cast new light on how the simple forms are interrelated. Although we have just noted that it might be difficult to recognize a Chinese or a North American legend as such, we would still expect to be able to recognize a saying in Chinese or Algonquian, even if we are relatively unfamiliar with the internal and external structure of the Chinese or Algonquian languages. This is easily explained. Roughly speaking, in our legends the verbal gesture constitutes only a part of the form. This is, to be sure, the structuring part, the part that embodies the sense and the essence of the mental disposition, and which allows us to recognize the legend as legend. Yet in between these individual verbal gestures we find other elements effecting transitions and connections without fulfilling or being fulfilled by the mental disposition to the extent we observe with the verbal gestures proper. We saw similar things with all of the longer narrative forms, such as the *Sage* and the fairy tale. With the case, we even showed how the simple form can be converted into a literary form with the aid of 'interchangeable' mediating elements. The characteristic differences that we perceived in various actualizations of the same simple form depend to a large extent on the relative flexibility of these elements. In the saying, by contrast, the verbal gesture made up the entire form; it bound the whole form so tightly together that here no word could be altered: the structure as a whole almost gave the impression of having a 'personal character'. Precisely this is what made the saying so easy to recognize.

Can this be generalized to our form 'legend'? Can we assume that these differences in how verbal gestures operate characterize the forms as such, and that in the legend, always and everywhere, there are elements that connect the verbal gestures, whereas in the saying, always and everywhere, the verbal gesture as such constitutes the whole?

Only an expanded, deepened study of the task, function and structure of the verbal gesture can answer this question. It might turn out that some forms are so constituted that their verbal gestures work as the main thread of meaning to define and assemble a significant structure without ambiguity under the sway of a mental disposition, while it is characteristic of other forms that they can be realized as a whole solely in the verbal gesture. It might also be the case that all of the simple forms are actually and originally realized only in the verbal gesture, and that with some of the forms the transitional and connective elements accrued to them in the course of a process of development towards the literary form, or were taken from the literary form. If the former is true, then these transitional and connective elements belong to the mental disposition and to the simple form as such; if the latter holds, then they will only have been a means of actualization.

In any event, observing the various activities of the verbal gestures is what has made it possible to classify our forms. Depending on whether the transitional and connective elements are present or absent, and depending on how the verbal gestures proper relate to these elements, we can designate the forms, with respect to their size, as *long forms* or *short forms*; with respect to movement, as *progressive forms* or *persistent forms*; and with respect to whether they are outwardly or inwardly oriented, as *open forms* or *closed forms*. If along with the verbal gestures the transitional and connective elements also belong to the simple forms proper, then we could regard this classification as a rigorous one; if they belong to the actualization, then the classification would still be significant with regard to the actualization.

Our study has thus to begin again with the verbal gesture. Provided that we avoid harmlessly listing and grouping the verbal gestures according to superficial traits and without sufficient linguistic knowledge, as 'motif research' has so often done, and that we regard the verbal gestures instead as the basic unit of meaning through which a structuring mental disposition announces itself – that is, if we construe them linguistically, in the deepest sense – then we can once again generate from within the very structure that we have just produced from without.

Index